THE NPR INTERVIEWS
1994

THE NPR
INTERVIEWS
1994

Edited and with an Introduction
by ROBERT SIEGEL

HOUGHTON MIFFLIN COMPANY

BOSTON · NEW YORK   1994

ISSN 1078-0211
ISBN 0-395-70741-2
ISBN 0-395-71373-0 (pbk.)

Printed in the United States of America

Book design by Robert Overholtzer

AGM 10 9 8 7 6 5 4 3 2 1

CONTENTS

America Talking
....

Enders
....

INTRODUCTION

Some mornings when I wake up to NPR and some evenings when I tune in after a day off, I hear one of our interviews as any listener might. It sounds like a fluent and intimate exchange, a spontaneous conversation between a deft interrogator and an insightful respondent. One good interview, and my disbelief in the magic of radio is suspended. As we like to say of our medium, "The pictures are better on radio," and the picture of an interview in the mind's eye is typically a simple, uncluttered scene of two people talking.

Here is a more accurate picture of a good interview and how it becomes part of an NPR program. In the beginning, there is a meeting. Our editors and producers meet often enough to make Rotarians look like loners. Staffs of individual programs meet, led by their producers and editors. Then they all meet together, joined by the "desks" (Washington, national, foreign, science, and cultural). Meetings are occasions for brainstorming, complaining, haggling among programs, and, ultimately, decisions of impeccable wisdom and fairness rendered by the managing editor or the still more august and infallible vice president for news and information programming.

At a typical program staff meeting, any member of the staff might propose an interesting idea for an interview. Someone has noted a brief item on one of the wire services: an inventor has discovered that Tabasco sauce can take the barnacles off a boat. Another has read the compelling work of a Mexican-American poet who was illiterate before entering prison. Another proposes a series of interviews with Muslim, Serb, and Croat refugees from the war in Bosnia. And yet another observes that the New York talk show host Joe Franklin is about to retire and might be coaxed into doing his Billy Crystal impression on national radio. The proposals are adopted, provided that there is a willing host and a general voice vote or mass mumble in favor, and they are assigned to the true unsung heroes (usually heroines) of broadcasting, the bookers.

Every program at National Public Radio has a booker, who often goes by the formal title editorial assistant. A booker is required to negotiate with publicists for touring authors and aides to politicians, as well as to find and book anyone from an Indiana farmer who teaches llamas how to square-dance to a war correspondent whose newspaper discourages radio interviews. She is heir to a vast collection of phone numbers organized idiosyncratically by past bookers. She has an ear for radio: Is this expert economist sufficiently animated, or too dull to carry four minutes? Is the telephone line from Bujumbura audible, or can we cadge a few minutes from the BBC satellite phone nearby? She knows which cities have studios with high-quality audio lines connecting them to Washington, at what hour Asian bureau chiefs are likely to retire, and which journalists in remote and dangerous places are glad to be on radio, if only their anxious parents in New Jersey are notified in advance of local airtime and the frequency of the nearest NPR station. Some bookers have gone on to jobs producing NPR programs. Others have gone berserk or, worse, gone back to graduate school.

Once the interview is booked, staff involvement starts to proliferate. The host reads everything available about or by the person to be interviewed and consults with the editor of the program about questions to ask. They take up their posts in the studio and control room. Then the engineer sets voice levels and positions microphones to make host and guest sound like equals (without simply suspending mikes smack in front of their faces and achieving the "interview in a banana tree effect"). The host is in the studio, the guest is seated opposite or in a remote studio or on a telephone, the engineer is working the faders of the console, and the editor is in the control room. Then the real worker enters the picture: the cutter.

Cutters enjoy all sorts of titles and occupy many different

ranks in the hierarchy, but when assigned to a story (often an idea they proposed) they all do the same thing: they cut tape. They do to recorded speech and sound what we all now do with the cut and paste functions of a word processor: take out those words, move this paragraph from the end to the middle, use the second version of the Q and A about Billy Crystal instead of the first, tack the end of answer seven onto answer four. In short, make nine rambling minutes recorded in the studio sound like four crisp minutes on the air. No edit may violate the pattern of voice inflections or misrepresent the intended point of a statement by shortening it. And it must all be done fast. A good cutter makes the difference between radio that sounds like it was edited with a knife and fork and radio so plausibly seamless as to suck in the likes of me. Cutters sometimes develop what I think of as Deadline Tourette's Syndrome: as airtime approaches, they shout incontrollably and blurt obscenities, which is one reason they do their cutting in soundproof booths.

After the interview is cut, there are still more hands whose work influences what we hear on the radio. The producer of the program listens to the cut version and finds that the joke about the Laffer Curve is mystifying unless a line previously cut to get down to three minutes forty-five seconds of tape is restored. The time must come out of another answer.

The director selects music to play after the interview. Picking up on the right mood, and not following every piece on agriculture with banjo plucking or every story on democratization in Latin America with Andean flute music, requires good taste and a fresh ear. Our directors are geniuses at this. They create the wallpaper patterns of sound, the aural background to what we do up front.

The interview that you hear as a result of all these efforts is no casual, spontaneous event. That it often sounds like one is a tribute to the talents of a great many people, all of whose work is reflected in this first annual collection of transcribed NPR interviews. They are drawn from the daily NPR news magazines — *Morning Edition; All Things Considered; Weekend All Things Considered; Weekend Edition, Saturday;* and *Weekend Edition, Sunday* — and were all broadcast in 1993. I selected the interviews after soliciting suggestions from producers as well as poring over rough, printed transcripts. My aim was to collect interviews that read well on the page. This meant excluding nearly all of our music interviews, which depend on hearing the music under discussion. I also wanted to reflect the breadth of subjects we addressed and to convey something of what the year 1993 was like. Thus, the war in Bosnia figures again and again, not only in the chapter devoted to it, "The Story of the Year," but also in the reflections of people who were being interviewed about other subjects, Octavio Paz and Desmond Tutu, for example. It casts a shadow of pessimism over much of what people are saying here about nationalism, war, peace, and brotherhood.

Another theme of 1993 was the inauguration of President Clinton which marked the first change of political party occupying the White House in twelve years. In many of these interviews, the new administration was no doubt the real intended audience. Bosnian Muslims, foreign policy wise men, and advocates of all causes spoke in 1993 with hopes of influencing a government that was just taking (or resisting) shape. Their remarks are about the new administration, as are those of the midwesterners whom Linda Wertheimer interviewed along Route 50, included here in "America Talking."

The NPR Interviews also reflects the year 1993 in terms of our personnel. Scott Simon spent much of the year on leave, working at NBC News. Bob Edwards likewise spent part of the year on leave writing *Fridays with Red: A Radio Friendship*. These absences permitted Neal Conan, Alex Chadwick, and Susan Stamberg to host a great many programs and conduct many excellent interviews, several of which are included. Katie Davis spent an impressive year hosting *Weekend All Things Considered* and performing missionary work for poetry on

radio. Linda Wertheimer, Noah Adams, and I hosted the week-
day program. Liane Hansen hosted *Weekend Edition, Sunday.*

While nearly all of these interviews were conducted by
hosts, I have included Nina Totenberg's extensive interview
with Justice Harry Blackmun, which she conducted with Ted
Koppel of ABC's *Nightline.* In addition, while I did not consider for inclusion host conversations with reporters (two-
ways, we call them), as they are often too choreographed to
qualify as interviews, I have included Susan Stamberg's interview with NPR correspondent Tom Gjelten about the war in
Bosnia, which strikes me as a reporter interview of a very different sort.

Although most of the chapters were easily defined and obvious to all, two require some explanation. I set aside a chapter for
interviews about "Animal Life," rather than incorporate some
into "Science," and others into "America Talking" because of
the great amount of time we devote on *All Things Considered*
to animal stories. An informal, in-house title for these items,
"Critter Corner," suggests that our intent is not entirely high-
minded. While I acknowledge there are grounds for skepticism
about such a chapter, there is also a good case for it. People have
always speculated about their relation to other animal species
and tried to determine to what degree animals possess whatever
qualities a given age might value in humans: a spine, a soul, a
brain, a legal personality.

The chapter titled "Enders" is a grab bag of mostly light interviews that would typically come at the end of a half hour on
All Things Considered. As different programs organize time
differently with segments of different length and rhythm, the
items in "Enders" did not actually all come at the end of a
program, or a segment. They could have. And they seem to
make sense coming at the end of this book.

One of the ironies of editing this collection was confronting
as an obstacle what I've always considered a great virtue of

public radio. For years, we have encouraged our staff to write for the ear, not the eye. We have held up fluent, clear, comfortable, and interesting speech as the model for our discourse, rather than the literate, highly punctuated language of the classroom. Making a book out of interviews that were conducted for the ear meant deciding just how offensive to the eye we were prepared to be in the interests of authenticity. The decision was to smooth out and sweeten, but not rewrite. My standard for verisimilitude was that the written versions would be a less exact transcription of the original tapes than a court reporter would make, more exact than if we were to render them into literate text, and closer to a playwright's script than to either of those extremes. I routinely corrected repetitions, omissions, and errors of grammar. I have also shamelessly changed to "yes" the many sounds of affirmation uttered by hosts and guests alike which approximate it (yep, yea, yeah, etc.) and which I deemed too painful for the eye to endure. Apart from such alterations, I believe this collection maintains one of NPR's knacks for recording and presenting the people of this country and the world, speaking as they do, without homogenizing them into a bland and predictable broadcast dialect of English.

The idea of an NPR publishing project that would benefit, in part, the NPR News Excellence Fund originated with John Dinges. Mary Morgan, NPR's very gifted director of promotion and public affairs, saw it through with the assistance of Gail Ross of Lichtman, Trister, Singer and Ross. At Houghton Mifflin, John Sterling proposed the idea of an annual collection of interviews and, with Janet Silver, turned an untested idea into a book. Jayne Yaffe brought such literacy and thoroughness to the task of editing the manuscript that I do not know whether I am more proud to count her as my editor or as a listener.

At NPR, Ori Hoffer provided computer expertise, and Necola Deskins-Staples, administrative support. Above all, I am forever indebted to Julia Redpath, whose good judgment and tireless dedication are evident to me on every page. If *The NPR*

Interviews is to survive as an annual project, it will be due largely to her enterprise in researching and assembling this first effort. Thanks as well to Jane, Erica, and Leah Siegel for putting up with my demands for time on the computer and my crankiness over deadlines of all sorts.

Arts and Letters

The seventy-year-old portrait photographer RICHARD
AVEDON, now a regular contributor to *The New Yorker,*
speaks with Susan Stamberg about his photography,
his life, and his "autobiography," *In Pictures.*
October 9, 1993

STAMBERG: I think we need to start with the physical size of
this book. Which weighs more? This book or your eight-by-ten
Deardorff view camera on a wooden tripod?

AVEDON: I'd be reluctant to carry either of them anywhere.
OK.

STAMBERG: It's big, 284 black-and-white photographs and
very few words. You call it an autobiography. You don't arrange
it chronologically, but it does include the first photograph you
ever took in 1931–32. Describe it to us.

AVEDON: I think there are two in the same year. One of my
sister and my mother when I was nine, with the Eastman
Kodak box Brownie. My father was a teacher before he became
a businessman. He loved to teach me everything he could, and
so the principles of photography were the first things. He
showed the way in which light burned by using the drapes
and how they would bleach, how a light-sensitive surface became a negative and then became a print, as he explained it.
Since my sister, being the beauty of the family, was photographed by all of us and by me all the time. We photographed
Louise with parasols and in clown costumes and standing in
the sunshine, and I thought, Well, skin is light-sensitive and
skin gets tan, so I took a negative of Louise and pasted it onto
my shoulder and went out to the beach. The next morning
I peeled it off and there was my sister on my shoulder. She
later died in a mental institution. I think her beauty had something to do with that. It's kind of an isolating experience.

STAMBERG: What an incredible story. What strikes me in these early pictures is that it's not just a story that shows your ingenuity, but that you were composing at the age of nine. You knew to get down in that rowboat and take a picture of your mother rowing so that it was framed perfectly and it fit right in the area of the picture. You knew all of that at that age.

AVEDON: I'm bad on the Bible, but wasn't there light before there was anything else? Weren't there days of light before there were rivers and mountains and trees and long before anyone spoke? And as a child, our way of experiencing the world is formed long before words. The things we are afraid of, I mean, to fall our of your crib is like Anuradhapura. To be hungry, with no way of getting food, it's starvation. You want the breast, that is where the food is, but maybe it jams into your mouth too quickly. I think the experience of being a child is so psychotic and the way we learn to deal with these things that can never be dealt with is visual, so I think I am arrested on the visual level. I think I never got much further than that.

STAMBERG: I said that the book was not arranged chronologically. The first image of the book, I wish you would describe for us and tell us why you chose to put it first.

AVEDON: If I remember correctly, the first photograph is a man on stilts.

STAMBERG: You must have worked hours to decide on the first photo in the book?

AVEDON: I'm just trying to be a little attractive. I don't know exactly what I did. It sort of came. It's a man on stilts in Sicily, in Palermo, and he must be from a little country circus and all the people in the town are following him. I put it first because it's a kind of perfect metaphor for the artist. Not above the crowd, but apart from the crowd, looking at everyone on very shaky feet. Those feet can go crashing at any moment and yet he's not down there with everyone, and you have to have that distance at all times. In other words, I'm looking through this booth here at the rest of the team and I'm watching their faces and learning more from the way, for instance, Melissa is trying to encourage me.

STAMBERG: It's Manoli [NPR New York Bureau engineer Manoli Wetherill].

AVEDON: Manoli. No wonder. Sounds like something delicious. She is trying to encourage me, but the nature of her encouragement is not natural. It's to make me feel good, and I can't stop thinking about how she is doing it while I'm talking to you.

STAMBERG: It's so funny. I made some plans for this conversation. The last question I was going to ask you was, "What are you looking at right now?" Because you are in our studio in New York and I am in Washington, I can't see you. Do you look at things differently from the rest of us, do you think? I'm looking at a microphone, but I bet you're looking at the same microphone there in New York differently.

AVEDON: I am looking at something very weird. There is a shelf, a little double shelf in front of me, and it's got one, two, three, four, five, six, seven, eight, nine, ten, something like twenty little glass balls that have snow in them that you turn upside down. One has a cow and one has the Nativity and one SAYS TEXAS SNOWMAN on it. One part of me is thinking about how would I photograph those if I had to.

STAMBERG: Yes.

AVEDON: I have just finished an issue of *The New Yorker* that has to do with the Kennedy years now that it's thirty years since the assassination, and there were certain people I could not photograph. They're dead and that is why I couldn't photograph them. Or for example, Nixon and Castro, who were unavailable, and I'm not good at still life. I am not good doing anything with someone I can't speak to. It's always between myself and another person. That is my gift and my strength, but since these people were unavailable, I found a man who collected Kennedy memorabilia, and he invited me down, and in a vitrine, in a glass case, were all these corks for whiskey carved out of wood. They're a little bit like these snowmen here, these glass balls. And there were heads of every head of state. Everyone I needed! So I took them down to a bar, stuck them in. I put Castro in a bottle of rum and I put Khrushchev in a bottle of vodka and did this still life. But I have to tell you, it was the only difficult picture I had to take in this entire issue of *The New Yorker.*

STAMBERG: You said something so interesting about your gift being not to take pictures of inanimate objects, but instead to take pictures of very animate ones indeed: Marian Anderson, that classic photograph, her hair streaming across the side of the photograph; Marilyn Monroe; and the nude Nastassja Kinski wrapped in a python. Everybody who's ever looked at a poster in a college dormitory knows that photograph of yours. And you once said that a portrait photo session involves "unearned intimacy." I never forgot that and I wish you'd explain what you mean about it.

AVEDON: I think it's very much like what you and I are doing now. We don't know each other. You have your agenda. I have mine. You have the right to ask me anything you want. We're the same person, Susan. We use people to express ourselves. There is no question you can't ask me in the next few minutes that I won't have to respond to. The result will be two of us dealing with this unearned intimacy. If you came over to me at a party and asked me the kinds of questions you could ask me or are asking me now, I would either turn away, or say, "Are you an anchorlady, or what is this?" You know? This is not a normal conversation, Susan.

STAMBERG: Right.

AVEDON: I don't talk about myself. You don't go around interviewing people, I hope, at dinner. You must understand me perfectly. You cannot interview the Empire State Building, but you can interview me, and we both must have this feeling about other people.

STAMBERG: But in a photography session, people can just, as they can in an interview, be lied to. Well, so can you.

AVEDON: That's right.

STAMBERG: There at your camera.

AVEDON: If someone lies to me in front of my camera, I think that's interesting. I don't want to get through anything. I think a person who's lying is really interesting, much more interesting than some bore who tells the truth.

STAMBERG: Or the fact that he or she is lying then becomes who they are in your photograph.

AVEDON: That's right. And that's interesting. That doesn't mean it's the last word. My truth isn't anybody else's truth. It's just, at bottom, a way of expressing my feelings through them, writing my autobiography with other people's faces.

STAMBERG: A reviewer in *Newsweek* writes, "There is no repose in Avedon's photographs." Do you agree with that?

AVEDON: There is no repose in my life. I get up a quarter of six. I jump out of bed. I go for the coffee machine, do last night's dishes, and start taking notes, and I'm in a rage when, at seven-thirty, people aren't at the studio working. I think, Don't they know the meaning of work? That's my life.

The spy novelist and erstwhile spy JOHN LE CARRÉ talks with Neal Conan about spy fiction after the cold war, the retirement of his spy protagonist George Smiley, and the publication of *The Night Manager.* July 21, 1993

CONAN: I wonder about George Smiley. Do you miss him?

LE CARRÉ: No. I'm very fond of him, but it was time he went. We spent thirty years together, in one way or another, and as I get older, I find it a little more difficult to write about the aging process. I like to write about younger and more vigorous people, and Smiley was also my stalking horse all through the cold war, and as the cold war began to fizzle out, so I moved away from him both in mind and, almost, in affection.

CONAN: In some respects, your new book is a departure from your earlier work; in others, it's very much an extension. In particular, there's the familiar battleground of the intelligence bureaucracies among those you describe as the "espiocrats." There's a scene between two characters I was hoping you could read for us. It's a conversation between Rex Goodhew, who is essentially a cop, if I'm not going too far, and a lawyer named Palfrey, who's describing a rival organization in British intelligence, people he calls "cold heads" left over from the cold war.

LE CARRÉ: Palfrey's a character part, so I'm going to give him a slightly wheezy, drunken voice, all right? This is his reply. He's describing the secret services now.

"Not *bad* chaps, Rex. Mustn't be too critical. Just a bit marooned. No more Thatcher. No more Russian bear to fight, no more Reds under the bed at home. One day they've got the whole world carved up for them — two legs good, four bad. Next day they get up in the morning, they're sort of — well, *you* know. . . ." He finished his premise with a shrug. "Well, nobody likes a vacuum, do they? Not even you like a vacuum. Well, do you? Be honest. You hate it."

"By vacuum you mean peace?" Goodhew suggested, not wishing in the least to sound censorious.

"Boredom, really. Smallness. Never did anyone any good, did it?" Another giggle, another long drink from the cigarette. "Couple of years ago, they were topnotch Cold Warriors. Best seats in the club, all that. Hard to stop running, once you've been wound up like that. You keep going. Natural."

"So what are they now?"

Palfrey rubbed his nose with the back of his hand, as if to correct an itch. "Just a fly on the wall, really, me."

"I know that. What are *they*?"

Palfrey spoke vaguely, perhaps in order to detach himself from his own judgments. "Atlantic men. Never trusted Europe. Europe's a Babel, dominated by Krauts. America's still the only place for them. Washington's still their Rome, even if Caesar's a bit of a frost." He made an embarrassed writhe. "Global salvationists. Playing the world's game. World-order boys, having their shot at history and making a few bob on the side, why not? Everybody else does." Another writhe. "They've gone a bit rotten, that's all. . . ."

CONAN: I don't mean to give too much away, but they turn out to be awfully corrupt. Is this something that is real to you?

LE CARRÉ: I never mind too much about real. I'm interested in what is credible and not what is authentic, and my use of the secret world is really to illustrate the overt world, and I believe that we are going through a period of great moral decline and moral indirection following the anticommunist crusade. I believe that we've seen evidence in both our continents of enormous corruption in high places, which is usually the consequence of indifferent government, poor leadership, administrative chaos. That's when people begin to help themselves from the till. They set up conspiracies, monitoring ceases, and that kind of stuff. And since I see my secret world as being where the trench warfare of the real world is fought, and I use it for that purpose like Agatha Christie used her country houses, and so on. Therefore, yes, I think they're corrupt as hell.

CONAN: You use Orwell's phrase several times in the book — "Two legs bad, four legs good" — as sort of a shorthand for the moral black and white of the cold war. Where do we look for the points of the compass, the moral compass, then?

LE CARRÉ: That's exactly the point, and I'm grateful for the question. I mean, we are busy retooling our prejudices. I happen to believe that one of the explanations for the most virulent form of the politically correct movement is that we are somehow filling the vacuum left behind by the anticommunist crusade. We're using words as dogma, words to bully people with. We're using these neo–Marxist-Leninist precepts on the assumption that if people speak properly, they will think properly. It's actually a disgusting theory. It's not natural to our Western culture at all. It's one of the bits of detritus which we're dealing with after the cold war trauma has passed.

CONAN: I see a strain of Christianity running through a lot of your books. I wonder if you see that as a possible lodestone.

LE CARRÉ: I was brought up a Christian. I'm not one now, but I certainly think that there is a moral pulse running through the stuff. There is a moral concern in this book, *The Night Manager*. I think there is a real moral outrage about the misuse of power and about people who have been appointed to really important positions misusing the trust the public has invested in them.

CONAN: In a sense, it's also a book about accountability and the lack of same.

LE CARRÉ: Yes, it is. Of course, that's why the secret services and that whole secret world were so useful to me because it raised the question of how much you owe to Caesar and how much you owe to yourself. It also raised the question of how much you can do in the name of freedom and democracy, and remain a state which can still be dignified by those descriptions.

CONAN: I understand that you are now the subject of a couple of biographers who are researching your life for books. I wonder if you find this a comfortable position or not?

LE CARRÉ: I don't like the idea very much of being written about, for several reasons. First of all, I like to be an observer and a watcher, and I don't like the floodlights being turned upon me very much. The other reason is there are chunks of my life which I cannot describe. If I were writing my autobiography, I would have to avoid them.

CONAN: For professional — when you were in the —

LE CARRÉ: When I was a spook, yes. So I just prefer to keep away from it. I don't think it's necessary, and anybody, actually, who takes my novels one by one, and knows a little about me, would know that great chunks of them are very close to the bone anyway.

CONAN: I was going to say, anybody who does read those books —

LE CARRÉ: *A Perfect Spy* seemed to me to be quite a good fictional representation of large chunks of my life. I never betrayed my country at the Czech secret service, but there were other areas where it was very close to the truth. I felt that I had known the lash upon my own body of that world. I had been ambivalent, I had been a chameleon, I had wrestled with my personal morality; at other times, I had simply swept it aside and thought, Screw it. And, so, the variation which I hope people find in my novels is, in a sense, the reflection of my own concerns about the possibilities, negative and positive, of my own character.

The soul music legend CURTIS MAYFIELD talks with Neal Conan about his music and his career. A 1990 accident left him paralyzed from the neck down, when he was struck at a concert by a lighting truss blown free of its moorings. May 8, 1993

MAYFIELD: My first writings started out when I was in high school, a little song called "Little Young Lover." All of a sudden everything I observed and I felt personally, whatever it was around me, I could make into song. From a good conversation, I could find reasons to get a hook line or pull something out of it to create a song. It went on like that for years. I actually used to sleep with my guitar. Before I knew it, I was writing five or ten songs every couple of weeks.

CONAN: I think one of the amazing things about your career is the degree to which you've been a catalyst for other musicians and provided not only material for them to perform, but ways to perform. And I wanted to ask you about a couple of people, one of whom, of course, is Jerry Butler.

MAYFIELD: I met Jerry when I was singing gospel. We were known as the Northern Jubilees. Jerry and some of his family had come to my grandmother's church. I think we must have sang one or two songs, and Jerry come back to the house and asked if he could join the group. We later became the Impressions. In '58, after a couple of years of woodshedding, Jerry and the Brooks brothers wrote this song known as "For Your Precious Love." We performed it for V-J Records. Everything else is history. Without our knowing it, the record was released as *Jerry Butler and the Impressions*. And, of course, it created quite a trauma with all the fellas because, while we were very pleased to hear the first piece of music being aired, they would close out with, "That was Jerry Butler." And, of course, that didn't do too much for the group itself. However, these things, as you look back, were blessings in disguise. The Impressions actually are somewhat famous for having Jerry Butler and Leroy Hudson and of course myself. When Jerry moved on, this only allowed me and my soft voice to be introduced. I was quite a writer at that time, and we came back with "Gypsy Woman" and began to start up a string of hits for the Impressions. Incidentally, years later, I was in concert in Germany, and after the concert I was invited across the street to a restaurant where there was about fifty to sixty Gypsies. They were all sitting in a circle with their women in the middle. As I came in, they gave me a great standing ovation, and the gentlemen who were about my age, they said, "Curtis, we've been waiting for you for twenty years." All because of that song which lent a little bit of pride for them as youngsters.

CONAN: Jerry Butler as a lead singer in the Impressions made some sort of sense. He has got a very different voice from yours.

MAYFIELD: Yes.

CONAN: I've always wanted to know Major Lance, for whom you had a couple of monster hits and wrote a lot of material. His voice is very similar to yours. Why did you decide to make material available to him as well?

MAYFIELD: Major was a close friend of ours. He also came up in Cabrini Green [a low-income housing project in Chicago], so did Billy Butler and Ben Chatters. Major was never too great a singer, so we would use him as lead to help him. But of course, the Impressions and myself, you probably heard us quite fluently singing in the background.

CONAN: Right, filling in all those holes.

MAYFIELD: That's right. So, as a result, he had a very similar sound, but the type of song being up-tempo in "The Monkey Time" and "Hey Little Girl," it was just a different type style.

CONAN: You talk about those, you know, sort of teen love songs, the greatest one of which that Major did was "Um, um,um,um,um,um," a funny title and a very wry song.

MAYFIELD: Major had a thing about coming to my house, and he would say, "Give me — I want to hear all the songs you don't like, Curtis." He always knew that there was something for him, even though I wasn't even showing people the songs because I wasn't that fond of them. And this particular song, Major heard the song, and he said, "I want that one."

CONAN: You reached, I guess, a pinnacle of success in the early 1970s when you made a decision to go out on your own as a solo artist, keeping the Impressions intact as a group but without you in it.

MAYFIELD: My original decision was to stay home and become an executive or something. However, that just didn't work. I recorded an album known as *Curtis*, and this sort of pulled me right back out as an individual, which was a blessing. I've never been one really to sit in one room and do anything. There we were once again, off and running with a different sound, still recognized as *Curtis*, but with depth of lyrics and something a bit more timely, songs like "We People Who Are Darker Than Blue" and "If There's Hell Below, We're All Going to Go." Still inspirational, but less fake, too.

CONAN: Then you move on to probably the most controversial thing you ever did as a performer and as a composer, which was "Superfly." That caused a lot of people to question why you did that.

MAYFIELD: To me, my first thought was that it was a commercial for cocaine because of all this glitter. And they were snorting the stuff so much in the movie. So it made me want to write in depth about things, so that's how "Freddie's Dead" came about, who was basically a good guy but got caught up with the wrong people. I mean, I tried to write in such manners as to how you really see it in the streets. A lot of good people with good intentions are just pulled astray with the wrong people and get caught up. And they usually become the goat of the situation.

CONAN: Did you ever sit down, finish writing a song, and say, "That's a hit, I'll tell ya, that's a hit"?

MAYFIELD: I felt that way with "It's All Right," which was really the recording that brought the Impressions back to being visible. And it's funny how I wrote this song. We were in between concerts in Nashville, Tennessee, at a club there. And we were sitting out in our car in front of the place, just sort of getting in some fresh air, and for some reason I was just running off at the mouth, and Fred, he was saying, "Well, all right." And I'd say something else, and he'd say, "Well, that's all right." And I say something else, and he'd say, "It's all right." Before we got out of the car, I was saying, "Say it's all right." By the time we went back to prepare for the other show, I had written this song, and we were singing it. We could have gone out for the final show and sang "It's All Right."

CONAN: You told us earlier that you're not a man to spend his life in one room, and yet inevitably now, that's mostly what you do. Where do you go from here?

MAYFIELD: It's hard to say where I go from here when I must take it day by day. However, I still have dreams. I think I may be fortunate as to the times, because there are many computers and new items which are voice-activating. Hopefully I will bring these things into my life, and hopefully through that, maybe I'll be able to write again.

CONAN: Finally, you personally, are you OK? Do you hurt all the time?

MAYFIELD: I don't hurt all the time. I'm OK but I'm not OK because I have a spinal injury, which has left me totally paralyzed. I can only use and move my neck and my head, and it doesn't appear as though things are going to get any better. So what do you do? You live with it. Whatever comes, I'll face it.

The cartoonist CHARLES SCHULZ talks with Robert Siegel about the end of the world's longest losing streak, when Charlie Brown hits a home run and sends his team to victory. March 30, 1993

SCHULZ: He came home, and he is leaping up and down and turning cartwheels and everything, finally ending up at the front doorstep, and he tells his sister, Sally, that he hit a home run in the ninth inning. And he says, "We won! We won! And I was the hero." And she says, "You?" [*laughs*]

SIEGEL: [*laughs*] His incredulous sister doubts his version of this heroic accomplishment of his. What has happened? Now, give us a little context here. This is not Charlie Brown as we know him.

SCHULZ: I think it's important, when we talk about cartooning, that we remember, and I've said this many times and I've written about it, that cartooning is still drawing funny pictures. And I think, if cartoonists forget this, then they are doing a disservice to themselves, because this whole thing came about simply because I could visualize this long panel of Charlie Brown doing these cartwheels. From this came the idea, Well, why not let him win? Of course, you have to have a little punch line at the end, which is Sally saying, "You?"

SIEGEL: So you are saying that the idea of this wonderful panel of drawings of Charlie Brown doing cartwheels in the air and totally upside down, vertical, jumping up and down, that was appealing enough to you that the character development that you've been working on for decades could be compromised in the interests of one great panel?

SCHULZ: Of course, now I'm in my forty-third year of drawing this, and as the years go on, you develop a lot of themes and variations, and you're always trying to improve on them. I think your faithful readers love the various themes that you play. Schroeder's pianistic performances and Lucy's psychiatric booth, Snoopy being the World War I flying ace. These are all the themes that your faithful readers like to see. But then, of course, you have to try to make it better each time. Your variations have to get better. This is a difficult proposition. So it is from these drawings and, now, after I finished that drawing, then I had no idea what was going to happen next. But I think you'll be a little bit surprised at how he happened to hit the home run and who was doing the pitching when he hit the home run.

SIEGEL: Aha! So there are more surprises in store. This doesn't have to do with the fact that this is the week of April 1?

SCHULZ: No.

SIEGEL: No trick here.

SCHULZ: I wasn't even looking at the calendar when I drew it.

SIEGEL: It is to be believed explicitly?

SCHULZ: Absolutely.

SIEGEL: Now we will have the prismatic reconstruction of what actually happened in this story.

SCHULZ: I think it's a mistake to be unfaithful to your readers, always to be letting them down. In this case, it has just kind of a slightly unique little twist at the end, but he does keep the home run and his team did win the first game.

SIEGEL: Really? Is this a whole departure? Is he going to start kicking fifty-yard field goals and getting dates and winning at everything now and being a great success in the world?

SCHULZ: No, I think that we get back to another premise which is very important, and that is that you should never destroy these basic themes. I always compare it to the old Jack Benny character. He had to stay within that theme. I refer sometimes back to — you remember the *Li'l Abner* comic strip? Or are you too young?

SIEGEL: No. Alas, I'm not.

SCHULZ: Al Capp made a terrible mistake when he let Li'l Abner marry Daisy Mae. The bottom fell out of the strip from then on, and that was unfortunate. But Al simply gave in to public pressure, and I don't think you should do that. So Charlie Brown can never kick the football, and all of these other themes must stay intact, I believe.

SIEGEL: Just one home run he gets?

SCHULZ: [*laughs*] One home run. Well, that's not asking too much.

The Nobel laureate poet OCTAVIO PAZ discusses poetry, language, and his Indian and Spanish ancestry with Katie Davis, who interviewed him after attending, and recording, a reading of his poetry. May 2, 1993

DAVIS: As I watched you read poetry last night, while the English translations of the poems or the English originals were being read, you often had a smile on your face, and it seemed to me that you really enjoyed hearing the words. Do you like just hearing poetry?

PAZ: Yes, well, I like hearing poetry. And, in this particular case, I was amused in some way, and also surprised to hear the sound of those poems, because when I translated them I was reading them. For me they were characters on a page, silent characters, and now finally they have a voice.

DAVIS: When you write, are your poems usually characters on a page? Or do you ever find yourself speaking them out loud?

PAZ: Yes, many times is speaking loud. Or, more, is speaking silently. Poetry is basically in the prose. When you write prose, you write in the page. No? And you hear poetry before writing it, in some way. You compose it, in some way, well, silent but aloud. You are hearing with the mind, the sounds. This is the great difference between, I think, prose and poetry.

DAVIS: When do you think you began hearing poetry in your mind? Were you a young boy?

PAZ: I think, yes. It's not only poetry. I think everybody, when they are children, we hear sounds, and that is poetry. That's why everybody, in some way, is a poet. Because poetry is words, but words and sound. And before writing, it's more primitive than writing.

DAVIS: You have also said — I believe it was during your

address when you received the Nobel Prize — that you hear voices of the myths and gods and culture that existed before Spain came to the Americas. You hear the voices of pre-Columbian Mexico. You said that you not only hear those voices, but as a poet you must speak with them.

PAZ: In some way, the writer must speak with them, especially Latin American writers, especially writers of a country where the Indian past is still a presence, is still alive. The United States is very different. But, yes, in our countries, we must learn to hear this voice, the silent voices of the past.

DAVIS: What do they say to you? Do they say things to you, and when you sit down you write "Sun Stone" or "Piedra del Sol"?

PAZ: No, no. They speak really. They speak, first, in a different tongue, in a language. I can say sounds or signs, to be more accurate, that we must interpret, that is, that we must translate. Perhaps this translation is not a real translation. We are using them as mask for, say, the things that we want to say. There is a strange relationship between the tradition and the writer. In some way, the translation must be direct, if it is a translation of the same language. But since our culture is not only Mexican, but American — every culture is a composite of many other tongues, many other languages, for instance, Latin, Greek for us. Then we hear also this past and we must translate. We don't know, really, what is, they say, the Greek or the Roman poets or even Nahuatl, the Indian language. But we must translate it and, in some ways, they are using us to be alive again and we are using them to say what they want to say.

DAVIS: You speak about a mixture of cultures and, certainly, in your personal being there is that mix. Your mother was from Andalusia. Your father was Mexican, but had Indian heritage. How does that mix of culture and language affect your voice as a writer? And how does it affect your language? The actual use of the language?

PAZ: As a human being it affected me a lot, because when I was a child I came to the United States and I learned English,

then I forgot, then I learned again. Then it was very complicated, my childhood in Mexico. It was Mexican, but I was not
entirely Mexican. I was a Spaniard; I was not a Spaniard. I was
a kind of *gringo* because I was coming from California and
things like that, no? It has been rather difficult, too, to deal with
all these problems of origins and contradictory cultures inside
yourself. On the other hand, it has been very good for me. I
think it has saved me of nationalism. That, for me, is one of the
things. For me it is one of the sins of modern world — nationalism.

DAVIS: We are certainly seeing that now around the world, in
Bosnia, of course, and in the former Soviet Union.

PAZ: This is strange, no? All this modernity style with universal ideas, the French Revolution and the revolution of the
United States. All was mankind — reason, human rights, universal ideas. Then the Communists also started with these universal ideas and now the only thing alive is nationalism. It's
very scary.

DAVIS: You, early on in your career, wrote a book that is now
referred to as the guidebook to the Mexican character. I don't
know if you're comfortable with that description, but it is the
book *The Labyrinth of Solitude,* and in it, in a sense, you interpret Mexico and the Mexicans for Western people. I have two
questions about that. Is that a burden for you to have to explain
Mexico to other people? Isn't it just better for people to go there?

PAZ: I think it's better for people to go there. I didn't write a
book to explain to the others. I wrote the book to explain to
myself what kind of person was I. In some ways this book is not
a picture only of Mexicans but of myself.

DAVIS: In writing the book *The Labyrinth of Solitude,* do you
fully understand what it means to be Mexican, or is that something you're still trying to define? In your mind? That mix of
culture? The history of violence?

PAZ: It's a point of departure. It's a way to see, but you cannot
see everything. There always remains a mystery in each country, in each human being. No, it's impossible to say "every-

thing" happily. There is many things to discover, and then the countries and human beings change. Not so much as people think. I think they change very slow. We are used now to modernity and also change. The Americans, especially, they love change, but if you go to New York and Europe and look at a newspaper, you find, for instance, horoscopes, and that's very old. People still are believing in astrology. They believe many old things.

DAVIS: The United States and Mexico and Canada are negotiating a free-trade agreement. There is a lot of talk, especially in Mexico, a kind of fearful talk that, if this agreement is signed, that Mexican culture will be imperiled. What do you think about that?

PAZ: I don't think so. I think it is absolutely not. No, the culture will not be imperiled. If a culture is imperiled, it's because the culture is weak. After all, we are a weak country in the political and the economic sense. We have been neighbors since the beginning.

DAVIS: At certain times, Mexico has actually inhabited more parts of the United States.

PAZ: Not only that. In some moments, Mexico City was more important than Philadelphia or Boston or New York, as a city. But we have seen, in two centuries, this marvelous birth of United States, how it was born, how it developed and became a very powerful country, a world power, and, finally, the world power. We have seen it and we survived. Then, if we have survived this, we can survive the trade agreement. I am not afraid, no. I think the cultures are always breeding?

DAVIS: Interacting with other cultures?

PAZ: Yes. In biology and history, in everything. And then, in the country I am very glad that Mexicans can understand better the American civilization because it's a civilization. Also, perhaps, we can give something, some salt, some flavor to the Protestant culture.

DAVIS: How do you feel connected to your generation?

PAZ: In Mexico or in all over the world?

DAVIS: All over the world and in Mexico.

PAZ: In Mexico there has been sometimes a misunderstanding with my own generation. I have been a loner. I have been a critic of many attitudes — nationalism, Marxism, many things for my major point of view, diseases of the Mexican mind. Diseases of the American mind. But, on the other hand, I think it's very important for a writer to have contradiction, to have dialogue. If there is total agreement, it's death. Total agreement, even in love, is not very good. If a couple doesn't quarrel sometimes it's —

DAVIS: I'm turning and looking at Señora Paz, who is laughing.

PAZ: Don't you think so?

DAVIS: I do agree, actually.

PAZ: Life is contradiction. If you don't have contradiction, you are death.

The poet DONALD HALL's latest books are *Life Work,* a journal, and the poetry collection *The Museum of Clear Ideas.* He speaks with Noah Adams about poetry, depression, cancer, the deaths of friends, life with the poet Jane Kenyon, and his writing habits. November 26, 1993

ADAMS: You write about when you are really working on something like the poem "Another Elegy," waking up at two and three in the morning, looking at the clock and hoping for four-thirty A.M. to come so you can get up and write.

HALL: Well, I enjoy what I do. I am very fortunate that way. I love what I do. It's very exciting. Not always, of course, not uniformly, but I do like to work anyway. But there are times I can't wait to get to the desk and get on with something.

ADAMS: So what's the routine? You get up and make some coffee . . .

HALL: I get up and make some coffee and feed the cats. Then I run down to a local store and pick up a copy of the *Boston Globe.* I have an arrangement with the store. They don't open until six, bunch of slugabeds. But I come back with the *Globe* and I wake up while drinking coffee, having breakfast, reading the *Globe,* and then I go into my study and get to work. Actually, the first thing I do when I come back, before I read the paper, is take a cup of coffee in to Jane. She sleeps a little later than me, but not a whole lot, and for her to wake up to the smell of coffee beside the bed, she thinks that's bliss.

ADAMS: Have you always worked that early in the morning?

HALL: Well, during the good parts of my life. There was a patch in my life, in midlife, where things went very bad. I remember thinking at the time, Oh well, you've been scheduled all of your life, why schedule now? And I went off of it. But I just went off of everything, and I didn't write much. I went through two years where I didn't write poetry at all. I was able to write some prose. I wrote a play, but I couldn't write poems. And of course poems are the most important. So I was punishing myself by refraining from what I loved most.

ADAMS: A time of depression?

HALL: Yes, I was depressed for quite a while.

ADAMS: I wonder if anyone has written poetry while depressed.

HALL: A lot of poetry is written, I think, when the poet is coming out of the depression, possibly even into mania, but remembering depression. A lot of poetry is about dealing with depression. It deals with it by expressing it, by sharing it. You're not the only one in the world who feels bad, who laments, who loses, and so on. Jane has a poem called "Having It Out with Melancholy" in her new book called *Constance* that has had an incredible response because it's a whole poem about depression. She is manic-depressive, but in effect, almost entirely depressive. Few manic episodes. And she has written out of this. I have watched her. I am quite bipolar. My lows have not been so low as some of Jane's have. After we moved here, after I wrote *Kicking the Leaves*, I went through a kind of mild, six-year depression, where I wasn't extremely miserable and I wasn't, you know, suicidal for heaven's sake or anything, but I worked every day. This must be an exaggeration, but it doesn't feel like one. I worked every day on my work without feeling that it was any good, and then toward the end of this period, things began to fall together, and I came up in general mood, and I found the missing words for poems I had been working on five or six years that tied them together.

ADAMS: Really.

HALL: The inspiration came at the end, not at the beginning. I think in my poem about cows, "Great Day in the Cows' House," which I like a lot now and like to read. I like to read it partly because I get to moo like a cow.

ADAMS: Yes, there are good sounds in it.

HALL: But that poem was just dead meat for five years, and then I don't think it is now, and I still like it quite a few years later.

ADAMS: This poem makes me just grin to read it.

HALL: Here we go. "Great Day in the Cows' House."

In the dark tie-up, seven huge Holsteins
lower their heads to feed, chained loosely to old saplings
with whitewashed bark still on them.
They are long dead; they survive, in the great day
that cancels the successiveness of creatures.
Now she stretches her wrinkly neck, her turnip eye
rolls in her skull, she sucks up breath,
and stretching her long mouth mid-chew
she expels: *mm-mmm-mmmmm-mmmmmmmm-
ugghwanchhh.*
— Sweet bellowers enormous and interchangeable,
your dolorous ululations
swell out barnsides, fill spaces inside haymows,
resound down valleys. Moos of revenant cattle
shake ancient timbers and timbers still damp with sap.

That's the first part of the poem.

ADAMS: You write about Henry Moore, the sculptor, meeting him and talking to him. And he said, the secret of life is to have a task. Something you devote your entire life to every minute of the day for your whole life. And the most important thing was, and this is what surprised me, because that is ordinary — it must be something you cannot possibly do.

HALL: That's the kicker. He was a wonderful man and a good talker. He was incredibly articulate. I wrote down at one point a longer version of that and he went on to emphasize that the most important thing is that you cannot possibly do it. And he knew that is where he was going to end up.

ADAMS: Was he exaggerating when he said that?

HALL: Well, no. Because his desire was for something he couldn't possibly know. That is, he wanted to know that he was better than Donatello, Michelangelo, that his work was the greatest sculpture ever made. And you may follow that as your task, but it's not something you can possibly know. And, when you finish the work, finally, and you've spent a lot of time going back to it, day after day, making little tiny changes, tiny changes. Finally it goes off to the bronze founder and then you see it and you see this is pretty good, but that's not quite as great as I intended it to be. I can't find out from this piece that I am better than Donatello and Michelangelo. I will try with the next piece.

ADAMS: But you have said that you really would like to write the greatest poem in the world.

HALL: I am not telling you that I think it's probable. I do see or meet a lot of people who seem to me to be satisfied with small triumphs. With publishing a poem in a magazine, or publishing a poem in a particular magazine, or winning a prize, or this and that. These seem to me ambitions that are much too modest. By having great ambitions you say nothing whatsoever about your ability to accomplish the great ambition, but it's possible that if I want to suggest that if you try merely to be good, you are less likely to be good than if you try to be great.

ADAMS: I want to ask about "Another Elegy," which is quite a long poem, in memory of William Trout. It took something like six hundred drafts over a period of ten or eleven years?

HALL: Right. "Another Elegy" started as an elegy for one poet, for my dear friend James Wright. For many years I tried to write it as an elegy for him. There is Jim Wright in this William Trout figure, but not only him. There is also Ray Carver, who was a bit younger than me, and whom I knew well and was very fond of. And there was John Logan, there was Dick Hugo. Then there are also the living in there. There is a bit of Galway Kinnell, who is a dear friend, in there. There is Robert Bly and Louis Simpson. Robert Bly is my oldest friend, and Louis is very close. And there is certainly me in that as well, finally. I had him come from Pocatello in Idaho. Simply, I like the town. I've been there a few times. I have a friend there I particularly like.

Idaho made him, Pocatello of hobos and freightyards —
clangor of iron, fetor of coalsmoke. With his brothers
he listened for the Mountain Bluebird as he dropped worms
into the Snake River, harvesting catfish for a Saturday
supper in the nineteen thirties.
    Two sisters of the Sacred Heart
cossetted him when he strayed from the boys' flock
to scan the unchanging dactyls of Ovid. Landowska set out
the Goldberg Variations on a hand-wound Victrola.

When he was fifteen he stayed home from fishing to number
feet that promenaded to a Union Pacific tune, ABAB
pentameters. At the university his teacher the disappointed
novelist nodded his head — in admiration, envy, and pity —
while Bill sat late at a yellow dormitory desk, daydreaming
that his poems lifted through night sky to become stars
fixed in heaven, as Keats's poems rose from Hampstead
lanes and talks with Hunt and Haydon.

ADAMS: I would like you to read from the middle of the
poem.

HALL:

    But the maker of bronzes
dies decapitated in the carwreck; the whitefaced mime
dozes tied to the wheelchair; the saint babbles and drools;
carcinoma refines chemist, farmer, wino, professor, poet,
imbecile, and banker into a passion of three nerves
and a feeding tube.
    At the Bayside Hospice Bill's body
heaved as it worked for air; IVs dripped; bloody phlegm
boiled from the hole punched like a grommet in his throat.

ADAMS: Goodness, that is bleak.

HALL: Yes, it is bleak. It is a bleak thought of aging and
disease that I am afraid is a human necessity. It is not the last
word, but it is a word that I speak of in the first part of this
poem.

ADAMS: In general terms, do you think it is necessary that
there be this much pain in a poet's life?

HALL: I think that there is pain in everybody's life, not just poets' lives. I see it everywhere. It's not constant, it's intermittent. Poets tend to be very up and very down, very joyous and very depressed. Wordsworth wrote the couplet, "We poets in our youth begin in gladness; but thereof come in the end despondency and madness." If you write poems that embody the range of human emotion, you cannot turn the volume down. When there is a sufficiency of cause, poets must not turn their eyes away or plug their ears, but listen to it all, feel it all in order to render it all.

ADAMS: May I tell you the significant paragraphs for me from your new book *Life Work*?

HALL: Yes.

ADAMS: The first one is the one that makes me truly happy. "On this best day Jane is home and I have no errands. We wake from our naps at the same time, and by earlier agreement know what we will do next. How nice to be old enough, living together, and alone, to make love in daylight with no more precaution than taking the phone off the hook."

HALL: [*laughs*] I enjoyed writing that too. Thank you. You know that it's amusing now when people call me up and they say, "Well, your phone was busy half an hour ago." They snicker. The phone is busy more often than we're up to that, I should say.

ADAMS: And elsewhere you have talked about "endorphins followed by endearments."

HALL: Right.

ADAMS: The saddest part for me was the paragraph that begins "Two and one half years ago I lost half my colon to a carcinoma. When I learned of my illness I wept for myself and for my old mother, for my children and grandchildren, and for Jane. And I wept to think that I would have to stop working." When that happened, did you ever think about not writing about that part of your life?

HALL: When I became sick with cancer the first time, and then the second time, I didn't think about it. It wasn't an issue not to speak of it. I didn't hire space in the paper and write about it, but I sat down at my desk, and lines of poetry came, or this book, *Life Work,* was already started. Lines of prose came in about my illness. And perhaps I'm insufficiently private, but I can only say that I don't feel as if I had a choice. That in order to deal with it for myself, I had to deal with it in the public way of language. Of course, at the time, I wrote pieces in which I did not refer to it, but during the same day, I was dealing with it by writing about it in other forms. That freed me, then, at other moments, to write without reference to it. I speak of the time, say before the operation, or when I began to write again afterwards. And I am thinking now of the second one, which was a little more dire than the first one. The first seemed dire enough at the time.

ADAMS: Oh, I bet.

HALL: But the second one was losing two-thirds of my liver, which is a big organ. And I feel fine right now. I feel wonderful. My tests are good. It's encouraging. I know perfectly well with my head that next month I could have a bad test and be on the way out, but I tell you, I don't feel that way. I feel very good, and I feel I'm not obsessing about my illness or approaching death now. I feel good.

The poet MAY SARTON talks with Katie Davis about her life, her work, her cat, and her new book *Journal of a Solitude*, in which she explains her visceral need to have solitude. In her last journal, the one she kept when she was eighty, May Sarton chronicled her struggle with illness and frailty. October 3, 1993

SARTON: My doctor said, "Why don't you just stop, May, and don't you think you've had enough." He said, "You'll never be well, you're eighty-one. So why don't you just, more or less, give up." Well, at that point, the next day I started a new journal. I was so angry, and so upset. It was a death sentence, and I wasn't going to have it. So that is why I'm doing another. It doesn't matter if it's never published. What the journal does is make you see what is really happening to you, and to some extent, in my case, I think it's actually made me do certain things on a certain day because of the journal.

DAVIS: It shapes your life in a certain way.

SARTON: Yes, in a way it does, and reading also. Many people tell me that they get the books that I recommend, and that that's meant a great deal to them, and so I don't read anything much that I'd feel would be of no use to people. I don't mean books of how-to, of course.

DAVIS: Not self-help books.

SARTON: I can't stand self-help books.

DAVIS: You have said before that writing your journal helps you live more intensely.

SARTON: Absolutely. It's true. Partly you are trying to find words for things, a certain light or whatever it may be, or a certain drawer. It's a terrible deprivation for me that I can't garden because writing is very intense and you're tired at the end of a morning's work, very tired, and if I could go out in the garden after my rest in the afternoon, get my hands in the earth, I immediately felt happy, relaxed, all the tension gone. Now I can't do that.

DAVIS: You have said before, "It's like cleansing yourself of your anguish. I can go out in the garden and work my anguish out."

SARTON: That's true, and anger too.

DAVIS: It's also time to reflect.

SARTON: Yes.

DAVIS: I would like to ask you to read from your first published journal, *Journal of a Solitude.*

SARTON: I think it's the best.

DAVIS: This first paragraph right here.

September 15th:
   Begin here. It is raining. I look out on the maple, where a few leaves have turned yellow, and listen to Punch, the parrot, talking to himself and to the rain ticking gently against the windows. I am here alone for the first time in weeks, to take up my "real" life again at last. That is what is strange — that friends, even passionate love, are not my real life, unless there is time alone in which to explore and to discover what is happening or has happened. Without the interruptions, nourishing and maddening, this life would become arid. Yet I taste it fully only when I am alone here and "the house and I resume old conversations."

That last line is a quote from a poem, of course. Yes, I think it was a good beginning.

DAVIS: You talk about solitude with such relish, and yet there have been times when the solitude —

SARTON: Becomes loneliness. Yes, I have said it somewhere that solitude is the richness of self, and loneliness is the poverty of self. There are times, of course, when you have a bad time with one thing or another, a bad relationship or a terrible disappointment of some kind in your work or anything else, and there are times when I've been lonely here, but very rarely, I must say. Partly because I have a cat, of course. A magnificent

Himalayan called Piero, and without him I couldn't live here. I have to have an animal.

DAVIS: You said, very recently, that your cat is the reason that you're still writing.

SARTON: Yes, that's true.

DAVIS: I would like to know why.

SARTON: Well, it's now ceased to last. It was that he, at about one in the morning, had to come in. He'd be out, you see they're nocturnal animals, cats, as you know. So he always goes out. Then I would hear this loud desperate mewing at the door. So I would have to wake up and try to go down the stairs without falling, with my eyes closed, and get him in. Then I was wide awake. And lines of poems began to run through my head. So I would make notes, and then the next day I would write the poem. So there is a whole book of poems that should be dedicated to Piero.

DAVIS: Why isn't it?

SARTON: Maybe it will be. I haven't decided yet.

DAVIS: Oh, this is the one that's coming.

SARTON: Yes, it will be next year. But now a dear friend has made a cat door for him. So this doesn't happen anymore, because he comes in and out of his own accord.

DAVIS: You have lost your muse, you said?

SARTON: I have lost my mews, actually. Mews is spelled m-e-w-s as well as m-u-s-e.

DAVIS: [*laughs*] I would like to ask you to read another of your poems. This is a shorter one.

SARTON: "A Light Left On." This is for Judy.

> In the evening we came back
> Into our yellow room,
> For a moment taken aback
> To find the light left on,
> Falling on silent flowers,
> Table, book, empty chair,
> While we had gone elsewhere,
> Had been away for hours.

> When we came home together
> We found the inside weather.
> All of our love unended
> The quiet light demanded,
> And we gave in a look at
> Yellow walls and open book,
> The deepest world we share
> And do not talk about
> But have to have, was there,
> And by that light found out.

I still like that poem.

DAVIS: It's beautiful. When you finish a poem like that, what kind of feeling do you have?

SARTON: I have a feeling of joy. Writing poetry is the thing I'm really meant to do, and that's what I am is a poet. Everything else doesn't matter compared to the poetry. If I were in solitary confinement, I would write poems, but I wouldn't write novels, and I wouldn't keep a journal.

DAVIS: You've written several times that you would like to die before you're eighty-five.

SARTON: Oh yes.

DAVIS: You seem to be marking that as a date.

SARTON: I sometimes feel, Hurry up, Sarton, what's keeping you? Because Margot Peters's book will not come out until I'm dead. That's in the contract.

DAVIS: That's the biography.

SARTON: That was by my wish and hers. There will be tons of letters. There is no doubt that there will be a great deal after I die.

DAVIS: But it's not as if you don't already have a wonderful body of work.

SARTON: But I am hoping that the serious critics will come along. There are, now, two books by university presses of critical essays on my work, and this I've waited for a long time, and I'm very happy about it.

DAVIS: It has bothered you sometimes, the reaction of critics to your work.

SARTON: Oh, very much so.

DAVIS: One, I'm thinking of, you reacted to a review, and you wrote about it in *Journal of a Solitude*. It devastated you. You went into a bad depression.

SARTON: I will tell you what it was. It was the first *Collected Poems*, four books were collected, and Karl Shapiro, who then had a big name, wrote in the Sunday *Times* and I read it on Christmas Eve. I was living with Judy then. It began, "May Sarton is a bad poet." And it ended, "I'm sorry to have to do this."

DAVIS: It was scathing.

SARTON: Listen, I wasn't wrong to mind. The *Times* has not reviewed a book of poems of mine since. Thirty years. He killed it for thirty years. You see, it matters. You can't help it. People say, "Why do you pay attention?" Why do you pay attention? Because books have to sell. And if somebody says it's bad it won't sell. And not only that, it meant I wasn't in the anthologies. That stuck to me forever. He is dead now and more people read me than ever read him, but the critics still maybe not. I do feel very bitterly. I have reason to. I really do. Partly it's that I am a lesbian, and partly it's that I'm a woman. It's a man's world. The poetry establishment is very much a man's world, I think.

DAVIS: I would, actually, like to ask you to read one more poem, "Now I Become Myself."

SARTON: I have got to get into a position where I have a lot of breath for this.

> Now I become myself. It's taken
> Time, many years and places;
> I have been dissolved and shaken,
> Worn other people's faces,
> Run madly, as if Time were there,
> Terribly old, crying a warning,

"Hurry, you'll be dead before — "
(What? Before you reach the morning?
Or the end of the poem is clear?
Or love safe in the walled city?)
Now to stand still, to be here.
Feel my own weight and density!
The black shadow on the paper
Is my hand; the shadow of a word
As thought shapes the shaper
Falls heavy on the page, is heard.
All fuses now, falls into place
From wish to action, word to silence,
My work, my love, my time, my face
Gathered into one intense
Gesture of growing like a plant.
As slowly as the ripening fruit
Fertile, detached, and always spent,
Falls but does not exhaust the root,
So all the poem is, can give,
Grows in me to become the song,
Made so and rooted so my love.
Now there is time and Time is young.
O, in this single hour I live
All of myself and do not move.
I, the pursued, who madly ran,
Stand still, stand still, and stop the sun!

....

The poet JIMMY SANTIAGO BACA speaks with Katie
Davis about his home in South Valley, New Mexico,
his poetry, and the profound effect jail had in shaping
his life as a writer. June 5, 1993

BACA: I have been thinking about my house today and the
peace I've created here and the violence that forged this peace.
And I was thinking about how prison played a part. Why did
I come here? Why did I pick this spot? Why did I refuse to
have them cut the trees down [around my house]? And I
realize in a lot of poems that I have, in every single poem, in
every stanza and every line, it's like a bar, a prison bar, and
I've overlaid the prison bar with the ivy of my poetry because you never forget it. I was thinking how if I described
the snow, I would be describing the snow with the language
of iron, and with the language of concrete, and with the language of being oppressed. And it makes it a political poem, in-
herently, although it's not. I was thinking about that all day
today.

DAVIS: Do you try to forget the people you knew in prison?

BACA: No. I saw many of them stand in line and die, very
young. And I saw many of them who had been in prison twenty-
five years who had been slaughtered.

DAVIS: Literally?

BACA: Literally slaughtered, yes. Piranha knives taken to
them or beaten by guards and dragged and buried in the back.
I've had a hard time dealing with that because I was out on the
mesas the other day and I was thinking about how I always
want to progress? I was on the mesas, running, and I looked up
and I saw a hawk and it was caught in an updraft and it was
flying backwards. It wasn't going forward, and I thought to myself, Well, that's good. It was a symbol for me that I can go back

and still fly. I don't have to go back. When I record something,
I don't have to go back and think it's a regression. I can still fly
backwards.

DAVIS: You are making me think of a poem you wrote that
was in your book *Black Mesa Poems.* I don't know if you would
want to read "Tomás Lucero."

BACA: "Tomás Lucero," yes. This is a very interesting poem
that you picked. You don't know the personal history of this
poem. This poem is entitled "Tomás Lucero," and it is from
Black Mesa Poems.

I wept when the police escorted you to the train.
For years, when the train darkly whipped across the *llano*
at midnight, shuddering my cot, the trembling ground
was your voice still the morning your brother
killed in your yard by the police.
I wept when your small son was engulfed in a blast of steam,
as the Santa Fe train chugged off he stood there,
choking, breast heaving with tears, a dark small shadow
in ghostly smoke.

You have given me hope, Tomás,
I knew you were not a strong man. When you knelt
clutching your bloody brother in your front yard,
across from my house I saw
how you wept, begging the blood back, the bullet holes healed,
the terrible nightmare erased. The dark cloudy
features of your face were an omen —
        you looked up at the policeman,
        took your brother's gun and shot him —
because of that one tragic moment
you had to become who you are not.
Sniff air, a hunted coyote,
try to charm the moon —
now hunted, you held alien weight of your brother's gun
in your hands
instead of your son's little body,
now earth became your bed, *arroyos* your paths,

instead of your wife's arms,
now you rest on canyon rockrim that overlooks
Estancia, Tajíque and Willard.
You must have wept for a return, to just sit on your porch,
watch your children playing in the yard
as you scold your oldest son for trampling chile plants
in the garden.

We sent you food, and every day
I have walked to your house to see how your family is doing.
When the police came to ask of you,
our silence asked them to leave our yard.
When you were finally caught,
I looked into your son's face,
watching you embark the train for prison.
I saw the most beautiful, inexpressible love and adoration
burst over and effuse his sorrowful face.
And then months after, a mysterious nobility
filled his eyes, two dark wounds bleeding your image
on everything they looked on —
Never have I seen anything as beautiful, Tomás,
as your son who is becoming a man.

DAVIS: You have said before, and this really is striking, that
poetry prepares you for a spiritual quest, to get you close to God,
and that fiction doesn't, fiction is irreligious. But there is something about poetry that is very spiritual.

BACA: Poetry puts you back on the footing with the first
people who stepped on earth. Those people who were the first
human beings must have believed that all things were God.
When I write, I could be in a boxcar like the Mexicans who
come to this country, and I would probably be etching a poem
with a nail on the hot iron boxcar from the inside to describe
what we were there for, and it would be speaking to God. It's a
funny thing. In unequivocal terms I can say that I would not be
here talking to you had it not been for poetry because I would
have become a warrior. There were many times in prison when

I had to choose between *el filero*, [the shank] and my pencil and paper. Almost every single time I had to go back imploding and take up the pen and pencil and I had to write. I had to find another way because I knew that what I was seeing and experiencing and sensing was not right. The carnage of what blacks do to blacks and whites to blacks and blacks to whites and Chicanos to Indians, what we all do to each other. I knew that there had to be some other way. If it meant becoming the pariah, I would do it.

DAVIS: Were you mocked when you began writing in prison?

BACA: You have to understand that to this day, my sister considers bookstores to be enemy territory because we were taught not to go into bookstores and that they were not for us. We passed fields with people working in cotton, tomatoes, and avocados, and yet we would stand there and look at them because they would tell us that's where we were going to go one day. So we were taught that was the place.

DAVIS: She won't go in because she feels that she wouldn't be welcome there?

BACA: Here's the thing. You're taught from birth that books are not for you. There's no books in your house except the Bible. Books are very alien. You go around bookstores, you don't go in them. I never thought I would be a writer. But when I found myself loving books more than I love my own life, that I would actually find myself, that I would give my life for a book, I celebrated that in the dance of surrender. I really went into this crazy dance and song. The convicts would say, "Jesus Christ, the guy is crazy, man. Leave him alone." So my love for books, in some ways, saved my life. When they came up to me, and I would ask them, "but have you read this?" They would all look at me with eyes saying "What?" And I would say, "I am asking you, have you read this?" I was totally naked and I meant every word of it. I loved it so much. All of us talked, the Polish writers [I was reading], the African writers [I was reading]. I would ask, "How could you write that?" or "God, what an incredible line." The people there next to me in the cell would say, "Who's in there with you?" And I would say, "Everybody is in here with me." So I became known as somewhat of a nut. The other side of that coin is when you do you become literate then you have to go on this other journey of recreating yourself by pulling in all the roots that are dangling. Somehow weeding all of that into this extraordinary emotional mosaic, so that when you speak you carry your own voice, not the voice of someone else.

DAVIS: Finding your voice, that was a sort of epic struggle.

BACA: It really was. I can remember as a little minnow poet, writing everybody, "Can you please help me?" but getting no letters back. And the only letters that I did get from people were "You have to write like me." I would say, "I can't write like you."

DAVIS: But somebody wrote you back. You're making me think of another poem. Maybe you could just read a little bit of "It Started." This is when you were first beginning to write poetry, perhaps you were even still in prison when you wrote it.

BACA: I wrote this when I was in prison. But let me just tell you very briefly what happened. I went to prison, seven and a half years, the whole thing, for possession with the intent to sell drugs. I had marijuana, heroin, and all that. I wasn't selling it. I never sold it. I was always using it for my own purposes. I never sold it, but they caught the guy in front of me, Mr. McKinney, for the third time with about five kilos of heroin. He told me don't worry about it. When he went up in front of the judge, they let him go. I thought, Well, I got it made because I wasn't even selling, I was just within three hundred yards of the commission of a crime. They had arrested all the people in that area. So I figured I had nothing to worry about. I got fifty years in a maximum-security prison. No parole board. Nothing. I knew that he had just given me the death sentence and I was only eighteen years old. I couldn't read or write. And I thought, Why, why? So my thing was to try to learn how to read and write to figure out why he did that. I wanted to know why. I went there, I went in front of a thing called the reclassification committee and I told them to please let me go to school. They said, "You got it. Two months in the kitchen, washing dishes, and then you go to school to the GED." I was happy because I was going to get to learn how to read and write. So I went to the kitchen for two months and went back to the reclassification committee and I was really pumped. This guy stood up and yelled at me and cursed at me and said, "What do you think this is? Tomorrow morning you're up at five and you go to the fields." That's when I said I'll never work for you again ever. They had to carry me out of the room because I refused ever to work for the prison system again. Consequently, I was put in the dungeon for years and years and years.

DAVIS: Solitary confinement.

BACA: All of that stuff went on. I got electroshock there, beatings, all that stuff. They burned all my stuff. They did everything. The warden said, "This is mine. You're mine. I'm going to break you. You're going to die." I really thought I was. So that's where this poem comes from. I was working in my cell, about two years after I learned how to read and write, and I wrote this one. It's called "It Started."

A little state-funded barrack
in the desert, in a prison. A poetry workshop,
an epicenter of originality, companionship,
pain, and openness.

For some,
the first time in their life writing,
for others the first time saying openly what they felt,
the first time finding something in themselves,
worthwhile, ugly and beautiful.
I think of you and me. Last night I was
thinking of you. I am your friend. I don't want you
to think otherwise.
I was thinking, when we first wrote to each other.
I remember instances, of tremendous joy
when receiving your letters,

what cells I was in,
what emotional state, under
what circumstances.
Your letters always fell like meteorites
into my lap.
You were my first friendship
engendered in this state, perhaps,
all my past life.
I showed you my first poem ever written,
  "They Only Came to See the Zoo"
But you didn't treat me like a wild ape
or an elephant, you treated me like Jimmy.
And who was Jimmy?
A mass of molten fury in this furnace of steel,
and yet, my thoughts became ladles, sifting carefully
through my life, the pain and endurance,
to the essence of my being,
    I gently, into the long night, unmolding
    my shielded heart, the fierce figures
    of war and loss, I remolding them,
    my despair and anger into a cry and a song,
I took the path alone, nuded myself to my own caged animals,
and learned their tongues and learned their spirits,
and roamed the desert, went to my place of birth . . .
    Now tonight, I am the burning bush,
    my bones a grill of fire,
    I burn these words in praise,
    of our meeting, our friendship.

I hadn't read that in so long. It has been ten or fifteen years since
I read that. That's amazing. I love that.

DAVIS: What do you think the fact that you came to writing
late, literally writing late, has done or does to your use of language, the way you hear things and the way you use words?

BACA: This is interesting because I was learning how to read
and write. I was learning and I was using language because I
wanted to make an epitaph for myself. I wanted to tell the world
I had been here.

DAVIS: Because you were so sure you were going to die.

BACA: I was going to die every day. I got shot, I got stabbed, whatever. But I was sure that I was going to die. I knew I was, it was just there. And I had to tell somebody that I was here, and that this was happening. If I could just write a letter to the world and then die that would have been cool. But I couldn't leave this world without anybody knowing I was here. It's a horrible thing. It's unthinkable to come to a universe, to live as a human being, and then to die and not have anyone ever know you were there. It's hard to comprehend that. When I started to write in my journal *Immigrants in Our Own Land*, those were not really poems as much as they were journal entries, and I was saying that if I die, you will find this in my box and this will explain who I am. That's all I wanted. I had no idea I was going to be a poet. I had no idea I was ever going to be published. This is just who I am.

DAVIS: *Yo existo.*

BACA: *Sí. Yo existo, aquí.* It's what I want to do. On the other hand, everybody else around me couldn't read or write. So they were coming up to me, "Crazy one. You were the craziness. Could you write my mother a letter?" I'd say yes, but he gave me two packs of cigarettes. I'd write him a letter and he would read it and this man who was the most feared in society and he would start to weep. I'd see the power of "Hey, man, I've got this girl in Georgia, man, could you write her a letter 'cause I want her to come visit me, but I don't know how to tell her." I'd say, "Don't worry about it," and two weeks later she's visiting.

DAVIS: You became the place's scribe.

BACA: Yes. There were a lot of blacks, a lot of Chicanos. It was like a country without rich Anglo people. So I became a scribe. It's no big deal. I wasn't sitting negotiating in New York, saying, "All right, when do you want your foreign rights, kid? I'll tell you what, I'll soft-cover, we're gonna go two and a half percent." There was none of that. I'd say, "You give me a box of pencils, I'll write you the poem for your girlfriend." And what happened to me was the people that wanted to beat me up were then coming up to me, saying, "Hey, you know what, man? You're all right, you're a clean dude, man." They became my friends. Ultimately, I became the spokesman and leader for those very people who said I was a coward because I didn't want to work. I became, after five years, their leader. They would come to me, and say, "Santiago, would you please lead the food strike tomorrow?" And I said, "Yeah, it would be an honor," and I saw what language could do.

The poet KATHA POLLITT talks, tongue in cheek,
with Linda Wertheimer about what it takes to be a great
and frequently anthologized poet. For *The New Yorker*
Pollitt reviewed *The Top 500 Poems*, a volume
edited by William Harmon, which identifies the most
anthologized poems in English. February 18, 1993

POLLITT: The first thing you have to do is have the right name. Now, it turns out that the best name to have is William. Of the poets who have published ten or more poems apiece in this grand contest, fully one-third are named William. And amazingly, this same preponderance of Williams holds through throughout the entire volume. So, clearly, if your name is not William, it must become William.

WERTHEIMER: William Butler Yeats, William Wordsworth, William Shakespeare.

POLLITT: William Blake.

WERTHEIMER: William Blake.

POLLITT: Yes, a very important William.

WERTHEIMER: The number-one poem is William Blake.

POLLITT: That's right.

WERTHEIMER: "Tyger! Tyger! burning bright in the forests of the night." So, OK, you are a poet named Bill.

POLLITT: Yes, and it helps to be sir. Sir William is good. That's my name now.

WERTHEIMER: [*laughs*] The other thing that you suggest is that the poem be short.

POLLITT: Very short. Think of it, the first poem, "The Tyger" by Blake, twenty-four lines but four of them are repetitions. So it's really twenty lines plus one-word-long. That's very good. It's like a memo. It should be short. It should be terse. You don't want to tax your busy reader's time or patience.

WERTHEIMER: So, good to be William, good to be short, good to be dead.

POLLITT: Very good to be dead. There are very few living poets in this volume. The youngest poet, actually, is Sylvia Plath, who is very dead indeed. And the next youngest poet, born in 1926, which is amazing to think of, is Allen Ginsberg. Now, of course, Allen Ginsberg is famous for "Howl," a very long, very wonderful poem, but he is represented here by a poem called, "A Supermarket in California," which has the primary virtue: it's short.

WERTHEIMER: I see, yes. OK then, you suggest that in looking at all these poems, you find that there are successful themes that work for being the top five hundred poems.

POLLITT: Yes, there are four successful themes. They are sex, death, poetry, and imaginary girlfriends. The amazing thing is that almost any combination of these four very powerful themes will work. So you could write a poem in which you could explain to your imaginary girlfriend why she should have sex with you before you both die, and then you get "To His Coy Mistress" by Andrew Marvell. You could explain why she should make love with you before you get too old for her, and then you get the top-rated Shakespeare sonnet, number seventy-three, "That time of year thou mayst in me behold." Beautiful sonnet.

WERTHEIMER: "When yellow leaves, or none, or few, do hang upon those boughs. . . ." That is a beautiful one.

POLLITT: That's right.

WERTHEIMER: The perfect poem to get into this anthology that you are planning to write, Sir William Pollitt, is?

POLLITT: Well, I am going to write one of two poems, and it's based on my analysis of the most popular images, settings, occasions, and seasons, and weather that occur in English and American poetry. So my poem is going to be called, "On Glimpsing a Snowy Owl at Midnight While Laying a Daffodil on Lincoln's Grave." And the other poem I am going to write draws on the fact that the most popular linguistic variation or dialect besides standard English is Scots. It's very good to write in the Scots dialect if you wish to be immortal. And my other poem is going to be called, "Wha' Bonny Spider Springs Along the Beach." It will be twenty lines long, maybe nineteen. Maybe I will put in some repetition so it will seem more like Blake or Frost, and I will send it out as Sir William Pollitt, and I think I will be in the next edition.

TELEVISION, RADIO, AND FILM

CARL REINER talks with Susan Stamberg about the two loves of his life: his wife, Estelle, and comedy, as well as his first novel, *All Kinds of Love.*
April 17, 1993

STAMBERG: Would you tell me please what a seventy-one-year-old family man like yourself is doing writing lesbian love scenes?

REINER: Well, there are also regular love scenes. There are nymphomaniacal love scenes, there are parental love scenes, there are grandparental love scenes, there are juvenile love scenes with older women, there are many kinds of love scenes. It intrigued me, and I searched into the corners, the crevices, of my mind, and I have wanted to know about that so I told myself about it and wrote about it.

STAMBERG: And you did it in print. That's why it's called *All Kinds of Love*, I guess.

REINER: That's right.

STAMBERG: So how many books do you think we just helped you sell through this list of naughty scenes?

REINER: I hope more than we printed, so that we will have a second printing.

STAMBERG: Well, books are always a combination of a fantasy and autobiography. You have been married for fifty years.

REINER: It's forty-nine and will be, as every two-thousand-year-old man might say, not yet. It will be on Christmas Eve, it will be fifty, yes.

STAMBERG: You have three children, and one of them, Rob, your son Rob the director, put your wife, Estelle, in his film *When Harry Met Sally.* She was the lady in the deli where Sally fakes an orgasm.

REINER: I laugh every time I hear it. You know how many

times we have eaten in the restaurant and people come over to Estelle, and say, "I'll have." They say it almost wrong. "I want what she got," or something, but they'll get it close enough. She became famous for one line and she should be famous for many more things than that one line.

STAMBERG: Did you have anything to do with that line?

REINER: Nothing. It was Billy Crystal who had ad-libbed it while they were rehearsing and writing the script, and Rob called his mother, and he said, "Ma, I got a line. You got to do it. It's one line. It may not be in the picture, but it's the funniest line that we have written." He flew her to New York, he had a trailer for her, and she felt so silly, and she was so nervous because when you have one line in the picture it's very hard to score, and she scored.

STAMBERG: She scored big.

REINER: She had a bull's-eye.

STAMBERG: I want to talk about you, and I wonder whether you remember the first laugh you ever got?

REINER: The first laugh I ever got probably when I was in the third grade. I had the ability to put my legs behind my neck and walk around on my hands and make funny sounds, and people laughed at that, and then I was able to put one leg behind my head and stand on the other leg and walk around like that. I was very limber. The second laughs I got was to jump from high heights and land without doing a plié, just clunk, plummeting to earth and just standing.

STAMBERG: That's very hard on the feet, you know.

REINER: I found out years later that it's hard on the knees too.

STAMBERG: Oh, gee. So, if your first laugh was putting your legs over your head, could you do that for us now, by the way?

REINER: No, I can't, but I get pretty close. I can't. I would hurt myself and you.

STAMBERG: You have worked with an awful lot of funny women whom we all cherish: Imogene Coca, Pat Carroll, Mary Tyler Moore, Lily Tomlin. But I want to ask you about some of the funny men you have worked with, and I think we need to start with Sid Caesar, *Your Show of Shows* on NBC in the 1950s. You were the ultimate second banana for him. He came here to NPR a few years ago and he told us how, when he was seven or eight years old, he would try out various accents in this restaurant his father ran. Nothing he said made sense. These weren't real languages.

REINER: No, and that's why we were symbiotic, because I was a comedian and I heard Sid Caesar, and I said, "Wait a minute, if I'm comedian, what's that?" When I got on the *Show of Shows*, I had done my act "Foreign Double-talk" in Italian, French, and German. I listened to him, and I said, "Oh, I'll never be able to do that here." I was the one who came up with the idea to do "Foreign Movies" so two people can talk double-talk, and so we made a wonderful relationship playing those kinds of things.

STAMBERG: You were the characters in this movie.

REINER: Right, and so if somebody had to talk French or German, we'd do that kind of double-talk.

STAMBERG: Do you remember any of those?

REINER: What do you want? Italian, French, what, German?

STAMBERG: French would be nice.

REINER: French would be nice. *Mesdames et messieurs donc l'addition l'heure bleu la boîte et sa fière. Et leur riant et heure piqueur on pipicheur son font tutu sa créature pas enlevée. Mon ha-ha-ha. Vous vous commencez vé-vé bourrant.*

See, that's what we used to do.

STAMBERG: [*laughs*] That's so impressive being able to recite the Gettysburg Address that way just off the top of your head.

REINER: You know something? To me it's very amusing. I used to do this in French, English, Italian, Japanese. I remember we did these Japanese movies. So one evening my mother called me, and she said, "You know, I met Mrs. Fineshriver, Mrs. Whatever-her-name. She said, 'Your son must be so smart, he speaks all those languages.' " I said, "Well, Ma, didn't you tell her I'm double-talking them?" She says, "What do they have to know." And I said, "Ma, but they pay me a lot of money because I can't talk those, I can make fun." She says, "They don't have to know." She would rather I was intelligent and could speak those languages than to fool. But she did appreciate it. She thought I was the best one every place I worked.

STAMBERG: We are talking about funny men. Mel Brooks.

REINER: Mel Brooks is the funniest man I know.

STAMBERG: Together in the 1960s you did "The 2,000-Year-Old Man." You started this as party entertainment, the two of you, right?

REINER: Yes, it started actually — if the truth be told, you like the truth, the absolute truth?

STAMBERG: Always.

REINER: There was a program on television called *We, the People*, very early in television. Dan Seymour was his name. Here was a man who was actually in Stalin's toilet when he heard Stalin say, "I'm going to blow up the world Thursday," and I got furious. I came into the office that day. I knew it was a fake. I turned to Mel, and I say here was a man who was actually at the scene of the crucifixion two thousand years ago, isn't that true, sir? And he said, "Oh boy." That was it. That started ten years of asking him questions, a thin lad. I would say, "You know Jesus?" He would say, "Oh yes, a thin lad."

STAMBERG: But did you have to bite your lips to keep from laughing?

REINER: All the time I turned away from the mike, that's what I did. I remember sometimes Mel said things that I couldn't stop laughing, and I turned away from the mike and I just waited. When you edit the tape you can take out the offending giggles.

STAMBERG: Of course you worked with Dick Van Dyke. You produced, wrote, and costarred in *The Dick Van Dyke Show* in the 1960s, and then movies. George Burns in *Oh, God*, Steve Martin in three comedies, including *All of Me*. This is a

different kind of humor from anybody that we have been talking about so far.

REINER: Steve is an original. There is no question about it.
He is sly. He looks like an insurance salesman. He is an abstract
human being. He wrote a book called *Cruel Shoes*, and one of
the chapters was "How to Fold Soup." Just so you will have it.
Who thinks in those terms?

STAMBERG: But all these people we have been talking about
have kind humor. They are not funny at the expense of others.

REINER: No, it's not ridicule humor. It's self-ridicule in
many cases. The 2,000-Year-Old Man ridicules, but he ridicules
society for being dumb because he knows everything they don't.
Sid's humor was very human. It was based on human emotion
and that's why people cotton to him, because if he felt pain he
illustrated it so clearly. Any kind of pain, physical pain or emotional pain, he suffered so much and so real. He is one of the
most real actors I have ever worked with, and he wasn't a
schooled actor.

STAMBERG: Do you think humor is a young man's game?
Does it get harder and harder to be funny as you get older?

REINER: If you have a funny bent in you, you can't stop.
George Burns cannot stop. He's still making jokes. It's a young
man's game in that if you have to produce humor every week,
like a *Dick Van Dyke Show*, which was thirty-three weeks a
year, or the *Show of Shows* was thirty-nine weeks a year, you
had to come up with new stuff every week, and that was live.
You need a lot of spunk and spirit and energy, and right now I
can do a picture a year. That's a lot of work. It's two or three
months of very hard concentrated work, but after that you can
say, "I'll go edit the picture now" or "I'll go have lunch with
Mel next door." Mel and I just did two pictures side by side. He
was doing a picture called *Robin Hood: Men in Tights*, and I was
doing *Fatal Instinct*, and we're saying, "Look, two Jews from
New York doing pictures for the world."

FRED ROGERS speaks with Linda Wertheimer about
what has changed and what has stayed the same
in twenty-five years at *Mister Rogers' Neighborhood*
on PBS. February 19, 1993

ROGERS: If anyone had told me twenty-five years ago that we
would be producing a whole week about divorce, for instance,
I would have thought they were fallacious, or if anybody had
told me that we would produce a whole week on child care. But
within these twenty-five years, these things have touched the
lives of all children, either directly or indirectly.

WERTHEIMER: I suppose almost as many children are living
with divorced parents as are living with parents not divorced, or
maybe even more?

ROGERS: Even if they aren't, they have friends who are.

WERTHEIMER: And they worry.

ROGERS: They worry that it may have been their fault. The
more I live, the more I realize how much children long to belong. There are many children today who really don't know
what they belong to.

WERTHEIMER: Susan Stamberg told me that not too far into
this project of *Mister Rogers' Neighborhood*, you decided to go
back to school, to divinity school.

ROGERS: I went to Pittsburgh Theological Seminary on my
lunch hour, and it took me eight years to get the master of
divinity degree and to get ordained, but I did it.

WERTHEIMER: Do you view what you do as a ministry?

ROGERS: Oh, I think everything that we do is some form of
ministry. You know, I think that the space between the television set, or the radio, if you will, and the person who is listening is hallowed ground, and those messages that we purvey

can be translated to the needs of the listener in ways that are unknown to us.

WERTHEIMER: Mr. Rogers, I want to ask you a dumb question. We were wondering, in twenty-five seasons on television, how many cardigan sweaters you actually have had? And how long they last?

ROGERS: I don't know whether you know it, but my mother made most of my cardigan sweaters while she was alive. In fact, the one that's at the Smithsonian is one that she made. Those have all worn out and we have some others now. I would imagine that there have been a couple dozen of those zipper sweaters. We use them every day. The same way with those blue sneakers.

WERTHEIMER: Why does it work so well, the neighborhood?

ROGERS: I think that we all want to be in touch with honesty. I think that someone who comes in, like a neighbor, or an uncle, or a grandfather, who wants to let the children know that they have value and that they matter — I hope that is what comes through to them in that they are able to sense that there is something within them that, just by their very being here, is worthy.

The columnist RUSSELL BAKER talks to Robert Siegel
about taking over as the new host of *Masterpiece
Theatre,* replacing the eighty-four-year-old English-born
Alistair Cooke. Baker writes "The Observer" column
for the *New York Times.* February 23, 1993

BAKER: The opportunity to make a fool of yourself before
millions of people is almost irresistible to me, I would say.

SIEGEL: [*laughs*] I see. You feel that the column in the *Times*
hasn't given you ample room to embarrass yourself yet?

BAKER: Well, it gave me a lot of room. The *Times* is very good
about that. For years, they gave me great leeway. The *Times* is
wonderful that way. I finally got it to the point where I could do
it without making a fool of myself. I hope if I live long enough,
I can do this that way.

SIEGEL: When Alistair Cooke signed off, when he retired
from this job, he said that he thought it was time for, and I
quote, "somebody young, new, and frisky."

BAKER: [*pause*] What does Alistair Cooke know about what
it takes to do this job? [*laughs*]

SIEGEL: [*laughs*] Well —

BAKER: Say that again. Young?

SIEGEL: Somebody young, new, and frisky.

BAKER: New and frisky.

SIEGEL: I think you have got the new and frisky down.

BAKER: Well, new and frisky, indeed. It's been a long time
since I have been frisky. I will be candid with you. I don't think
that's what it takes at all to do this job.

SIEGEL: What do you think it takes?

BAKER: Can I be serious for a moment? What does it take? It
takes some grasp of literature, really. You have to have some
feel for what makes a story, and Cooke always had that. He

would always lead you in onto what was interesting about this particular book they were dramatizing, even when it was a book that you had spent your whole life struggling not to read.

SIEGEL: Of course, one of the very specific tasks that he faced was to tell an American audience what typically an English writer was getting at and what would be evident to every viewer in Britain of this program and might not be evident to an American.

BAKER: I don't think that's terribly essential to it. Cooke has spent his life — Mr. Cooke, I should say, shouldn't I have to show proper deference to this man I'm in awe of? — has spent his life interpreting, really, Americans to the English. That's been his great contribution to journalism. I have spent half my life now interpreting America to Americans. Though, really, it's an interpretive job. I don't think it takes a knowledge of England so deep that it can't be readily handled by somebody who got a gentleman's C in English literature in college, which is the case with me.

SIEGEL: Do you know what the stories are for next fall?

BAKER: No, I don't.

SIEGEL: When you find out, are you going to make a small course out of this?

BAKER: Yes.

SIEGEL: And then study them?

BAKER: I will not only read the books very closely and outline them, but I will study the biography of the authors and read some of the history of the time in which they are set. I really believe in being excessively prepared. One consequence of that, of course, it makes you a terrible bore. But I am promised by the producers that they will not let me become too tedious.

SIEGEL: [laughs] What is it about this that you find most challenging at the moment, the most difficult?

BAKER: I don't think of it in terms of challenging or difficulty. I think it's very interesting to be associated with something that's really an enduring ornament of American culture. This thing has been running for twenty to twenty-five years. For all the abuse that television gets, this is one of the things that justifies television, ennobles it somehow. I like being identified with that. That's good. What is challenging about it is to maintain that level of quality. Can I do that as Alistair Cooke has done? He has helped to maintain it, perhaps contributed to it. I, at least, would like to get out of it without lowering it.

SIEGEL: Were you asked about your appearance today at the announcement press conference?

BAKER: About my physical appearance?

SIEGEL: Yes.

BAKER: Well, some wise-guy reporter, after looking at me for twenty minutes, asked me if I was going to, I believe the question was, Was I going to get some decent clothes to wear on television? [laughs]

SIEGEL: [laughs] Those reporters will do that.

BAKER: I said I was not worried that much about what my clothes look like. I was more concerned about my hair because for about twenty-five or thirty years, I have cut my own hair. I have not been to a barber since, oh, I don't know, the Eisenhower administration. I remember I quit going to the barber because my barber went from two dollars a haircut to two dollars and a quarter.

SIEGEL: [laughs] That's where you got off?

BAKER: I thought, that's just too much to get a haircut, particularly for the kind of haircuts you got in those days. I said I could do this myself, and I have been doing it ever since. It's always interesting what my hair looks like. I am in some fear of these television people. You know how important hair is on television.

SIEGEL: [laughs] Yes.

BAKER: I am afraid they're going to insist that I put in mousses. Is that what that stuff is? Mousse?

SIEGEL: I guess so.

BAKER: Mousse. It's mousse.

SIEGEL: Is this a point of principle with you, or is it just cheaper not to go to a barber?

BAKER: Well, you know what? You've got to put me down as just a plain American boy. The idea that a real American boy would get a blow-dry hairdo and put in gels to puff up his pompadour is offensive to me. I know we all do, but I like to think I am just plain mud-between-the-toes American, and I am not going to be pushed around like that by television.

WALTER BERNSTEIN and ABRAHAM POLONSKY talk to Robert Siegel about writing the early CBS television program *You Are There* when they were blacklisted during the McCarthy era. The two men, together with the late Arnold Manoff, submitted scripts through fronts, individuals who lent their politically acceptable by-lines to the banned writers' works, to the producer Charles Russell, who was in on the ruse. Polonsky's long-unacknowledged *You Are There* teleplays were assembled and published by California State University at Northridge. June 14, 1993

POLONSKY: It's very bad and very sad that Arnold Manoff and Charles Russell are dead. It's very sad that all the scripts, the wonderful scripts, that Arnie wrote shouldn't be made available with the name of the proper author on them. His show on Socrates, remember, Walter? I think that was picked by the Museum of Modern Art as one of the better shows that they had, right?

BERNSTEIN: Yes.

POLONSKY: They got some prize or something. So I think these things should be made known. Walter and I can defend ourselves with lies, but he can't.

SIEGEL: Walter Bernstein, what did you do as the outside man?

BERNSTEIN: I had been working in television. It was then live television, before Abe and Arnie Manoff came from the coast. I had had certain credits under my own name and I knew certain producers, like Russell, so I was able to go to Russell in particular, and say, "I have these two friends who are here and they are very good writers and how about using them on the show?" He was very amenable to it.

SIEGEL: Did he know that you were blacklisted?

BERNSTEIN: He was the one who told me when he was the producer of *Danger*, which was the show before *You Are There*. Oh, yes, he knew we were all blacklisted.

SIEGEL: Your friends from the coast? He knew that when you were speaking of Polonsky and Manoff that they too were blacklisted?

BERNSTEIN: Oh, I told him that, and his concern was only that he be able to tell his bosses upstairs that there was a real, live person whom they could see on demand.

SIEGEL: So the three of you would be able to write this new television program, *You Are There*, provided that you each had a front who would be the body?

BERNSTEIN: Yes, that was an absolute requisite.

SIEGEL: Did the three of you meet frequently?

BERNSTEIN: As often as possible. We would meet in Steinberg's Dairy Restaurant on Broadway.

POLONSKY: And don't forget Max the waiter.

BERNSTEIN: We had a waiter named Max who couldn't figure out who we were because we looked like bums but we would occasionally throw around big numbers and money and things like that. We would be talking about scripts, but he wouldn't know. He came to us one day and he said he had finally figured out who we were and what we did, and we said, "What?" and he said, "You're in the wholesale fruit business."

POLONSKY: [*laughs*] That's right.

BERNSTEIN: [*laughs*] I don't know how he put that together.

POLONSKY: Because Arnie looked like he worked at the produce market.

SIEGEL: Arnold Manoff?

BERNSTEIN: Yes. But we would meet regularly, usually there or at one of our houses.

SIEGEL: For people who don't remember this program at all, for those who are too young or who didn't watch television at the time, we should say that after an introduction by Walter

Cronkite [who was not yet the anchorman of the evening news], CBS news correspondents like Mike Wallace and Bill Leonard would cover an event as if it were a live television event. One of them was "The Crisis of Galileo." That's in your collection of screenplays, Mr. Polonsky. Did you choose that subject?

POLONSKY: It came up in a discussion probably at the restaurant one day, and I got it because I knew who Galileo was. The others weren't quite sure.

BERNSTEIN: That was not a subject that CBS would have chosen.

SIEGEL: Yes, tell me about writing Galileo for CBS.

POLONSKY: I understood his scientific importance and I understood also the moral problem involved in his life, which was very similar to the moral problems involved in the lives of many people around us at that time. So it was historically accurate, even though it was told in terms of the nature of those times, and I did not move away from what happened historically. Nevertheless, it was significant at that moment in terms of what was going on in the United States. The significant event in his life was when he was challenged by the church to say he didn't believe in his own theory and that he would report anybody to the church who in any way violated the rules of the church about the nature of the universe at that time, and Galileo said he would do that.

BERNSTEIN: After they showed him the instruments of torture, I believe. Do you remember that?

POLONSKY: In the original script I wrote, they threatened him, but Charlie Russell, the producer, when he had the show written, he ran down to the Catholic Church headquarters in New York and said that it was too violent or something.

SIEGEL: You mean they ran the script past the archdiocese to see if they would object to your depiction?

POLONSKY: Bill Dozier did, the executive producer, and then told Charlie what he had done. Charlie got around the problem by having the conference take place in front of the instruments of torture. So it was obvious what was going to happen to Galileo if he did not change his opinion.

SIEGEL: When you wrote a program like that, you must have been consciously, if in a muted way, protesting against the McCarthy era of the day.

POLONSKY: I would characterize our writing of all those scripts as the only guerrilla warfare waged against McCarthyism at that time on television.

SIEGEL: Three of you, blacklisted, working through fronts in cahoots with the producer Charles Russell.

BERNSTEIN: And the director, Sidney Lumet.

SIEGEL: You were able to write in "The Tragedy of John Milton," or Arnold Manoff in "The Salem Witch Trials," about many a historical incident that was equally about the 1950s.

POLONSKY: Walter did too, a great many of the shows.

BERNSTEIN: "The Death of Socrates" we did. What Abe said was essentially true. We were very consciously trying to say something about the period we were living in.

SIEGEL: How did this system come to an end?

POLONSKY: Walter, you tell him.

BERNSTEIN: It came to an end when two things happened, mainly. They moved the show to California and put it on film; our shows were live. Lumet was no longer associated with it, nor was Russell, and we remained in New York, where we lived.

POLONSKY: Bill Dozier, as a matter of fact, Walter, was going to the West Coast.

SIEGEL: He was the executive producer who took it out to California?

POLONSKY: Yes, it was for a big job at CBS out there. He wanted to take one of the shows with him and he wanted to take *You Are There*, which was a prestigious show at that time, but the CBS executives in New York didn't want to let him do that, so Dozier said, "Well, these shows are being written by blacklisted writers." He knew that all along, as a matter of fact.

BERNSTEIN: Yes, he always did.

POLONSKY: In fact, I think it was on the jazz show, he once told Charlie, "That's a good script Abe wrote." I don't know how he knew that.

SIEGEL: But you are saying that he disclosed that so that he could get the show moved to California with him.

POLONSKY: They were eager to get rid of everybody connected to the show and go out to the West Coast, and then Dozier discovered out there that it wasn't so easy doing the show.

BERNSTEIN: No.

POLONSKY: He also discovered that the best thing was not to treat any subject that had any significance whatsoever.

BERNSTEIN: This show was not successful out there, once it moved to the coast, for a number of reasons.

POLONSKY: The main reason was they abandoned the subject matter.

BERNSTEIN: They wouldn't deal with historical conflict; they wouldn't touch anything.

SIEGEL: For many of us growing up after the war, *You Are There* was the program where we first encountered Walter Cronkite, reading an introduction and a conclusion to every program that summarized what it was about.

BERNSTEIN: Abe wrote that final marvelous thing that Cronkite said at the end.

SIEGEL: Which I would like to hear the true writer of read for us in a moment, but first, did Walter Cronkite know, Abe Polonsky, that you, that a blacklisted writer, were the author of these immortal words?

POLONSKY: I don't think he knew. He may have suspected, but it was better not to know. That was the age of it being better not to know anything.

SIEGEL: Abraham Polonsky, could you read for us the line that Walter Cronkite used to say?

POLONSKY: I would be happy to read, but I don't have it here, but let's see if I can remember it. "It was a day like all days, filled with — "

BERNSTEIN: Excuse me. He started by saying, "What kind of a day was it?"

POLONSKY: Thank you, Walter. "What kind of a day was it? A day like all days, filled with those events that alter and illuminate our times . . . and you were there."

HARRY SHEARER talks with Alex Chadwick about
the ins and outs of Los Angeles and *Man Bites Town,*
a collection of his columns that has appeared in the
Los Angeles Times Magazine. Shearer hosts *Le Show,*
a public radio show in Santa Monica, portions of
which can be heard on *All Things Considered.* He is
a voice on *The Simpsons* and a member of the fictitious
rock group Spinal Tap. May 29, 1993

CHADWICK: You say a lot in your columns that you are from
Los Angeles, and you note it with some pride. You're a true fan
of the city.

SHEARER: The strange thing about Los Angeles is that it's a
place like New York used to be, where a lot of people come for
the sake of their ambitions and they don't tend to be extremely
curious or oriented toward setting down roots here. I, on the
other hand, did grow up here. I know why I'm here. I like it here.
I say in one of the pieces in the book that this is a strange place
for anybody to visit as a tourist. It's sort of like a Siamese cat of
a city. Its charms become evident only upon close and long-
term examination.

CHADWICK: Many of the visitors or transplants that you find
there are so far from thinking they can put down roots, seem to
think that dry and sandy soil simply wouldn't hold any roots at
all, no matter what.

SHEARER: It's true. But I've grown many a crop in this dry,
sandy soil. It is a desert and it takes some care and some water
and as much water as we can steal from the north.

CHADWICK: You write at one point in the book about the
Hollywood-Washington connection. You tell a story about
coming to the White House for a Christmas party a couple of
years ago. A lot of people are talking now about the Hollywood–

Los Angeles connection with Mr. Clinton in the White House and the welcome mat out, I guess, for most anyone who's been in film or television or anything else out there.

SHEARER: It's interesting. The part of this that gets the great media attention is, of course, the celebrity side of it. The part that seems to be ridiculously under-covered is the fact that Hollywood is an industry and has interests, like many other industries, and like many other industries, when it contributes to political campaigns, expects those interests to be favored. While everybody is sort of yakking it up — "Oh, Barbra Streisand's going to be giving policy advice on Bosnia" — the Justice Department recently reversed an FCC ruling that had the effect of favoring the networks over the Hollywood studios, and the Justice Department just very recently announced that "We're going to be taking another look at this." The networks didn't give money to the Clinton campaign, the Hollywood studios did. Gee, I wonder how that happened? This is the nexus that really counts and, of course, it's buried under all the Streisand bashing. I think that these two towns are remarkably alike, they're remarkably self-obsessed. Except that I think the denizens here may be just slightly more secure. After all, Warren Beatty didn't destroy his career trying to be Gary Hart.

CHADWICK: How is it that the *Los Angeles Times* asked you to begin writing this column?

SHEARER: Alex, I am not privy to two things: why they asked me to write it and why they asked me to stop. But they did both things sort of out of the blue. I was interested in the idea because I had written columns when I was a kid for the UCLA student newspaper and since that time all my writing had been designed to come out of the mouths of characters in comedy, TV, movies, and things, and so the idea of like writing for a character called myself that wasn't spoken, that was just sitting there in print, was appealing to me.

CHADWICK: There is a kind of darker aspect to many of your columns. That is, you take on the reality of life in South Los

Angeles. You talk about how the city has changed, not always very comfortably.

SHEARER: There are individual streets that are now proposing to gate themselves, to separate themselves from the fabric of the city, and that impulse is very strong here right now. It's understandable. We have withstood an amazing wave of immigration. I think nothing since the beginning of the century in New York compares to it, and we weren't prepared for it and we didn't have any leadership to sort of guide us through it, so we've all had to sort of struggle through it on our own. A natural impulse is just to put up walls and gates. Los Angeles is going through a very dire period right now. This is a city that always imagined itself recession-proof. We had recession-proof industries. Everybody always wants to be entertained and everybody always wants jet bombers. Those two assumptions have been proven wrong. So, it, combined with the riot last year, which was widely misunderstood, has made this town very jittery about itself right now, but I think it's almost the stage where you can say in the history of this place of sort of the nervous adolescence that's going to be grown out of very soon. The pimples will go away.

CHADWICK: You are in a possibly unique situation. Here you are, a man who is a gifted mimic, able to create a number of voices, and with your own weekly radio show. Now, you know that anyone who writes a book likes to go on radio programs and be interviewed about the book. Here you are on ours. Are you going to interview Harry Shearer on *Le Show*?

SHEARER: No, I did that once a long time ago, just to prove it could be done and to prove why it should never be done again. But I don't view my radio show as a platform for selling my stuff, oddly enough.

CHADWICK: How do you view that show?

SHEARER: It's my sandbox. It's a place where I can play with notions and ideas and new characters and basically have a one-to-one relationship with a kind of mass audience.

CHADWICK: It's a remarkable effort because it's so written,

if you will — it's very funny, very clever, very fast. There is a lot of back and forth in it.

SHEARER: Thanks. I guess because I had a little training in journalism and still retain some interest in it, my sense of how to do these characters is rather than to grotesque them up and caricature them, is to find out what is real about them and to make fun of that. What makes me proudest, whether it's when people see *Spinal Tap* or when people hear me doing George Bush, is that for that split second at the beginning they think it's the real thing. That to me is the highest compliment.

After forty-three years, 21,425 shows, and more than
three hundred thousand guests, the talk show host
JOE FRANKLIN retired from television. Before his final
broadcast, on superstation WWOR, Franklin talks
with Liane Hansen from his Manhattan office about
never missing a show. August 1, 1993

FRANKLIN: Never one single show. Never one day, one
show.

HANSEN: But I heard you were late sometimes?

FRANKLIN: Well, I was. Sometimes I'd walk in while the
theme song was being played. Every night about this time, we
say, "Have we got a show for you, a good one. Provocative,
fascinating, interesting and exciting people."

HANSEN: Your first guest was Eddie Cantor.

FRANKLIN: Eddie Cantor was my very first guest. He had
heard about my program. He read about me someplace in *TV
Guide.* And at that very same time, there was a little accident
in the Bronx, somebody actually bombed a synagogue, and he
came on appealing for funds to rebuild the synagogue. I thought
maybe he might raise three dollars, or twelve dollars, and he
raised something like a hundred thousand dollars from one time
on TV, on my show, and that's when I first realized that TV was
a really powerful medium.

HANSEN: You worked with him when you were a teenager.
You were a writer for his radio show?

FRANKLIN: I sure was. I was Eddie Cantor's writer.

HANSEN: What was that like for you now, to be master of
your own talk show and talking to somebody that you used to
work for?

FRANKLIN: It was quite a kick. I idolized Eddie Cantor, and
when I list my golden guests, he's always there with me. Of

course, my favorite golden guests are the ones where I read these people who never did a talk show. I have got the photographs or the kinescopes. I will read of where Charlie Chaplin never did one, where Cary Grant never did one; I read where James Cagney, where John Wayne, never did one. I have got the proof that I have had three hundred thousand guests. I have had everybody that I ever wanted except Greta Garbo. But we used to meet in the street and we'd smile. I know that if she ever had done a show, it would have been mine.

HANSEN: But she didn't talk, Joe. She really sort of made it part of her persona and her mystique, that she just didn't talk. It would have really been a coup for you to be able to talk to her.

FRANKLIN: That's right. But she gave me a couple of her souvenirs. I have got an archive of memorabilia. I have got a pair of Greta Garbo's shoes.

HANSEN: Where would you get those?

FRANKLIN: It's a funny thing that she went into a health food store one day to have some juice at the bar and she took off her high-heeled shoes there by mistake, and the clerk at the bar sold me those shoes for about thirty dollars, which I've been told today I could probably sell for three hundred thousand dollars.

HANSEN: You are your own booker, right?

FRANKLIN: I am. I tried talent coordinators. I tried bookers and they get that power feeling. They get a little bit smug and sometimes they start to think that they're me, so by me doing my own work and booking my own guests I somehow, I have become what you would call the master chemist or the master catalyst. I can feel in my mind who will go well on which panels and who will intermingle well and I guess I've got it down to a science.

HANSEN: Jim Florio, New Jersey governor, is going to be your guest on the show?

FRANKLIN: My very final guest will be Governor Florio and he's proclaiming August ninth as Joe Franklin Day, and he reminisces with me on that show about twenty or thirty times he was on my show in the past as a congressman but never as governor. He mentions he was on twice with Tiny Tim and I reminded him that Ronald Reagan was on my show five times. Also never as president, never even as governor. He was on five times as a TV and radio host. Once or twice with *Death Valley Days* and three times with the *G.E. Theater.*

HANSEN: You must have thought that somehow the governor of New Jersey, though not when he was a governor, but Jim Florio and Tiny Tim made a good panel or you wouldn't have booked them together.

FRANKLIN: What a mix!

HANSEN: I am going to exercise my prerogative here as a talk show host and ask you questions that I have wanted to ask. People who do this for a living and certainly someone who has done this for a living as long as you have, do you think that if somebody agrees to come on a show and do an interview, that anything goes? That you can ask that person anything you want?

FRANKLIN: Nowadays, apparently, yes. Nowadays, it's gotten very explicit, gotten very pornographic. And, look, you can't knock it. It gets the ratings.

HANSEN: I know ratings determine business, but sometimes ratings aren't the bottom line.

FRANKLIN: I can't believe some of the things I see, but people out there volunteer to go on those shows. Most Geraldos and most Sally Jessys and most Donahues and Oprahs, they tell me that they don't go after those guests. Those guests come to them with their fanatical way of life, and apparently when they go on these shows it's their outlet and it makes them less inhibited. I don't know what the theory is that people want to volunteer to go on these programs, and apparently the ratings show that people watch these programs.

HANSEN: You sound like my colleague Susan Stamberg, who was talking about her broadcasting experience when she began twenty years ago. She said it used to be that it was very difficult to get people to talk into a microphone. They would be nervous, you would have to warm them up, you would have to ingratiate yourself somewhat. Now they're going to elbow people out of the way to get to the microphone.

FRANKLIN: It's a world of mad exhibitionists out there, right?

HANSEN: You asked Montel Williams, who now does his own daily show. You asked him what he thought the role of a talk show host was in these days and how much influence a talk show host could have. I want to ask you that same question. What do you think the role of a talk show host is? How, maybe, that role has changed over the years?

FRANKLIN: I think it hasn't changed that much. I think some of them feel they've got a power that they don't have. They are strictly entertainers. I have seen, without naming names, that there are a couple out there who have let that little bit of notoriety and fame go to their heads, but when they get behind a certain campaign or a crusade or a politician, they don't have that kind of power. I have always had the theory that talent is secondary. You have got to have the right agent. You take David Letterman, with a forty-two-million-dollar contract. His agent is Michael Ovitz. I never had an agent. I have always been like a mom and pop candy store. I guess I have felt intimidated by some of the agents who wanted to work with me. I hear from two, three agents a week now. They want to submit me and repackage me. I tell them that I have got to rest and then I'll decide what to do, but it's a business. It's a show. It's show business and it's not like the old days when it was from the heart and lovable and huggable and kissable. Now it's gotten too bottom-line, that's my uninformed appraisal. Do I sound bitter or cynical?

HANSEN: Oh, no!

FRANKLIN: Maybe just disappointed.

HANSEN: Billy Crystal does a parody of you. I know you know this. You like it very much. Why do you think you like his parody of you so much?

FRANKLIN: Billy Crystal, I think, made me into a superstar. I taught Rich Little how to do me. I taught Frank Gorshin how to do me. There were Joe Franklin sound-alike concepts happening all over the country now where people say, "Hello, this is Joe Franklin for Martin Paint. We are pushing the late, great Al Jolson's records." I encourage them. The first time I heard Billy Crystal do me, I said, "One of us is lousy." But I loved it. He did me for four years. People tell me that subconsciously, down deep, without realizing, he is me now. He has done me so many times that he is me now without knowing it.

HANSEN: I thought maybe the reason you liked it so much is, certainly — given *Mr. Saturday Night* and what he did with that particular movie. He has a real respect — and you will forgive me for saying this, but a real respect for guys of your generation and that generation of show business that existed in New York, the Walter Winchell, the up-off-the-street, back-toward-Damon-Runyon kind of guys.

FRANKLIN: Yes, the Irving Berlins, the Eddie Cantors, the people from the East Side who made it big, Georgie Jessel, names like that.

SCIENCE

The geophysicist ANDREW McFARLANE describes to Noah Adams the ordeal of escaping the erupting Galeras volcano in Colombia. On January 14, 1993, a team of United Nations scientists were inside the outer rim when the volcano erupted, killing nine people and injuring ten others. January 26, 1993

MCFARLANE: We had started down from the rim and were making our way down the big boulders and loose ash that make up the crater. We were on the outer wall of the active crater and inside the surrounding caldera rim, and there was a loud boom. I turned around and looked over my shoulder, back at the top of the crater, and I could see a dark cloud rising over the top of the crater. At that point, for just a second, it was hard to tell how serious it was, but we knew it wasn't good, and we started running. Within seconds, these blocks of hot rock were falling all around us, and I was nicked by one. And I saw one of the Colombians get basically crushed by one. At that point, it seemed very unlikely that any of us were going to get out alive.

ADAMS: Were you knocked down? Were you, in fact, lying there?

MCFARLANE: I was not knocked down by that. We were running down a very difficult terrain, and I think we all fell and got up and fell and got up several times. The big blocks of rock, as they hit on this soft ash, they tended to make pits where they struck. And if you fell, you tended to roll into these pits, so you would be on top of the hot rock and would be thereby compelled to get up and keep going. I had burns on my hands from climbing over some of this stuff.

ADAMS: Did you eventually give up trying to get out?

MCFARLANE: No, we didn't. We wound up in a group near

the bottom of the cone and were kind of resting there for a little while, when a rain started to fall that was full of ash. And so, we were pretty much soaked with this muddy rain. And we set out together and crossed the moat between the crater and the caldera wall and started climbing up the caldera wall, as far and fast as we could. At that point, we were holding our packs over our heads to keep from getting knocked out by flying projectiles.

ADAMS: And then what happened?

MCFARLANE: We just made it as far up the caldera wall as we could, within our strength. We were all exhausted and in shock, and running and falling at that high altitude took a lot out of us.

ADAMS: Did you make it to the top of the outer rim by yourself?

MCFARLANE: I would estimate I got about a third of the way up before I just couldn't go any further, and I was reached by the Colombian Red Cross there. The Red Cross got there with pretty amazing speed, and a couple of guys got to me and offered me some water and tried to help me walk. I got a few more steps and folded up completely, and they strapped me into one of those metal mountaineering stretcher-type deals and hauled me bodily up to the rim of the caldera.

ADAMS: Did you, while all this was going on, ever start talking to yourself, along the lines of, "Well, I picked this career, I sort of asked for it, in a way"?

MCFARLANE: A lot of thoughts like that were going through my mind, especially at first. I was surprised, a little bit, at the chaotic nature of my thoughts. I was thinking things like, Boy, my dad's really going to be upset if I get killed up here. And I forced myself to concentrate on what I was doing. My mind would wander off, for a second, on something else, and I would sort of jerk my concentration back to getting down the mountainside.

ADAMS: Did it ever occur to you that it was a great opportunity for somebody in your particular field of science?

MCFARLANE: Not really. It was interesting to be there, but

the danger was so extreme. I have been in some dangerous positions before, but never in one that I really didn't see any way I could get out of, and that sort of robbed the scientific aspect of it of much value.

ADAMS: Sure. One of your colleagues who died was from the Kamchatka Volcanic Institute in Russia.

MCFARLANE: He was one of the people who was down inside the crater, and, as we were leaving, I remember looking down, taking a last look at the crater. I noticed that he appeared to have finished his sampling and was standing more or less out in the middle of the crater floor, having a cigarette and enjoying the view. The wind had come in and sort of blown the fog out of the crater a little bit, and it was a nice view. He looked quite satisfied and seemed to be enjoying himself there, which, I guess, was as poetic a way to go as he might have hoped for.

ADAMS: Do you think that the team could have overlooked some warning sign? There had been no eruption in six months and no seismic activity. Was there anything else that could have been overlooked?

MCFARLANE: Really, I doubt it. I think further instrumentation might have been helpful. It was funny, after the event, because a lot of people in town came to me in the hospital, and several of them seemed to be trying to get me to tell them that there was really no hazard to the town, that you can have these little eruptions around the vent, but the town is basically safe. And I think some people wanted to be reassured for personal reasons and, perhaps, some people for more political reasons wanted me to say something like this. It's just not true.

ADAMS: The town is six miles away.

MCFARLANE: They're very fond of pointing out that no one in the town has been killed by the volcano in five hundred years. But the fact is, you could say that about any number of other volcanoes that have erupted. People just need to grasp the idea that volcanoes do not operate on a human time scale.

DIANA MCGOWIN, an Alzheimer's victim, speaks with Linda Wertheimer about her experience of succumbing to the destruction of personality and intellect. McGowin is the author of *Living in the Labyrinth*, a journal describing her self-aware journey into this terrifying disease, which began when she was forty-five years old and went to the doctor looking for a diagnosis of what she describes as "bizarre" behavior.
September 17, 1993

MCGOWIN: The one that sent me into a neurologist's office was when I was on what should have been a twenty-minute errand near my home and I became lost. I couldn't find my home and I was lost for over four hours. I drove out a tankful of gasoline just trying to find my own house, and I have lived there over twenty-six years. When that happened, I realized that was not absentmindedness and that was not preoccupation. It wasn't anyone else's fault. I just had to realize that I had a physical problem and so I went to my doctor.

WERTHEIMER: In reading the book, there is a sort of a mixture of panic and coping. Where on the one hand you're just completely horrified by what is happening and on the other hand, you're constantly devising all these ways to make it work.

MCGOWIN: That's how each of us do. I'm not unique in that. *Living in the Labyrinth*, the way I see it, while it does have some coping strategies in it, they are the type of coping as in how to jump out a window if the building's on fire. I feel it deals with the initial stage of grief.

WERTHEIMER: Yes, that is exactly the word I would use.

MCGOWIN: I cannot abide people who say, "Into each life some rain must fall," "Just get through one day at a time," "It's always darkest before the dawn." Well, so what, you know, that doesn't help me a bit. Don't tell me to live one day at a time when I don't know if I can get through this afternoon. And I think most people who have their backs against the wall feel that way and some of them jump because they feel that way.

WERTHEIMER: I think that the thing that is the most terrifying thing about Alzheimer's is the sense that you're losing yourself and what you were talking about, the reaction of grief. Could you just tell me what you meant by that?

MCGOWIN: It's the grief of your own loss, the loss of your own self. Everyone has lost someone near and dear to them and they're familiar with that grief process. An Alzheimer's patient is witnessing their own demise and you feel grief for yourself, for your own loss. You feel grief for your family, for what they're going to endure because of you and you feel grief for yourself for what you are going to miss in them. When I was first diagnosed, I thought it was a disease of the elderly. I didn't know younger people, even in their twenties, had this. So I went through really hard denial, so did my family. My husband wanted me just to buck up and shape up and snap out of whatever was wrong with me. My son, who at that time was just leaving his teens, kept searching the house for either alcohol or drugs because he thought Mom was on one or the other. This is what you see. They were presented with a puzzle with no solution. And anyway, that is the grief process, the grief of our own loss, our own death is impending and before we die, we know we're going to lose our cognitive ability and be a burden to someone. None of us want to do that.

WERTHEIMER: This is the ultimate terror of Alzheimer's, for me, that loss of cognitive ability. This is the most uncomfortable question I'm going to ask you, but can you imagine having this conversation with me ten years ago? What you would have been able to do and say and think about? Can you feel the difference?

MCGOWIN: Oh my, yes. Ten months ago, we don't have to go back ten years ago. When you awaken each morning, you take inventory. We laugh about it, but that is what we do. We take inventory.

WERTHEIMER: Like?

MCGOWIN: Mental inventory. You go through your family's names. You go through what you're supposed to do that day. You go through your address. Can you remember the phone number? Now, you're not going to have the answers to all these, but by the time you're through doing these things you have a fair inventory and then you know if you are going to have a good day or a bad day because on bad days, you don't have many of those answers.

WERTHEIMER: Tell me what your situation is. Tell me your state of health and how you deal with the condition you're in now.

MCGOWIN: Initially, I went through a fairly rapid deterioration that was very frightening because it did indicate to everyone, doctors, me, everyone, that I was going to be one of the quick ones, but, thank God, I hit a plateau and it leveled off and I'm there and God knew what he was doing when he didn't affect my speech first because it could have been the other way. Some people are much brighter and higher-functioning than I am, but their ability to speak is affected and it gives them the appearance of being more devastated and it's very frustrating to them. I'm sorry, I forgot the second part of your question.

WERTHEIMER: How do you cope each day? You talk a little bit about how to cope in the book, with the lists and your journal and writing all your questions down so that when you don't remember what they are, you can go look.

MCGOWIN: Yes. And I draw maps, I have hand-drawn maps because the commercial maps contain too much information for me, they are very confusing, as though someone were speaking much too rapidly. I can't assimilate that information so I draw little hand-drawn maps and I only go to places that are within my long-term memory unescorted, because short-term memory isn't reliable. If I'm in a restaurant and I go to the ladies room, how do I get back to the table?

WERTHEIMER: In spite of the terror of the whole thing, you approach this with the attitude that you had done a lot in your life and you ought to be able to bring a lot of that same gutsiness to this experience.

MCGOWIN: My attitude, frankly, is I refuse to be terrified by this thing. It's depressing as heck. I'm not going to sit here and say that it doesn't bother me. Anyone who knows me will tell you, I am no Pollyanna. My attitude is, and I say it over and over and over again and I truly mean it in all my heart, Alzheimer's can be fun if you know how to play it. There is one idiom that I don't think is trite and that's "You play with the cards what's dealt you." This is what was dealt me, and so I intend to make full use of whatever capacities I still have because I am very aware of every one of them and I'm very aware that they may not be there tomorrow.

The paleoanthropologist RICHARD LEAKEY talks with
Alex Chadwick about a one-and-a-half-million-year-
old fossilized *Homo erectus* skeleton found near Lake
Turkana in Africa in 1984. The son of the renowned
anthropologists Louis and Mary Nichol Leakey, he
uncovered the largest collection of early human remains
ever found. The so-called Turkana Boy is believed to
be the first human species to cross out of Africa.
Dr. Leakey, along with Richard Lewin, wrote *Origins
Reconsidered*, a scientific detective story that attempts
to assemble evidence from this skeleton, starting
with rings on the teeth. January 2, 1993

LEAKEY: It seems that like rings in a tree, you can actually
age quite specifically how long a tooth has been in existence
while it's forming. From that, it was possible to say this individual with second molars just coming into place, was, in fact,
nine years. If at nine years, it already had a cranial capacity of
X and we project forward an adult cranial capacity from other
examples that have been found, you can project backwards what
it was like to be in the birth canal because you can measure the
birth canal, and from that you can work out some of the biology
that is so important in answering these questions.

CHADWICK: How do you know the size of the birth canal?
Do you have other adult specimens of *Homo erectus* from that
time? Females? And can figure out how large the birth canal
was then?

LEAKEY: The evidence is there, and although we don't have
a complete female pelvis, we do have some evidence, and on the
statistical comparisons with modern humans and with modern
chimps. I think a second question that is also very important,

related to the teeth, is the question of the stage at which infants are born. In humans, we're born, to all intents and purposes, a number of months too soon. We are absolutely helpless at birth, unlike other primates which within a few days have the capacity to grip onto their mothers and are stronger in terms of their dealing with the external environment. By knowing the age at which this skeleton died, and by being able to measure the birth canal in *Homo erectus*, we were able to predict *Homo erectus* was born as human children are, in a very early condition, needing a lot of parental care and mothering. That sets up a system where you have got to have a lot of other care for the mother, because if she is looking after, the whole time, a helpless child, she is certainly in no position to fend for herself or to seek food. So there are series of patterns there that interrelate that make us sure we're dealing with something much more like ourselves than a chimp.

CHADWICK: But don't chimp mothers mother their infant chimps?

LEAKEY: Yes, but a human child, which can't hang on, has got to be carried and held on to tightly. It can't be left anywhere. A chimp child, very quickly, within a few weeks, can grip onto its mother, and the mother can go off in any direction doing her thing and it's no longer a burden. Human children are much more burdensome to their parents than animal children.

CHADWICK: From this you look back at *Homo erectus* and say that this is the beginning of human society?

LEAKEY: There are a lot of characteristics in *Homo erectus* that we now know for sure suggest that it was already much more similar to ourselves, that is, modern humans, than it was to the other apes. Science has gone through periods of uncertainty. The pendulum has swung from looking to a very early date for the onset of these characteristics to a very late date. This has always been open to speculation. Now we have some evidence that suggests that there is no need to speculate. We know that certain very human qualities were well established at least a million and a half years ago.

CHADWICK: Were these qualities human in the way that we think of human? That is, we think primarily of consciousness and a sense of self as the central human characteristic.

LEAKEY: That's a question we would love to answer, and in the book we speculate on those issues. We will never know the answer. All one can say is that the evidence for the biology of these creatures is there. We do know that tool-making technology, or if you like a home base pattern, the evidence for people going back to one place, were established. And I think it's more likely that one can now speak of self-awareness and consciousness having quite an earlier start-up time than it was before.

CHADWICK: When you speak about the Turkana Boy, who is this nine-year-old, I note that you refer to, what I call *him*, as *it*, an impersonal pronoun. Is that because you feel that humanity should not be conferred on this? Is this a conscious choice on your part or something you are not really aware of?

LEAKEY: No, I think there is a conscious attempt on my part to speak of the species rather than the individual fossil. Although the Turkana Boy is a young male, the information that it confers is information about the species and about its type rather than it as an individual. And I think it's often easier to depersonalize it in that sense, and one is, if you like, slipping back and forth from an individual discussion to a discussion about a stage in evolution that is important.

CHADWICK: Is there any sense of individuality that you get from discovering those bones and holding on to them and pulling from them the secrets of *Homo erectus*?

LEAKEY: In a strange way I think there is. I think there is definitely a sense that this is an individual who one almost knows because there is so much of him there. His death and subsequent preservation took place in environmental circumstances that can be documented to a back quarter of a small swamp. One can reconstruct, rather like a forensic scientist, a lot about the conditions immediately after death, and from that and an understanding and greater clarity of the biology, the life history. I think one gets to a point where one has a much stronger personal feeling for this fossil than one would for most.

The medical anthropologist CAROL JENKINS of
Goroka, Papua New Guinea, and Professor ANDREW
STRATHERN of the University of Pittsburgh, talk with
Liane Hansen about the improbability of the 1993
discovery of the Liawps, a "lost tribe" in Papua New
Guinea. The tribesmen have been accused of lying to
PNG government officials to facilitate trade.
August 1, 1993

HANSEN: Every few years there are reports about "lost
tribes" being "discovered" in remote areas of the world. In
Papua New Guinea, in the late 1980s, the Hagahai was reputed
to be a lost tribe, but anthropologists proved otherwise. How do
these stories get started and how are they perpetuated? Do you
mind if we start, briefly, with some definitions here? What is it
we mean by "lost tribe"?

STRATHERN: Let me just jump in here by saying that this is
the whole problem. Usually, when we say something was lost,
we mean that at some previous time is was not lost. What is
usually meant by these descriptions of lost tribes is just some
people living in relatively remote circumstances on the fringes
of regular administrative contact with the outside world.

JENKINS: All of these groups in the last thirty to fifty years,
that the reports come out about, are groups that have been
contacted somehow by others in the past. But then they're lost
again to the bureaucracies. They are very remote, and they're
living very simply. They are living very traditionally.

HANSEN: Do you think it's possible that the Liawps, indeed,
have not had contact with the outside world, Dr. Jenkins?

JENKINS: If the outside world includes other Papua New
Guineans, it's impossible.

HANSEN: Professor Strathern, you have spent a lot of time in the area where the Liawps live in the Telefomin region of Papua New Guinea. Tell us a little bit about what that is like and why it's a little inconceivable that the Liawps would not have had contact with anybody else.

STRATHERN: It's not totally inconceivable, but it's unlikely. It is a very mountainous area with vast stretches of rainforests, deep valleys, like high mountain ranges. There are probably numbers of groups out there that don't have absolutely regular contact with the administration, especially if we reflect that since Papua New Guinea's independence, the kind of patrolling that used to take place in colonial times has probably been less frequent than it had been. So it's very likely there are some people who have drifted out of the administrative sphere. On the other hand, if you look at the size that is reported for some of these groups, anything from about fifteen to twenty people up to currently about seventy for this group, it's pretty obvious that a group of that kind is unlikely to have been entirely self-sufficient over a time. It probably had to have marriage contacts with other groups, trading contacts, and it probably had to have a subsistence cycle in which it moved around in search of supplies, which would bring it, from time to time, in contact with other groups of Papua New Guineans. This, I think, is probably the kind of thing that Carol is referring to there.

HANSEN: In this case, it was a government patrol that made contact with the tribe. Why would the government agent think it was an undiscovered tribe? Simply because, as you say, it had dropped out of the bureaucracy?

STRATHERN: This is one of the interesting things about the reports, which, from my distance, are not possible to evaluate. I read remarks that the people were fascinated by the clothes of a patrol. They were interested in the kinds of tools that they carried. They were interested in the kind of so-called modern foods which could be made available to them. My guess is that this was not entirely a spontaneous reaction but more a matter of trying to gain the attention of the government patrol by a kind of dramatic behavior that Papua New Guineans are rather good at, in order, quite simply, to plug into whatever services they had been missing out on in the previous years.

JENKINS: In 1984, when I was with the Madang government patrol that went into census the Hagahai once again, as they had tried ten years before and ten years before that, we heard similar things. That is, the Hagahai said, "We didn't know there were outside people." They literally said that to me and we couldn't believe what they were saying. When we questioned, they would say they saw smoke from fires over the hills. It was literally untrue. They were simply lying. They had been marrying their neighboring groups off and on for quite a while, but it is an attempt to get attention. It is an attempt to get the government to pay some attention to them, and people like patrol officers or missionaries jump to this and create a bit of a media frenzy partly out of a certain type of romanticism that urban Papua New Guineans have about these remote groups who, in some way, represent the way their ancestors lived.

HANSEN: There seems to be, sometimes, a tendency to put in a bit of detail that is intriguing. I'm looking at a story that appeared on June 25, 1993, from the Reuters News Service, in which another journalist in Papua New Guinea had mentioned that the Liawps are reported to worship a stone that they carry on their journey, which really plays into a sort of mythological kind of idea, does it not?

JENKINS: [*laughs*] Stones, Andrew can tell you some more about stones. Stones are not uncommon in Papua New Guinea, as objects of reverence.

STRATHERN: Surely, in all the areas neighboring this area, there are stones which are important repositories of ritual force, sometimes associated with the sun or associated with the earth itself or they're the petrified forms of certain powerful ancestors, stones which are also held by the people to be able to travel through the crowd and come up at a certain point and be associated with the origins of a group. In other words, there is a whole complex of ideas in that whole area which is very well known and very well documented, but what is interesting is to see the extremely exoticizing way in which this is presented, as though it were something utterly weird.

HANSEN: Is there something about that part of the world that would make these stories believable to the rest of us?

STRATHERN: It partly goes back to the history of earlier exploration in that part of the world, where there is no doubt that in the late 1920s and 1930s, there were "enormous discoveries," discoveries made of very large populations in the interior of New Guinea. It's also known that New Guinea is the home of very many diverse, small pockets of languages and cultures, which makes it statistically possible that, from time to time, something of this sort would turn up. In addition to that, I think that it's interesting what Carol has said about the romanticism of urban Papua New Guineans. They have obviously inherited an earlier colonial romanticism, in a certain sense, which was projected on New Guinea as a whole during the times of colonial administration and is very much a part of the overall fascination of the West and of Europe with the primitive frontier. So it's interesting to find, in a sense, today's educated Papua New Guineans somehow take on the mantle of that in relation to their remote areas, but probably with a different emotional tone to it.

HANSEN: Dr. Jenkins, did you know that the Hagahai were lying right away? And if so, how did you go about proving that the tribe was indeed lying?

JENKINS: The oral histories, even at the very first, began to contradict them. There were individuals among them who had already made contact with a cattle camp that was several days' walk away and I had found cattle tags, little metal tags with numbers, around women's necks, so there were visible contradictions to these statements. But the main thing that we did because we were very frightened of some sort of accusation of fraud or something would come up later like it did later. We bled everyone as soon as we could. Within six months of that first patrol, we bled everyone and looked for antibodies to their exposure to diseases, to try to see what level of contact they had

had by looking at what prior diseases had come through and at what time.

HANSEN: These are remote tribes of people that live in this part of the world. What should we be doing about contact with them, maybe, Dr. Jenkins, from a health standpoint? Is it dangerous for people to be constantly going in and checking some of these remote tribes out?

JENKINS: It's, of course, dangerous. One of the first things they have to do is immunize these people. They have not been exposed to tuberculosis. TB is rife in Papua New Guinea. They have not been exposed to a number of things that urban Papua New Guineans carry. We found in the first few years that the Hagahai were undergoing this sustained contact with missionaries and others that they experienced a lot of devastating epidemics. We worked very hard to immunize them, but cold chains are very difficult to maintain in remote areas. It takes a great deal of money. The government does not have that kind of money, and we had to secure funds from Save the Children and UNICEF and a number of outside agencies in order to immunize these people.

HANSEN: Professor Strathern, what about from the cultural standpoint? Interaction between those in the outside world who would like to go in and, more or less, examine these remote tribes?

STRATHERN: I have no doubt there will be a push from various sources to want to do that. One should also note that the missionaries have already gone in there. I was interested to see that at least one of the missionaries from the Baptist mission, who seems to be a Papua New Guinean himself, takes the line that they should not go in and do the sorts of things that missionaries did in colonial times, just rush in and attempt to destroy all the rituals and beliefs of those people. I do feel very strongly that whether there is going to be a detailed study of them or not, we have no right whatsoever to go in and make a destruction of that kind in the name of any kind of belief system that we, ourselves, follow. So I hope there will be a chance for some social scientists, shall we say, to be involved in early work in contacting these people. I entirely agree with Carol that the absolute imperative is to get some kind of medical contact in there and get them in some way protected from diseases from the outside. But I would hope that some cultural anthropologist also might be interested in going along with medical patrols. Perfect would be a medical anthropologist such as Carol herself who does both of these things, and so we would be able to place these people more accurately, shall we say, in the cultural and linguistic picture. One thing that really puzzles me about the reports at present is that these are said to be near the Indonesian border. On the other hand, they're said to be somehow between Oksapmen and Telefomin and Telefomin is nearer to the Indonesian border than Oksapmen is. They're probably somewhere in the Sibic foothills and some are out from the population, as the Hawa population, but details of this kind are very hazy to me, and I think if you send an anthropologist in there pretty soon that one would get them sorted out.

HANSEN: Do you think it is possible somewhere in the world that there is a civilization, a tribe perhaps, that, indeed, has not had any contact with anyone else but their own tribe?

STRATHERN: I would say no, because it's a human tendency always to make contact with others in addition to oneself. I think there is tremendous concern with the problem itself, a problem which comes from the history of colonial and western European expansion, essentially. It's a form of romanticism or frontier mentality in which we're fascinated to try to find what is beyond our spheres of knowledge, and I think it's relatively unlikely, in fact, that a thing of that sort would be found, nor do I think it's the important job of anthropology to go out there searching for this, in fact.

HANSEN: Would you agree, Dr. Jenkins?

JENKINS: Absolutely. And I would say I don't know what you people see, but I saw an article that said that there were seventy-five of these folks. It makes me think, I would never call that a civilization or even a tribe. It's much more likely to be a clan group, a related group of people who are separated for various reasons from larger groups that may have died out, the leftovers from an epidemic or a fight.

JULIE MARAVICH opted for a preventive mastectomy
after her mother, JO CUNNINGHAM, and twenty-
five-year-old younger sister CHARLENE developed
breast cancer. The three women talk with Katie Davis.
August 8, 1993

JULIE: You almost start to think of your breasts as the enemy, like not truly a part of your body. I still think they could
potentially be dangerous to you. . . . At the age of twenty-six, I
didn't want to start thinking about having mammograms every
six months. I thought that would be too much radiation, and I
thought immediately if a woman has breast cancer and she
wants to have the other breast removed, they call that prophy-
lactic mastectomy. I figured, why can't I have it done? It's not
unheard of. I had heard cases of it prior to that, and I just thought
that would be a good option for me.

DAVIS: It's not something that somebody suggested to you?
You came up with it on your own?

JULIE: When I told my surgeon and my gynecologist about it,
they basically said, my gynecologist in particular, said, the
question for me is not whether you should or should not have
it done, but how long can you afford to wait? And I agreed one
hundred percent, because once you have cancer, you have it.
You still have to address it. You have to get the chemotherapy,
the surgery, everything, and I just felt that it would happen to
me because Charlene's and my lives have paralleled each other,
you know, so much, since we were kids, and I just felt certain
that it would happen to me at one time.

DAVIS: Sort of an intuitive thing?

JULIE: I don't know, it's strange. We had our tonsils out
almost together, had our wisdom teeth out together, and we

have identical birthmarks on our legs. We're sort of telepathic. We are thinking about each other constantly. Like, I'll call, and she'll say, "Oh, I was just getting ready to call you." It happens often, really often. I guess it was a mental thing. I just felt almost certain about it. And doctors estimated that I did have a fifty percent chance. It's not a hundred percent chance, but I thought that the numbers were much too high.

JO: Katie [who was not interviewed] is my second daughter. She is thirty now, and, of course, she had the same fears that Julie did, and when she went to her gynecologist and had a mammogram, her doctor suggested Julie's procedure immediately.

DAVIS: The preventive mastectomy?

JO: Yes, and, of course, our faces just dropped. I kept saying, "Oh, no. He's crazy." What doctor in his right mind would suggest such a thing? And then all of the doctors started saying the same thing, so Katie basically had the same fears that Julie did.

DAVIS: You thought to yourself the doctor is crazy because it does seem like a radical thing to do.

JO: It is. It's very radical. My daughters are all very, as you can see, very good looking, very well proportioned, voluptuous women, you know? And they were all very good looking, and to do this deliberately to your body when you're not sick. They have never been sick. They have never really been through the childhood illnesses.

DAVIS: Did you try to talk Julie or Katie out of it?

JO: Definitely. Oh, I was the biggest objector.

JULIE: She told me I was crazy.

JO: Right up until the last minute she was going in the operating room.

DAVIS: Why?

JO: I kept trying to talk them out of it because they didn't have cancer.

JULIE: Mom made the surgery much easier for us. As soon as we woke up, she was there doing all the little things. We didn't

even have to call the nurses into the room. She just did everything for us. It was amazing. She was there for us to scream at,
and everything. She just catered to us. It was wonderful. It's nice
to have a mom.

JO: You do things like that for your children.

DAVIS: Julie, do you feel safe now?

JULIE: Not entirely. I feel safer. I certainly do feel safer. Pro-
phylactic mastectomy is not one hundred percent, you know,
sure. But they do remove about ninety-five percent of the tissue,
but some of it still remains. But in my mind I can think, therefore, maybe I'm back down into the normal range, like one in
nine for the rest of women, or maybe even ninety-five percent
less likely to get breast cancer. I don't know, but I just thought
that I had to have it done.

DAVIS: Some doctors have criticized this surgery because
they say there haven't been any studies done that say if you do
this, you lessen your chances of cancer. What would you say to
that?

JULIE: I think common sense would tell you if there is less
breast tissue there, then your chances have to be lower. I can
feel all of the breast tissue that I have. The implant is under-
neath the muscle. It's not obscuring anything, and it's all there,
right there where I can see it and feel it, and I feel very confident
about that.

DAVIS: Have you thought about it in terms of your daughter?

JULIE: I try not to think about it because I really don't think
that this is something you would have done lightly. We had a
very strong family history, very strong, and psychologically, it
was detrimental for me having this constant fear. I just hope by
the time she is fifteen or so, that, as I say, we have more options.

DAVIS: Did this whole experience make you think differently about your body and your breasts?

JULIE: I think yes. This may sound a little bit strong, but it's
a completely different attitude. You don't think of them as
much as a sexual object, you know, something to show off as
much as something to be afraid of.

DAVIS: What do you think, Charlene?

CHARLENE: I agree. I had no doubt in my mind that I wanted them removed as soon as I found out that I had cancer and I knew that I could live without having real breasts, you know? I would much rather be alive. So they're not as important. So I don't think about them too much anymore. I miss them. I miss having real ones, but I'm much happier now. Even though I still have cancer, I'm much happier knowing that I did what I did to have them removed.

JO: You would think why does God even give us breasts if we're going to have so much trouble with them? God, I don't know.

JULIE: The way I look at it is Charlene saved our lives, the rest of us. If it weren't for her, I certainly never would have had anything done. We had to use the scare tactics to get Mom to get a mammogram.

JO: Yes.

JULIE: And it worked, and lo and behold, she had it.

JO: Because I never believed in going to doctors unless you were sick, and I didn't want to go for mammograms if I didn't need them, you know?

DAVIS: The other thing that is striking to me is the openness about it. Is that a decision that you made to talk to people about it? I assume you're quite open with friends, and to talk to the media about it?

CHARLENE: I don't like anyone to feel uncomfortable around me and I just want everything to be open. If people have questions, please ask, and I'll be glad to answer. I won't give advice, but I will certainly answer anything that they want to know. It's important. It has to be talked about more, you know? It's something that is happening to so many women. If I know that women can learn from me, from what I have been through, and maybe even have a different attitude about how to survive through chemotherapy and radiation and try to be happy and live your life and not mope around and be sad every second because you have cancer. You know? It has its bad moments, but it also has its good moments, too, and I'm enjoying it. I am. I was just talking to a friend yesterday, and I really would not change places with anyone. I would not want this to happen to anyone else and I'm surviving and I'm having a great time, in spite of everything.

The British physician Dr. FRANK RYAN speaks with
Linda Wertheimer about the scientists who found
the cure for tuberculosis and the frightening fact that
TB is back. Dr. Ryan is the author of *The Forgotten
Plague: How the Battle Against Tuberculosis
Was Won — and Lost.* July 1, 1993

RYAN: Tuberculosis is the most dangerous infectious disease that ever existed on earth. Its history goes back into the Stone Age, and wherever it arrives in a community, it tends to come in very insidiously. It doesn't arrive like cholera or influenza. It arrives very slowly, and an epidemic often lasts a century or possibly even multiples of a century, so it behaves quite differently to other diseases. In this century and the previous century, to give you some idea, I have estimated that a thousand million human beings died from tuberculosis in those two centuries alone, so we are dealing with a disease of enormous potential, and obviously a very dangerous condition indeed.

WERTHEIMER: We Americans would say a billion people, a thousand million.

RYAN: Yes, that is true.

WERTHEIMER: When there were no drugs to treat tuberculosis, how was it treated?

RYAN: The big movement, of course, was the sanatorium movement. Now, I would like you to imagine what it was like for a young person. I have described tuberculosis in the book as rather like a Miltonic Satan because it was despotic in its character. It's a very strange disease, a very curious disease. It only lives in human beings. It doesn't exist anywhere else, so we are its pasture, if you like. And this young person would lie on the ward. They wouldn't be in hospital for two weeks or one week. They would be in hospital for a year, possibly two years, possibly three years, for much of this time, lying on their back being spoon-fed, not even allowed out of bed. Meanwhile, this extraordinary battle would take place inside them, which would decide whether they lived or died. That tiny little bacteria might grow and kill them, or for reasons that were quite unknown at that time, it might shrivel up and disappear, and they would seemingly get better, and about fifty percent got better and fifty percent died.

WERTHEIMER: Dr. Ryan, the book is an account of all of the people who attacked the disease from all different directions and managed to put together a package of drugs which ultimately were successful against tuberculosis. But I wanted to just ask you about one of those people, René Dubos, who you call the philosophical scientist, and who came up with not a scientific but kind of a philosophical construct upon which he began his work. You mention this, on page sixty-two in the book. I wonder if you could just read that little section.

RYAN: Certainly. "Every substance of living extraction was broken down in soil. It was a self-evident truth based upon one of the best known precepts of the Bible. 'Dust thou art and unto dust thou shalt return.' Now he was faced with a much more difficult task of making that philosophy work."

WERTHEIMER: What an extraordinary thing to have a person just have an idea which must have come to him from pulpits in his youth or from attending funerals as a child and suddenly to know that there is where he would find the answer.

RYAN: This was an extraordinary revelation because of his deeply philosophical turn of mind. He realized that this was his window onto a universal truth, and this was the inspiration for all of the work that came later. It's quite true that Dubos realized Pasteur had said that one day we will find that good bacteria will fight bad bacteria. Dubos was a deeply spiritual and religious man, too, and he believed in this concept of the Bible.

If you think of it, everything nasty in nature, everything that lives, if it's put in the soil, it's destroyed there. Now Dubos was working at this time with a man called Oswald Avery of the Rockfeller in New York, and Avery had been searching. Avery was a medical doctor, and had been searching for twenty years fruitlessly for something that would kill nasty bacteria. He turned to this young man of very tender years, and said, "Could you help me?" and Dubos, who was very confident at this time, said, "Yes, I think I can." The reason why he said "I think I can" was exactly that precept from the Bible, which is quite extraordinary.

WERTHEIMER: In the very last chapter of your book, after you deal with the discovery of the cure for tuberculosis and the essential triumph over the disease, virtually eradicating it from the Western European countries, you then say that once again, we have lost control of tuberculosis. What do you think was the single most important factor or factors?

RYAN: All over the world, where tuberculosis is now rising again, is the AIDS virus. Essentially, it's a very strange phenomenon about tuberculosis. It's actually a benign disease, because ninety-five percent of the people who contract tuberulosis show no symptoms of disease. They never develop the full-blown disease, but the germ becomes dormant in them, and they develop a latent form of tuberculosis. What happens is that there are little cells in the body, lymphocytes, if you want, white cells, which control tuberculosis and hold it in their bands in a tiny little focus in the body. The AIDS virus infects those very cells. It actually chooses the very type of cell which controls tuberculosis.

WERTHEIMER: You have a view of tuberculosis that few people have. Do you have any notion about what ought to be done about this new epidemic?

RYAN: I think we do need new antibiotics. We need to come to terms with what the disease is, we need to understand it, and very few people do. We have got to find an effective strategy, we have got to fund it adequately, and stick to it. I think we have got to deal effectively with the AIDS crisis, which is very important. We have to deal with noncompliance, in other words, people failing to take the medicines properly, and I think that is, again, very important. We have got to help the Third World because if we allow it to continue to rampage there, it's going to come back into our own back yards and haunt us.

The medical historian SHERWIN NULAND discusses with Neal Conan his publication *The Face of Mercy: A Photographic History of Medicine at War*, in which he traces the history of the art of military medicine from the siege of Troy to the siege of Sarajevo. Dr. Nuland is also a clinical professor of surgery at Yale University. October 28, 1993

CONAN: In the first part of your book, I was fascinated by the way military medicine was forced to change almost completely due to the development of gunpowder.

NULAND: That is true. After the Battle of Crécy in 1346, which was the first battle in which gunpowder and actually guns first appeared, suddenly there arrived on the scene this extraordinary means of killing large numbers of people and what may be even worse, perpetrating on them some extraordinary kinds of wounds.

CONAN: Before that, the penetrating wounds by spears or arrows were fairly straightforward.

NULAND: That's right. It was literally and figuratively straightforward because the path of course of an arrow or a spear is rather direct. As bullets and various kinds of projectiles came into being, it became pretty clear that their pathways were not direct. They would bounce off structures, they would tumble through the body, they would veer off in one way or another without anyone being able to be sure where exactly they had gone and how much damage they had perpetrated.

CONAN: In your book, you don't let us forget that until very recent times, soldiers were far more likely to die from disease than anything they would encounter on the battlefield.

NULAND: That's certainly true. If we look at our own civil war, the most commonly quoted statistic, and it's only for the

North because we don't really have good statistics for the South, is that twice as many men died because of pestilence, malnutrition, things of that nature, than of gunshot wounds of any kind.

CONAN: It's shocking to read how unprepared both sides' medical corps, if that is an appropriate word, were for the U.S. Civil War, and that while the generals were intimately familiar with Napoleonic tactics, their medical staffs were utterly ignorant, or greatly ignorant, of the great advances made by Napoleon's doctors.

NULAND: The most important advance that they were ignorant of was the advance of how to get the wounded off the battlefield quickly and get them to treatment as soon as possible. At the first Battle of Bull Run, many troops were left lying on the field, and were unable to get away from the field because there was no system of medical military transport, and some of them took days before they got to any sort of medical care.

CONAN: What kind of role did military doctors play in the development of what we now regard as proper hygiene and proper sanitation?

NULAND: There was no real understanding about the dangers of garrisoning of troops in close quarters, whether it had to do with water supply, whether it had to do with *excretio*, or whether it had to do with personal contact and ticks and lice and all this kind of thing until eventually it became developed from trial and error, as a result of military campaigns that had fallen on their faces because so many men died before the battle actually occurred.

CONAN: This idea of the military and public health, I guess, would go all the way to Walter Reed and his efforts to fight yellow fever in Cuba.

NULAND: This is just what happened with the situation after the Spanish American War when Walter Reed was confronted with the massive epidemics of yellow fever around the time of the building of the Panama Canal. It was by his extraordinary efforts that it was finally understood that yellow fever was carried by the *Aedes aegypti* mosquito, and from then on, it was a simple matter to wipe the mosquito out. They already had the sanitation methods. They had to know what to do with them.

CONAN: You describe the extraordinary bravery of the troops who volunteered to be the living guinea pigs, the human pigs, to test Walter Reed's theory.

NULAND: What actually happened is that several of the men came forward beyond the number of volunteers that he wanted, and even when he explained how dangerous this was and how likely some of them were to die, they refused to turn around and go back. They said this is something we do for other people and for our country, and as you know several of them did die, including one of the doctors.

CONAN: I don't mean to denigrate your narrative in any way, but some of the most remarkable things in this book are the pictures. I'm looking at one now, the very last picture in the book in fact, and one of the most moving. It's a gathering of the Ruined Faces Club, of men who were disfigured during the First World War.

NULAND: The First World War was really the first time I would have to say when everybody wore a helmet, and helmets seemed like a great idea, and they were a great idea. They saved many lives, but the result was that shrapnel, bullets, would ricochet off helmets, be diverted by helmets, and went into the face. The helmets themselves were often knocked into the face, and so there were many facial injuries. Now we also have a war in which a man with a facial injury is likely to survive because in previous wars, the other injuries that he got might kill him. Whereas by the First World War many of these men were being saved, so they were coming back with damaged faces. Not only that, but of course the First World War was the one in which the infant specialty of plastic surgery came out of its swaddling clothes. Suddenly there was an enormous understanding of what could be done with skin grafts and flaps and other reconstructive techniques and with burn treatment.

CONAN: At several points, you describe a race as healers

struggle to come up with ways to deal with the news that weaponry can damage people.

NULAND: Unfortunately, the healers are never as ingenious as those who create that weaponry. You must remember that most medical effort is designed toward civilian use. Virtually all destructive effort is designed toward military use, and in between wars engineers, gun designers, whatever, are constantly figuring out new ways to kill and maim. We go into a burst when the war starts, thinking again of how to treat wounds, and we are always far behind. They are always way ahead of us.

Arthur C. Clarke, the inventor and science fiction author, talks with Susan Stamberg from his home in Sri Lanka about great technological advances of the twentieth century, from telephones to walking on the moon. Dr. Clarke is the author of such science fiction classics as *Childhood's End*, *Rendezvous with Rama*, and — with the director Stanley Kubrick — the film *2001: A Space Odyssey*. His 1945 article "Extraterrestrial Relays" proposed the idea of communications satellites. A recent novel, *The Hammer of God*, was published in 1993. July 24, 1993

STAMBERG: Thanks for agreeing to talk with us, Dr. Clarke.

CLARKE: Nice to talk to you. You sound as if you are on the other side of the room, it is so clear.

STAMBERG: As opposed to being on the other side of the earth. How are you speaking with us?

CLARKE: AT&T has given me one of their wonderful new video phones, which has a little TV screen, about two inches by two inches, and it works over ordinary telephone lines. It's an incredible thing. Now, it's not television in the sense, you don't see a continuous moving image. The image is refreshed every five seconds or so. I think everybody should get one, and I am already dissatisfied with old-fashioned screen telephones.

STAMBERG: How do I look on your phone?

CLARKE: Unfortunately, you don't have one at your end, so I can't tell.

STAMBERG: To me it's a terrific advantage.

CLARKE: You can turn off the camera if you want.

STAMBERG: Oh, that's good. To what extent has the work

that you did in 1945, inventing the communications satellite, permitted us to be speaking right now.

CLARKE: It's really the key to the whole thing. Of course, I can see the communications satellite largely as a television broadcasting device that could cover whole areas of the earth, and so three of them, in fact, would be able to cover the entire earth. The use of telephones was secondary. We did get the first stage of global telecommunications with the satellites, but now the cables, fiber optic cables, have come along and they control much of the terrestrial telephones. So the two are really complementary, the fiber optics cable and the satellites.

STAMBERG: Dr. Clarke, for most of your writing life and maybe even before you started writing, you have been interested in the idea of meteors hitting the earth and this new novel of yours, *The Hammer of God*, tells the story of one that is heading in the future towards the earth and an attempt to head it off. You have been writing about this at least since *Rendezvous with Rama* in 1973 and thinking about it even longer. Why are you so fascinated by that?

CLARKE: It's one of the most dramatic things that could happen. And I have a sort of personal reason because my friend, the late Luis Alvarez, and his son Walter brought up the theory of the dinosaurs being wiped out by an asteroid, so I had a particular interest from that point of view. And, it just reminded me, it's also raised in the *Titanic* and I didn't know all about raising the *Titanic*. I guess I am sort of rather fond of disasters of various kinds. And in a way, the *Titanic* and the iceberg and the earth and asteroids, there is a certain parallel.

STAMBERG: I have been reading a new biography of you and enjoying it very much, by Neil McAleer, and from it, it seems that you were destined to be a great communicator. You were born into a post office family in Somerset, England, right?

CLARKE: I think our background is probably more farming than engineering, but my father was a post office engineer and my mother was a post office telegraph operator, and she could still read Morse code into her old age.

STAMBERG: Is that so? And she took you flying just before your ninth birthday. What do you remember about that?

CLARKE: I really don't recall that at all vividly, but what I do remember is my first Concorde flight. I remember that very vividly because it was such a steep takeoff that the curtains between us and the pilot swung back at such a steep angle, and you realize how steeply you were rising up into the sky. I do recall that very vividly.

STAMBERG: Not too fast for you, then?

CLARKE: I would like to go even faster one day.

STAMBERG: You were there helping Walter Cronkite anchor the Apollo moon landings at the end of the 1960s and into the early 1970s. But you never got a chance to go to the moon yourself.

CLARKE: No, I'm afraid not. At one time, of course, we thought that there might be space stores about now. But that was in the euphoria immediately after Apollo, and then there were the shuttle disasters. I don't think there will be any commercial space stores in this century, but of course, it will be inevitable in the next.

STAMBERG: It will be, you believe?

CLARKE: Oh yes, no question. The same will happen in space that is happening in aviation. It will take a little longer, but some time in the next century the cost of a ticket to the moon will be no more than an around-the-world jet ticket today.

STAMBERG: But you need the political will to make the commitments for the money that it's going to take to expand the technology. Do you sense that kind of political willingness around the world these days?

CLARKE: No, it doesn't exist now. And, of course, in a way the Apollo program is sort of a historic collaboration caused entirely by the cold war. One day we will be really glad that it did happen, but we've got to look probably fifty years ahead of schedule. But we won't be going back to the moon, and won't be going on to Mars, except on a very small scale, until we have cheap methods of space propulsion.

STAMBERG: In 1970, you told Alan Watts, the philosopher and theologian, that the purpose of the universe is the perpetual astonishment of mankind. Twenty-three years later, do you have any change or addition for that?

CLARKE: No, in fact, it's much more astonishing now. When I said that to Alan in the dear old hotel Chelsea, we didn't know half of the incredible things; pulsars were just being discovered, neutron stars, with the black hole still in the future, and these incredible things we are finding now, particularly gamma ray bursts, which are tremendous explosions. Suddenly, something switches on several million sun powers of gamma rays, and no one knows what it is. Some scientists and writers have suggested that it may be industrial accidents.

STAMBERG: That sounds to me, though, like a very, I don't know if ethnocentric is the right word, but humancentric interpretation of why we are all here.

CLARKE: No one knows why we are here. And, of course, the great question is, Is there anybody else anywhere out there?

STAMBERG: What is your bet? If there is that discovery of intelligent life elsewhere, will it be benign or malevolent?

CLARKE: Many of us optimistically hope that any malevolent civilization will self-destruct before it can reach us, but I wouldn't bet on it.

PATCH ADAMS talks with Alex Chadwick about his radical approach to treating terminally ill children. He dresses up as a clown and refuses to charge patients for their care. Dr. Adams wrote *Gesundheit* and is the founder of the Gesundheit Institute in northern Virginia. January 25, 1993

ADAMS: If doctors have to carry malpractice insurance, they practice their entire career in fear and mistrust. If doctors are bogged down in paperwork, they cannot spend the proper amount of time with patients. If doctors are going to be so near human suffering and dare to give of themselves and be vulnerable around other people's human suffering day in and day out without there being a context of joy to do this in, it will beat them down. I believe what happens is that they'll start overlooking the other person's suffering and stick to the lab values and the x-rays.

CHADWICK: Let me ask you about one aspect of medical care that you write about in the book, and that would be the final medical act. You talk about "fun death." Isn't that the opposite of what most people would think of as a doctor's concern?

ADAMS: By fun, I mean what is fun for the individual. It is not my definition of fun, but for each individual, their definition of fun. And, let me say why. When I was an intern at Georgetown, there was a young girl with a large bony tumor on her face. She was obviously going to die. It had disfigured her to the level of the Elephant Man, in horrendous ugliness. I went in, I talked with her, and I found out her great sadness, and it wasn't sadness about dying. It was a sadness of "Why, when my parents come to visit me, do they not stay very long, and why are they crying? Why do my friends not visit me anymore? Why is it hard for people to look at me? What have I done?" I looked at this young girl, and I said, "We're going to play. We're going to have fun." I spent the rest of her life having fun with her. I promised her I was going to be a person that is fun to be with, and I would not be afraid, and I would just fit death into one of the other things that has to happen in life.

CHADWICK: Doctors are usually taught to avoid personal closeness with their patients, but that is not the case at the Gesundheit Institute?

ADAMS: I think it is a gross error. I think that when people found a family doctor or primary care doctor that spent time with their patients, they would laugh at the concept of not getting close to one's patients. I think one of the reasons people aren't going into medicine now and that so many doctors are disgruntled, so many doctors are quitting medicine, so many doctors are really hurting, is because, indeed, in the climate of malpractice and in the climate of greed in medicine and the climate of all the paperwork and the controls, the only thing left is the intimacy with the patient.

CHADWICK: You don't carry malpractice insurance? You refuse to carry malpractice insurance?

ADAMS: Even if the law in the states where I practice demanded it, I would break the law. It is wrong. Everything to do with the system of malpractice is wrong.

CHADWICK: But if you make a mistake, then what happens?

ADAMS: It's ridiculous to somehow gloss over the fact that we doctors make mistakes every single day. We are imperfect. We are imperfect! I can tell you, I have done vast experiments with patients and made probably ten thousand or more gross mistakes, and have never been sued. Now maybe someday I will be sued, but I'll tell you this: I never meant harm to a patient. People that are bad doctors should not be treating people. It is not that they should have some kind of financial spanking and their premiums up; they should be taken out of medicine. Everyone else should have the privilege to make a mistake.

CHADWICK: Is your model, the way that you conduct medicine at the Gesundheit Institute, is this an answer or a solution that you realistically think can work all across the country? Is this what everyone should be doing in medicine?

ADAMS: I think it's far too simplistic in the modern age to think of anything being an answer for such a gigantic and complex situation. I think it's ridiculous to ever perceive that an answer for New York City is going to be an answer for Pocahontas County, West Virginia. What I would say is that yes, each community could get together and say, "How can we care for the health needs of our community to make it a true community hospital?" And that could be dramatically cheaper than the current version. . . . I attended a home birth last month, and this person put a big deal in the fact that at a very troubling time during the birth, I ran over, sat down next to her, and held her hand. For her, it was a giant thing; for me, it just seemed natural to do. So if somebody wants to say that I'm not a doctor by doing that — I don't need the doctor M.D. part of my life to feel good.

ANIMAL LIFE

JANINE BENYUS talks with Robert Siegel about the behavior of animals, from sleep to sex to self-preservation. Benyus wrote field guides to wildlife habitats in the United States before writing the book *Beastly Behaviors*, which she calls "a Berlitz guide to the zoo." March 15, 1993

BENYUS: When you're in the animal world, you're sort of in a foreign country. Animals have their own customs and their own language, their own body language, their own rituals and ceremonies. We wouldn't think of going to Tibet without reading a travel guide first. *Beastly Behaviors* I think of as the guide that gives you insights about the animal world before you travel there.

SIEGEL: One of the behaviors you report on, in all the different animals, is sleep. And it varies enormously. I'm very surprised by how different the sleep habits and, presumably, needs are, of different animals.

BENYUS: For instance, giraffes sleep about twenty minutes a night. They'll sleep four or five minutes deeply and then wake up. That's all throughout the whole night. If you add that all together, they get about twenty minutes, whereas, a lion will sleep twenty-one hours out of the day. Shrews, which are smaller than mice, don't sleep at all. They don't even rest. They are always moving because they have to eat their weight in earthworms every day, so they're constantly hunting.

SIEGEL: There's a saying that political writers sometimes invoke when two superpowers reach an agreement that disadvantages a little country. They say, "When elephants make love, the grass suffers." I must say that, until reading your description of elephants' mating habits, I didn't know the half of it. It's not just the elephants who are mating, it's all their friends and neighbors.

BENYUS: [*laughs*] That's right. There's a thing in elephant behavior called "mating pandemonium," and when a couple begins to mate, the entire family will surround them. There is sort of a hoopla that goes on. They scream and they trumpet and they urinate and defecate and move around, and it seems as if they are celebrating the couple's mating. What actually may be going on is that they're learning. Animals watch other animals mate to learn those night moves, and they're also supporting the procreation of another member of their herd.

SIEGEL: Cheering it on.

BENYUS: I think so.

SIEGEL: In a mating pandemonium.

BENYUS: Yes, mating pandemonium, it's called.

SIEGEL: So the African proverb about the grass being hurt would be very literal about what happens to the area.

BENYUS: [*laughs*] That's true.

SIEGEL: The behavior of zebras, when they sense an intruder in their midst, is just as fascinating. There is a formation that they assume.

BENYUS: They know exactly the flight distance that they need to get away. They know that — if they're watching a cat, they'll just stand, and they'll stare. And then, if the lion does get within their flight distance, then they will turn and run. And the lead stallion will take up the rear and kick backwards, to make sure that none of the other zebras are harmed. They have a very harmonious society, zebras do.

SIEGEL: The zebras travel, you write, when they are in a herd, at the pace of the slowest zebra, so no one should be left behind.

BENYUS: That's right. And if one of the zebras gets into trouble, they will send a rescue group back and come galloping back, circle the zebra that's in trouble, and gallop away with them. It's in their best interest to keep peace and harmony. That's why they have so many communication gestures. The kind of things that I write about in the book are communication gestures that help lubricate this social bond and that they're constantly doing. Even at the zoo, if you watch zebras, they're constantly nosing one another, licking, grooming one another, to keep up these bonds. It's the glue that keeps a society together and keeps the individual alive.

THEODORE XENOPHON BARBER, author of *The Human Nature of Birds*, tells Robert Siegel that birds are hardly the instinct-driven automatons they are often assumed to be. Rather, they are capable of affection, altruism, and deductive reasoning. September 1, 1993

BARBER: Birds are very intelligent and aware and very much like people in their emotions and feelings and in their ability to relate, in their erotic sexuality, in their play, in their fun games and ability to communicate with humans and among themselves. Researchers have found a tremendous amount of data that just isn't anything like anybody ever thought, and just overturns all of our preconceptions and thoughts.

SIEGEL: If you were to direct the attention of a skeptic to a particular bird or a particular story that would disabuse the skeptic of his belief in the strictly instinctual, robotic nature of bird intelligence, what bird would you direct me to?

BARBER: I suppose today it would be Alex the parrot, who is being thoroughly studied, and a tremendous amount of data show that Alex is a person. He understands, relates, and asks questions. Oh, he's learned to talk, by the way. He replies to abstract questions. He knows the name of everything around him and also uses numbers.

SIEGEL: What is it about this most remarkable of birds under study, Alex the parrot, that qualifies him for a humanlike intelligence? What is it about us that qualifies us as human?

BARBER: The ability to figure out things and to make deductions. He learns that a triangle is three-cornered, then he learns that a square is four-cornered. Then, when you give him a football, he comes up himself and deduces that it's two-cornered. Then, you give him a pentagon and he deduces that it's five-cornered.

SIEGEL: Even if you could assemble twenty or forty good stories about interesting relations between birds and people, and interesting insights into birds' intelligence, that would still be the tiniest sliver of the relations between people and birds. People have had thousands, probably millions, of birds as household pets. I have great affection for the parakeet in our household who spends a lot of time on my kids' shoulders and is a lovely little guy, but he doesn't possess human intelligence. That would be a stretch. Why don't we all detect this in the birds that we have?

BARBER: Because nobody has really looked at birds the way scientists have now. For instance, parakeets have been well studied. When they're free in the house, they are able to show what they can do, they can learn to speak, communicate. They can communicate with words but they can also communicate in other ways. When you have two of them, they're mated and fairly happy. They are entirely different than what people think they are when they keep them in cages and don't really interact.

SIEGEL: The phrase that seems to sum up the judgment of the ages on avian intelligence is the phrase "birdbrain." Birds have rather small brains, and they're lacking in the cerebral cortex to which we attribute all kinds of rational skills.

BARBER: Right. That is silly. It's really ridiculous for two reasons. First of all, we know darn well that we can miniaturize anything and it doesn't really change it. In other words, the size of something doesn't matter. They have small bodies; that's the main reason. But the bigger reason they don't have a highly developed cortex is because that's where the human specialties are. They have a highly developed hyperstriatum, another part of the brain where their specialties are localized. So what I'm saying is, you should look at it the other way around. You should say humans have a very odd brain. They don't have this highly developed thing that birds have. We think everything we look at, we look at through a very limited point of view, the human point of view.

SIEGEL: You write that you're fully aware of the criticism by scientists of anthropomorphizing, and of what would be, I think, an eagerness to see in other species humanlike traits.

BARBER: Right. I have been a scientist now for thirty-six years or so, and what is ruining and hurting us from understanding reality is this darned anthropomorphism. We're afraid. All scientists are afraid to say what they really find. When they find birds are like people, they can't say that. They would be excommunicated, they would be thrown out, they would be considered as unscientific. That's our problem. It's this anthropomorphic bias, taboo, that's so strong in science that we can't face reality. But if we do, we will see a whole new world around us, and we might even begin to react differently to the animals and nature and reality and maybe even save our planet that's now under destruction. Birds are one part of it.

EDWARD KUTAC, a bird watcher, tells Linda Wert-
heimer about the rare arrival of a blue-footed booby in
Granite Shoals, Texas, and about the hundreds of
birders who came to see this South American bird.
Kutac is the author of *The Birder's Guide to Texas.*
September 14, 1993

WERTHEIMER: If you were to describe the booby by saying
that it looks like another bird, does it —

KUTAC: It looks like another booby.

WERTHEIMER: [*laughs*] I thought that might be the case.

KUTAC: There are brown boobies and there are masked boobies and there is a red-footed booby. And these are all different
species.

WERTHEIMER: But does it look like a duck or does it look
like a gull?

KUTAC: It has webbed feet like a duck. It has a long bill for
catching fish like a heron. You might call it close to a small
heron in description, but not the feet. The feet would be more
like a duck in that they're webbed. When I was there, most of
the time the bird was asleep, but if somebody pecks on it it'll
come away or if somebody makes a noise it will look around
and stuff.

WERTHEIMER: Is that how it comes by the name booby?
Because it's a dozy bird?

KUTAC: Boobies got their name a very long time ago when
sailors from Europe were sailing around the world and, of
course, they had to add provisions as they went along, and so
they would stop at islands or places and kill things and that was
their food until they got to the next stop, and when they found
boobies around South America they could walk up to them
with a club and hit them in the head and the booby wouldn't

leave, so they thought this was kind of dumb, so they gave them the name booby and they've been boobies ever since.

WERTHEIMER: How does this booby spend its time?

KUTAC: Mostly just sitting on the end of that diving board and sleeping.

WERTHEIMER: There's a boat dock with a diving board on it?

KUTAC: Yes.

WERTHEIMER: And this creature is just out on the end of the diving board?

KUTAC: Yes.

WERTHEIMER: And does it dive?

KUTAC: I'm sure it does to feed. You could see bones around there that it has eaten, so it's obviously feeding on small fish.

WERTHEIMER: The people whose dock it is that this blue-footed booby is resting upon — how do they feel about hosting?

KUTAC: Apparently very cooperative. People are welcome to come up there and sit in their lawn chairs or walk up and photograph the booby or whatever they want to do. So I think they're kind of proud that they've got something special, which is good. Sometimes rare birds show up and people don't want anybody coming to see it. They don't want to be bothered because it is a mess.

WERTHEIMER: I suppose you could sell tickets.

KUTAC: That hasn't been suggested, so maybe we shouldn't bring that up yet.

WILLIAM LISHMAN tells Noah Adams about
Operation Migration, an experiment in which eighteen
goslings were trained to imprint on an ultralight
aircraft. Following two planes, the geese successfully
migrated 350 miles from Toronto, Canada, to
Warrenton, Virginia, in seven days. Lishman is the
director of Operation Migration in Warrenton.
October 26, 1993

LISHMAN: The further away we got from home, the closer
they would fly to us. In our own home area, where they fly, they
know the area, so if they break away they just go home; but
when we've flown fifty miles away, for example, then they
don't know the territory and we're the only thing they know
and so they stick with us. They're just following us, like, "Hey,
Mom, where are we going?"

ADAMS: You flew sometimes four and a half hours a day.
How did you know that was right? Could you see them getting
tired sometimes?

LISHMAN: Yesterday was the only time that really worried
me, because they were panting quite a lot. The thing is, we
were flying in warmer air, and they can fly a long distance in
cold air. The oxygen in the air is thicker and they get more
oxygen in.

ADAMS: Did you say you could hear the geese panting in
the air?

LISHMAN: No, you see them. They have got their mouths
open, their tongues stuck out. You can see it, but you can't hear
it, no.

ADAMS: So they just look exhausted?

LISHMAN: Yes. When they landed here yesterday, they were
ready to land.

ADAMS: I'll bet. I don't want to venture too much into the anthropomorphic area here, but I just couldn't help but wonder what your flight must have looked like to another normal flight of geese?

LISHMAN: It never crossed my mind what it would look like to them. I know that on one flight, when we were in Ontario, we were taking them on a short cross-country up there. A large flock of Canada geese passed in front of us, and our geese steered off to try and catch up with them. We were a little bit worried that they were going to take off with this wild flock, but they turned around and came back to us.

ADAMS: What's the plan now? They will winter here in Virginia?

LISHMAN: That's right.

ADAMS: And then how do they get back to Canada?

LISHMAN: The plan is we'll fly back. We'll retrace those steps with them in the spring, in April of 1994, and keep them up in Canada over the summer. Right now we're questioning whether we should just raise the second flock and bring two flocks down next year and then release them here and then see if they would return. If you think about how it happens in the wild, there is always a number of generations migrating together so that the new birds may fly with the older birds two or three times and they learn the route. Whether they'll learn the route with one flight down and back is a question in our mind at the moment, and maybe we should take them, to really make the experiment worthwhile, take them down one more time and then leave them on their own at the end of next fall.

ADAMS: To fully prove your theory here, they would have to be able to come back from Canada to Virginia one winter by themselves?

LISHMAN: Right.

ADAMS: Are you worried that they are so totally imprinted on the ultralight aircraft that they would require that?

LISHMAN: What happens when they reach maturity or when they are reaching breeding age, they don't want to have anything to do with their parents. So they're on their own at that point anyway. We just play this parental role in the same way that their natural parents would for the first two years.

STEVE PRINGLE, the general aviation liaison for the Anchorage International Airport, tells how three pigs named Larry, Moe, and Curly saved the day. On a small island at the airport, nesting gulls were creating a hazard for incoming planes. Mr. Pringle set the food chain to work, dispatching the pigs to the island to disrupt the nests, eat the eggs, and reduce the gull population. A year later Linda Wertheimer checked in with Mr. Pringle to find out how well the scheme had worked. August 4, 1993

WERTHEIMER: First of all, did the experiment work?

PRINGLE: It was a rousing success. In fact, it worked so well for us, we've committed to it for next year and probably two or three years after that.

WERTHEIMER: So did you really see a decrease in the gull population?

PRINGLE: Not so much in the adult birds. We did see a decrease in adult population for water fowl. The ducks and the geese, the Canada geese, got the message early on and they moved elsewhere to nest. The gulls were very determined to nest on the island, and they kept up their efforts.

WERTHEIMER: Did it take care of your hazard? Your hazard problem with birds flying up into the path of airplanes?

PRINGLE: Certainly we put a dent in the future population. The pigs found and destroyed over 350 gull nests out there.

WERTHEIMER: Now, Larry, Moe and Curly, the three pigs you put out on that island, have completed their work. Is that it?

PRINGLE: That's correct. Last Friday we removed them from the island, and we were instructed to return them to the farmer, and he was to do with them what he wanted.

WERTHEIMER: Which is?

PRINGLE: Ultimately their demise was to be slaughtered for consumption.

WERTHEIMER: So these pigs, after having spent the summer disrupting gull nests and presumably eating eggs, are about to be bacon?

PRINGLE: Or bacon and eggs, probably.

WERTHEIMER: When you put them out on the island they were, what, little pigs?

PRINGLE: Sixty pounds, and when we took them off they were all in excess of two hundred, two hundred twenty pounds. They continued to grow and grow and grow, and we were worried if we left them there much longer we'd have to use a helicopter for air support to lift these hogs off the island. They weren't pigs anymore. They were hogs.

WERTHEIMER: So did they get a last meal?

PRINGLE: Yes, in fact, they did. That's how we encouraged them into their transport pens. We gave them a variety of fruits and vegetables, of watermelons and cantaloupes and grapes and strawberries and things. So I guess you could say that was their last meal.

WERTHEIMER: Did you have any qualms at all about sending Larry, Moe, and Curly off to their unhappy fate?

PRINGLE: Oh, of course. Everyone involved with the experiment became attached to them. They each had their own personality and it was sad to see them go, but it's just one of those necessary things that needs to be done. We had so much community involvement with this. People would come out and set up large telephoto lenses with tripods and they would actually sit and wait for these pigs to walk out of the brush. The Princess Tours is quite a large company here, and they would run their tour buses around this island in hopes of glimpsing a pig, so it was crazy, but it was a lot of fun.

The anthropologist ELIZABETH MARSHALL THOMAS talks with Liane Hansen about canine behaviors, from why dogs chase cars to why wolves howl. She began researching for her book *The Hidden Life of Dogs* more than fifteen years ago when she cared for Misha, a neighbor's dog with an insatiable case of wanderlust. October 31, 1993

THOMAS: I would get complaints about him from far away, and by making a map of where his complaints came from, I saw that he had a huge range. And he could always find his way home. He was obviously navigating some very dangerous traffic. He was obviously crossing rivers on the ice, which is very dangerous for dogs. I decided to follow him, and I would follow him first on foot, then on a bike, and I kept this up for a couple of years, and I found many things that I wouldn't have ever dreamed of that he was doing. He was a very intelligent and capable dog.

HANSEN: What did you find out about why he was roaming in the first place?

THOMAS: It turned out that he was roaming in order to compare himself to other dogs. He wanted to reassure himself, I think, that he was the better dog.

HANSEN: Did you ever figure out why dogs chase cars?

THOMAS: I think they are trying to herd them. I think this is a shepherding reaction. I think dogs think of cars as they would think of large ungulates, like cattle or something like that, and they want to bring them under control. Also, the hunting reflex is there, too. They may think they are trying to get away. I know a dog who bit the tire of a car, to her sorrow. She was OK, but it was a terrible experience.

HANSEN: You have studied wolves, too, haven't you?

THOMAS: Yes.

HANSEN: And you found quite a few similarities between dogs and wolves? I'm interested in the whole idea of howling. Let's talk about culture. Do you know the movie *One Hundred and One Dalmations,* the cartoon?

THOMAS: I haven't, alas, seen it yet, but I hope to someday.

HANSEN: There is one scene where the dogs of the city are communicating to other dogs that something has happened, so it's a series of barks that goes from the city of London out into the countryside. How does that fit into the way dogs actually use their own powers of speech?

THOMAS: Howling, I think, is certainly a communication. Howling means many things. It's calling to others. It's a call for assembly. When the whole group howls together, it can be a loud signal to other groups of wolves, who are maybe at the periphery, to tell them, "Here we are, a large group." It also serves the function of a rallying call, making everybody feel good, making everybody feel together and cooperative, the same way that singing before a sports event might make us feel.

HANSEN: So they really weren't too far off in that cartoon movie about having this network of dog barks.

THOMAS: Probably not.

HANSEN: To what extent do you think our own knowledge of dog behavior is sort of influenced by the images we have? Of course, there is that hearty, perennial Lassie. "Go, Lassie, get help."

THOMAS: Yes, indeed. Some Lassies would know and might be able to do it, but perhaps that's the ultimate ideal of a human-dog relationship, from the human's point of view. Lassie doesn't seem to get all that much out of it, but the humans certainly do.

HANSEN: So what do you think? Are we trying to put human qualities on dogs, or should we just start trying, as you have done, to find out what those dog qualities are that we're looking at?

THOMAS: I don't think I'm putting human qualities on dogs. I think what happens here is that humans and dogs have similar qualities, and by looking at one's human qualities, one can make a guess as to what the dog is doing with his similar dog quality.

HANSEN: One of the last stories you tell toward the end of the book is about the dogs in your yard who dug a den. You said, "I would like to know what the world looks like to a dog, or sounds like or smells like. I would like to visit a dog's mind to know what he's thinking and feeling, to have another dog look at me and see not something different, but something the same, and to my great surprise, during those afternoons by the den, I felt I came close to achieving that." You sort of divested yourself of your primate experience and were able to experience a dog's life, as it were?

THOMAS: I tried to. I think many people have wanted very much to get out of their species experience and into another, if possible. Certainly people who observe animals would very much like to know what it is like to be another kind of animal. You can't get out of your own consciousness, but the only way you can approach it is to observe very closely and try to duplicate the experience as much as possible, which is not an easy thing to do. I don't know how close we will ever be able to get with that, but it's fun to try.

Dan Rosenberg tells Linda Wertheimer about the colt born to the 1980 Kentucky Derby winner, Genuine Risk. This was the sixteen-year-old mare's first successful pregnancy. Mr. Rosenberg is general manager at Three Chimneys Farm in Midway, Kentucky.
May 17, 1993

ROSENBERG: The foal was born on Saturday evening. We induced labor because ultrasound examination revealed that the fetus was in distress, and so the decision was made to induce labor, and the delivery itself was very rapid and very uneventful. And the foal stood and nursed and did all the things that foals are supposed to do, and the mare did all the things that mares are supposed to do. She was a wonderful mother, and there was a great deal of elation and jubilation. Yesterday evening, the foal became very uncomfortable. It has actually had a condition that is not uncommon in newborn foals, called muconium retention. Muconium is fecal material that all foals are born with, and they pass it, generally, quite easily, and sometimes require a little bit of assistance to do so. But sometimes it becomes impacted and requires surgery. And, in this case, it did require surgery.

WERTHEIMER: It's not quite twenty-four hours, then, since surgery?

ROSENBERG: Since the birth, it's been not quite forty-eight hours. We came out of surgery at probably seven-thirty or eight this morning.

WERTHEIMER: And how is he, now?

ROSENBERG: Oh, he's doing fine. He's in the stall with Genuine Risk, and he's a good, strong foal. The surgery went very well, and he came out of the surgery well. He doesn't feel great. He's recovered from major surgery, and he's a little bit depressed, but he's comfortable, and all his vital signs are normal. And we're very happy with his condition right now, considering what he's been through.

WERTHEIMER: Does abdominal surgery put a bit of a cloud over his racing possibilities?

ROSENBERG: No, it really shouldn't. Barring infection or other kinds of complications, he should just go on and never look back.

WERTHEIMER: Now, tell us some sort of happier news. What does he look like?

ROSENBERG: Oh, he's beautiful. He is just a beautiful colt. He is a chestnut, he is great big, he has got a really nice head and a beautiful shoulder and plenty of bone, and he is very well balanced. He's got a star and a stripe and three white stockings.

WERTHEIMER: So we will be able to tell which one he is.

ROSENBERG: Oh, yes. He's got a lot of chrome on him, he's very flashy.

WERTHEIMER: When do you think that this little horse will be out of the stall and into the pasture and we'll actually see him?

ROSENBERG: At this point we have to take it day by day. I would hope, if everything goes well, that it's a matter of days.

WERTHEIMER: What about Genuine Risk? How is she?

ROSENBERG: She's wonderful. She's really wonderful. She is a great mother. She is just very attentive to the foal and wants it right there in front of her all the time. She's not a nervous mother, but certainly a concerned mother. She nickers to the foal all the time and wasn't very happy when we took the foal away to go into the operating room and was relieved to have the foal back.

BILL BROCKNER, a bird watcher in Kittredge, Colorado,
talks with Noah Adams about the rare arrival of
the Siberian Baikal teal in his small town and of the
commotion its arrival caused for bird aficionados.
January 25, 1993

BROCKNER: I received a call on November 28, through my
wife, on an odd duck. And she had made notes on this bird and
gave me the notes and asked me what I thought it was, where-
upon I just about had a cardiac arrest because I knew instantly
what it was.

ADAMS: When she described it, what was the tip-off for you?

BROCKNER: She described a bird smaller than a mallard, teal
size, with two white dots at the base of the bill. That was the
dead giveaway.

ADAMS: Was the Baikal teal a bird that you had been dreaming about?

BROCKNER: I have been wanting to see the Baikal teal for all
my life.

ADAMS: Did your wife say, "You better come quick, it's
down here at the creek?"

BROCKNER: When my wife told me, I said, "Let's get up there
immediately." And so we roared up to the pond where the bird
was living with some mallards. Then I put on my telescope and
binoculars and my dreams were answered.

ADAMS: Isn't there something in birding called the "life
list"?

BROCKNER: Yes, correct.

ADAMS: In North America, how many birds are on the life
list?

BROCKNER: You have a potential in the neighborhood of
850 birds.

ADAMS: Would the Baikal teal be one of them?

BROCKNER: The Baikal teal is one of them.

ADAMS: And how many have you seen?

BROCKNER: I have seen 736.

ADAMS: You have got kind of a ways to go.

BROCKNER: I do, but once you pass 700 it becomes a bigger and bigger job all the way along the line.

ADAMS: How do you figure the Baikal teal got to Bear Creek, there in your part of Colorado?

BROCKNER: I feel that the bird got caught up in one of the north Pacific storms that were heading toward North America. And the bird just followed along with the storm and came over the Aleutian chain and perhaps down along the Pacific Coast and then worked back over across Idaho, Montana, perhaps, into Colorado.

ADAMS: Trying to go where?

BROCKNER: It just was looking for a good spot to get away from the rough weather.

ADAMS: Now, I want to clear something up. We read in the *Los Angeles Times* that the bird could be seen through the picture window of the Bear Creek Tavern, right?

BROCKNER: That is correct.

ADAMS: Is that the same bird?

BROCKNER: It is the same bird.

ADAMS: Kind of getting around there.

BROCKNER: It moves up and down. As the ice forms and it gets frozen in, it will follow a flock of mallards and show up at some other pond.

ADAMS: How many bird people have come there?

BROCKNER: Over four hundred twenty-five people have been here so far.

ADAMS: Four hundred twenty-five people have come to see this bird?

BROCKNER: Exactly.

ADAMS: From where?

BROCKNER: One of them came from England, and the rest are from San Diego to Boston.

ADAMS: Are these people with a great deal of money and time to spend?

BROCKNER: Some of them have little or no money, and some do have the money to hop an airplane and get over here and see the bird immediately.

ADAMS: That's amazing.

BROCKNER: It's a wild hobby.

GARY DIXON, a private investigator, talks to Robert Siegel about the case of Max, an African gray parrot, who was not allowed to testify in a murder trial in Sonoma County, California. A woman was smothered in her bedroom, and the only one believed to have witnessed the murder was Max, the victim's pet.
November 12, 1993

DIXON: Within two months of her death, the owner of a pet store [that had resold Max] had called in and reported that the bird was saying "Richard" and then three emphatic nos. "Richard, no, no, no." The defendant's name in this case is Gary, and he told me that the bird had never mentioned the name Gary in the year that he had the bird until he finally sold it. However, there is a Richard, which was a friend and a confidant of the victim, and he testified that he was with her two nights before her death and the night before her death and probably was the last person to see her alive.

SIEGEL: Now, were you actually able to see the bird, Max the parrot, and hear it actually say this?

DIXON: No, I never tracked down the bird itself. The bird was sold to some local residents who have since divorced, and the woman took custody of the bird. I don't know her whereabouts. But since this hit our local newspaper, a lot of people have called in that knew Max and have reported a bunch of different stories about this particular bird. Apparently, this is a very wise and intellectual bird, as far as African grays go. Apparently, a lady that was taking care of the bird at one time went over to feed it at Jane's house. She was trying to get the bird to say all kinds of things, and the bird wouldn't say anything. When she got exasperated, she looked at the bird, and said, "Max, you're just dumb." And she turned to walk away, and while her back was turned, the bird, Max, said, "I'm not dumb." She said it scared the hell out of her and she was unnerved for two weeks.

SIEGEL: We are getting up to that critical moment in court. The latter part of last week, you're on the stand, defense lawyer asks you, "Why did I ask you to follow up on the bird?"

DIXON: My statement was because the bird was making spontaneous statements to the handler. At which time, the prosecutor shot out of his chair and objected very vehemently to the court, and the objection was sustained by the judge, and so the statements made by the bird were never presented to the jury.

SIEGEL: This would have been, at best, I think hearsay. If one can say that the parrot was truly saying it.

DIXON: Or birdsay.

SIEGEL: Birdsay. Mr. Dixon, I'm very surprised that after all this and all this publicity, that Max himself is not to be found, that somebody hasn't stepped forward, and said, "I now am the owner of this bird."

DIXON: We just consider that Max is in the witness protection program now. That's just kidding, of course.

SIEGEL: Where might he be in that case?

DIXON: I was told by the handler, the pet store owner, who knows where the bird is, that the people are very private and apparently have not chosen to come forward.

The attorney HARRY AVRIL tells Linda Wertheimer how residents in Dania, Florida, stepped in to save a colony of free-roaming monkeys after poachers were hired to nap the band of monkeys. June 30, 1993

WERTHEIMER: So, Harry, what is a colony of monkeys doing living along the coast of Florida in the first place?

AVRIL: We had a chimpanzee farm up on U.S. 1 here in Dania in the 1950s, right after World War II, and it went out of business. And when it went out of business, it could not sell a number of small rhesus and spider monkeys, and the property owners turned them loose. Then they settled into a mangrove wetland preserve area and have been doing quite well for the last forty years. We never had any problems with them until about a month ago.

WERTHEIMER: What happened?

AVRIL: An individual was driving down Dania Beach Boulevard and apparently hit a monkey. He got out of his car to check on the monkey. He says a group of monkeys charged him. They didn't bite him or didn't scratch him, but they charged him and scared the dickens out of him. The property owner suddenly became suspicious, or worried, about their potential liability should someone be bitten while the monkeys are feeding in the afternoon. Then about a week ago I was driving home from the office, and I saw three or four individuals going into the mangrove with fatiguelike outfits on and blowguns and nets. I pulled over, and said, "What the heck's going on?" They told me that the property owners had given them permission to come on the land and remove the monkeys, and I was a bit incredulous because I knew some of the land was owned by the state and county. To make a long story short, we had our wildlife officers out here and police officers and, after about two hours, they came up to me and said, "Harry, these monkeys have to go. These fellows have their permits."

WERTHEIMER: So how did you work it out?

AVRIL: I did it the old-fashioned way. I rolled up my shirtsleeves and headed over to the law library and did some research. Surprisingly found a case from 1972 over in St. Petersburg in the Second District Court, said this is a case of first impression, and we are going to pass the following standards from now on for situations like this. Those standards are, quite simply: if warning signs are posted, the property owner did not bring the wildlife onto the property in the first place, and, finally, the property owner is not receiving any financial benefit. Then with those three things established, liability would not exist.

WERTHEIMER: So you actually found a monkey precedent?

AVRIL: Absolutely. The case concerned a property owner with an undeveloped piece of property through which a tribe of monkeys ran.

WERTHEIMER: So these monkeys are requiring a substantial amount of your support at this moment?

AVRIL: I am going to try to get it passed off as pro bono work this year. I don't know if the Supreme Court will agree to do that, but I think it's for the public good. It's certainly for the good of this community, and we feel real happy about the success we've had.

WERTHEIMER: Given the fact that people are taking an interest in the monkeys, good and bad, you think these monkeys are going to live happily every after?

AVRIL: They will certainly live to romp another day. As long as I am here in Dania, I am going to do my best to protect them.

PHILLIP LOBEL talks with Alex Chadwick about
a listening device called the "spawn-o-meter,"
which allows scientists to listen to the sounds of
fish spawning. Dr. Lobel is an oceanographer at the
Woods Hole Oceanographic Institution in Woods Hole,
Massachusetts. October 23, 1993

CHADWICK: Tell me, what is a spawn-o-meter?

LOBEL: The spawn-o-meter is a device coupled to a hydro-phone with a radio transmitter that allows us to have a listening ear in the ocean, transmit that data back to the lab, and to separate the sounds so we can distinguish fish spawning from the other noises that occur on the reefs.

CHADWICK: Did you develop this specifically to listen to fish spawning?

LOBEL: I developed it with two colleagues at the Oceano-graphic, Jim Bowlin and David Mann, and our purpose was to monitor the breeding activity of the domino damsel at Johnston Atoll, both to understand its reproductive habits and also to monitor the potential impact from the military activities on the atoll, the concept being that if some pollution or disturbance was occurring on the reef long before a fish would turn belly up and die, they would feel ill, and their spawning behaviors would be disrupted.

CHADWICK: A lot of us do think that fish don't make a sound. How does it occur to you that fish do make sounds and how can you make sense of them?

LOBEL: What I did was think that we could listen to the turbulent sounds that fish made. If you ever saw the movie *Hunt for Red October* or read Tom Clancy's book, one of the key elements of antisubmarine warfare was picking up the knuckling sound made by fast-moving bodies like a submarine through the water. When they turned rapidly, they would create a turbulent noise that we could hear with a hydrophone, and the hydrophone I am using was derived from the navy sonobuoys that were used for listening to submarines. I put it together with an underwater video, a coupled system. I packed up a unit, went to Jamaica in January 1988, and filmed some fish that myself and others had studied many times, but we never knew they made sounds. I was overwhelmed. I found that hamlet fish and parrot fish, fish that we commonly see spawning but could never hear, were in fact not just producing turbulent noise but biologically specific sounds such as the actual release of their eggs and sperm. There was the *click, click, click* that we heard, and that's the male fish signaling to the female, "Get ready." Then that squeal that we heard was the two fish coupled together in the spawning embrace and simultaneously releasing eggs and sperm.

CHADWICK: Is this a language that you are talking about? A fish language?

LOBEL: That's the exciting question right now. We are now trying to determine if these sounds occur repeatedly and in a stereotypical fashion with particular behaviors. If that's the case, then we need to take the next step and see how important sound is for precise communication.

CHADWICK: If I had a fish tank at home with goldfish in it, could I hear goldfish? Do goldfish make sounds?

LOBEL: It's really quite possible. In fact, goldfish belong to a group of fish called Ostariophysi, which are defined by a unique morphology related to their hearing that gives them the best hearing of all the types of fishes. So it's hard to believe that they are not using sounds. But we haven't kept a recording. This is a new field and the technology has only been developed in the last year, but fish tend to be discreet about when they produce their sounds, so many of them only make sounds when they are actually reproducing.

RELIGION

The pollster GEORGE GALLUP, JR., talks with Alex
Chadwick about his findings on Americans' religious
and spiritual beliefs, as well as his own. He is the head
of the George H. Gallup International Institute, and
the Princeton Religion Research Center in Princeton,
New Jersey. May 29, 1993

CHADWICK: Tell us first what you have learned about the
role that religion plays for many people.

GALLUP: It clearly and in very obvious ways plays a major
role in the high level of voluntarism in this country, and when
we dig deeper with more penetrating measurements, it's clear
that religious motivation in people's lives is perhaps a driving
force behind much of the behavior and attitudes of the American people.

CHADWICK: I was surprised, quite surprised, by your reporting that there is a substantial group of Americans, one-seventh
of the population, you say, that you would describe as "saints."
Would you expand on that a little?

GALLUP: Obviously such measurements are subjective to
some degree, of course, and nobody knows but God who are the
true saints, but these people were identified through a twelve-
item scale that we developed, and then we took all the persons
who fell on one side of the continuum and then looked at them
in terms of tolerance, ethical behavior, happiness, charitable
activity, and that sort of thing, and found some truly dramatic
differences, particularly in the area of charitable activity. Persons on the highly committed end of the scale were much more
likely to be involved in informal charity. That is, not necessarily belonging to volunteer groups, though it included a lot of
those, but also informal groups as well.

CHADWICK: You note also that a large number of Americans

really are virtually ignorant of the moral foundations and traditions that do underpin many of the beliefs of our secular system.

GALLUP: Yes, absolutely. When we ask what is the basis of their moral compass, if you will, many just simply say personal experience. Most people feel that the Ten Commandments are valid rules for living, but they are hard-pressed to name them. I think the stark truth is that most Americans really don't know what they believe and why, in the area of religion.

CHADWICK: You say that you have discovered two things about deeply spiritual people that run counter to stereotype. First, deeply spiritual people are extraordinarily open-minded, they are not bigoted and small-minded, and second, they are very happy.

GALLUP: We did discover that the deeper the faith, the more open, the more tolerant.

CHADWICK: Mr. Gallup, when you talk to news organizations and to news executives, people in the news media, and tell them about the importance of spiritual belief in people's lives, what is it that you tell them they are missing, that we, the news media, are missing, by not reporting this, and not finding it and covering it?

GALLUP: Basically that people are interested in religion. It rates high in terms of people's interest, but not necessarily the material or the kinds of articles that appear on the church page on Saturday. But they are interested, as far as we can tell, in people's spiritual journeys and what is going on beneath the surface of life. I think perhaps the media have not paid enough attention because perhaps they are not as interested as other segments of the populace in religion and spiritual matters, and perhaps they themselves in many cases are not very involved in religion.

CHADWICK: You are a deeply religious man yourself?

GALLUP: Yes.

CHADWICK: Is it possible that your views are colored by your own beliefs? Of course, you are supposedly an expert at removing that kind of consideration from your survey data, but in this case, isn't it possible?

GALLUP: No. We, in our field, remind ourselves constantly it would be dishonest to mislead people and not to present the data as absolutely fairly as possible.

CHADWICK: What would you say the rest of us can learn from the more spiritually inclined among us?

GALLUP: Prayer is absolutely essential, and I think that's a great message for the populace, really. Also, these people did not just fall into a deep faith. They worked at it. In many cases there were crises, so I guess another message might be to look for the deeper meanings in crises, and to hang in there in your spiritual journey.

Reform Rabbi ALEXANDER SHINDLER talks with Robert Siegel about renewing a call for the active pursuit of converts to Judaism. Although Jews do not traditionally pursue missionary activities, Rabbi Shindler disagrees and says their religion should reach out to those looking for spiritual guidance. Rabbi Shindler is president of the Union of American Hebrew Congregations. October 26, 1993

SHINDLER: From the very beginnings of our faith, we were active missionaries. Indeed, Abraham, who was the founder of the Jewish people, is lauded in Scripture itself for the seventy souls he made at Haran. And rabbinic literature says that his tent was open on four sides so that he might miss not a single nomad who passed by, so that he could invite them in and bring that nomad under the fluttering wings of God's presence. The prophetic literature is replete with calls for everyone to come to Judaism. This tradition of proselytizing continued until the Roman Empire became the Holy Roman Empire and subsequently the Muslim religion expanded and marched across North Africa into Spain. Restrictive legislation was introduced. Any Jew who accepted a non-Jew, or any non-Jew who came to Judaism, was burned at the stake. And if you'll allow me to mix a metaphor, this burning at the stake tended to cool our conversionary ardor.

SIEGEL: With great difficulty, it seems, over the years Jews have gotten some Christian churches, most notably the Roman Catholic Church, to hold off on a mission to convert the Jews. That seems to be part of what is at work here. Jews have been averse to other people's efforts to convert Jews.

SHINDLER: I don't envisage the proselytizing activity of the Jew to have this kind of triumphalism, which marks so many of the missionary groups that are directed at us. By triumphalism,

I mean religions that claim that you cannot achieve salvation unless you become a Christian. I want the message of Judaism to be introduced into the marketplace of ideas to those who are looking, not those who are committed to any other faith. I don't envisage sending our kids to the airports with leaflets and what-not or selling flowers. What I want is to overcome this notion that the Jewish community is an exclusive club for born Jews. I want to remove the NOT WELCOME signs from our syna-gogues and from our hearts. We are not going to target any group. We are targeting those many people who hunger for meaning in their lives.

SIEGEL: Some of the reactions to your proposals, I think some of the less enthusiastic ones, get to a difficult question, which is the degree to which a Jewish identity is a synagogue-based, spiritual, ritual practice, and to what extent it is an eth-nic affiliation that millions of Americans have and that is rec-ognized by Jewish authorities even in some who have never set foot in a synagogue.

SHINDLER: I understand that. But this, incidentally, is part of that which attracts many non-Jews to come to the synagogue, the fact that we are a close-knit community, a caring commu-nity. They become a part of a people. So I can't consider a sufficient ground for objecting to this effort.

SIEGEL: How do you respond to an Orthodox Jewish critique that Reform Judaism might be straining too hard, saying, "We are confident, we Reform Jews are confident about our values," but really meaning, "We are not so confident that we would watch our numbers diminish but know that whoever is going to temple is Jewish? Whoever wants to be Jewish is Jewish, and so be it." How do you respond to the critique that there is a bit of protesting too much here and wanting to make sure that people who found it difficult to affiliate as Jews once they marry a gentile should have an easy way to do so?

SHINDLER: I think that all synagogues ought to be open to that. Why should we exclude those who happen in this plural-istic society to marry out of the faith? Why should we exclude them? Why should we mourn them? This is absurd. We should bring them in. When I first proposed the outreach program, the Orthodox rabbinate said that not just the non-Jew who marries a Jew but the Jewish partner should be kicked out of the synagogue. That's absurd. It's self-defeating. It's not just.

KAREN ARMSTRONG discusses with Liane Hansen her bestseller, *A History of God,* an ambitious work that focuses on Judaism, Christianity, and Islam over the past four thousand years. Armstrong is a former Roman Catholic nun and now teaches at the Leo Baeck College for the Study of Judaism in London.
December 19, 1993

HANSEN: In your book, you write that God is a creation of human imagination, but it's not a product of that imagination. Would you explain?

ARMSTRONG: What I mean is that all monotheists, Jews, Christians, and Muslims, have been very careful to distinguish our experience and our way of thinking about the Divine and the reality itself, which is beyond any human description. So throughout the centuries people have found different ways for talking about this reality, which we have called God for convenience sake, but it's always been a canon of faith that our ideas of God bear very little relation to the ineffable, indescribable, and incomprehensible reality itself.

HANSEN: It's always interesting to go back to the beginning. Go back to the dawn of Judaism and tell us about Yahweh.

ARMSTRONG: Yahweh began life as a very aggressive tribal deity of the Israelites, a god of war, murderously partial to his own people, as we read in the Bible that he smote all the Egyptians who were the enemies of his people. There was very little universal about this God, and, indeed, the early Israelites were not monotheists in the sense in which we are today. They believed that other gods existed, but by the terms of their covenant, they agreed to worship only one god, Yahweh. But later, the prophets of Israel, who were writing centuries after the exodus from Egypt in about the seventh and sixth centuries

B.C., made this tribal god a symbol for the absolutely indescribable reality which other religious people were discovering in other parts of the world and calling by different names. In Buddhism, for example, this absolute reality was called Nirvana.

HANSEN: Tell us a little bit more, then, about the origin of the god of early Islam.

ARMSTRONG: Muhammad, when he began to preach his new religion, which would eventually be called Islam, in the seventh century A.D., was not intending to found a new religion. He believed that he was simply bringing the old religion of the Jews and the Christians to the Arabs, who had never had a messenger from God before. Throughout the Koran, there is a great emphasis that Muhammad is simply endorsing and continuing the line of prophecy that goes from Adam to Abraham, Moses, and Jesus, who is accounted a very great prophet in the Koran. Muhammad saw himself as continuing in this revelation and saw his god as identical to the god of the Jews and the Christians. As the Koran says, "There is only one divine being, so there can only ever be one religion." And "The religions of all traditions have their grain of truth and are cultural expressions of man's experience of the Divine."

HANSEN: I think I skipped a step here. Perhaps I should backtrack a little bit and have you describe the god of early Christianity.

ARMSTRONG: Jesus had no intention of founding a new religion. He believed that he was the Messiah who had long been promised to the Jewish people, but later, after his death and resurrection, Christians found in the person of Jesus a revelation of God. And gradually, in about the fourth century they decided, formally, that Jesus had been the incarnate son of God. That raised many questions, as you can imagine. If Jesus was divine, did that mean there were two gods? And what about the Holy Spirit, whom Jesus mentioned so often in the Gospel? Did that mean there were three gods? So in the 370s, three Eastern Orthodox theologians evolved the doctrine of the Trinity, that God as he is in himself is indescribable, unknowable, but he has revealed himself to man in three ways, as Father, Son, and Spirit.

HANSEN: So the whole idea of God changes through the centuries, depending on which humans are experiencing the mystery at the time.

ARMSTRONG: The idea of God has never been static. If it had been, the religion of this God would have died away long ago. What characterizes a world religion is its capacity to adapt and evolve to meet the challenge of different times and the challenge of very different cultural environments. Think of the way that Christianity has spread from being a Semitic religion into the Greek gentile world, and way over into Africa and Australia, which the early Christians had never heard of. The same with Islam, which began in very peculiar conditions in Arabia, but has become a universal religion, stretching all over the world. Constantly in the history of man's experience and conception of this one God in the three monotheistic religions, we can see Jews, Christians, and Muslims adapting and changing their idea of God to meet their particular circumstances. Thus, for example, at the time when the Jews were expelled from their home in Spain in 1492 by the Christian crusaders there, a tragedy that was regarded as one of the greatest tragedies to have befallen the Jewish people since they lost their Temple, the Jewish exiles evolved a theory of God, himself, going into exile and seeing the whole of creation as in some way displaced, dislocated. This kind of cabalistic mysticism became normative throughout the Jewish world and was a response to a particular tragedy and helped to comfort people and help them, despite the apparently hopeless conditions in which they were living, to believe that there was some ultimate meaning and point to their lives.

HANSEN: What about the Word, the Torah, the Koran, the Bible? Many say that each one of those contains everything that a believer needs to know, and then if you mix that with what might be described as faith. I remember the Christian parable of Doubting Thomas. "Blessed are they who do not see but believe." Those two things equal religion. Don't Fundamentalists, for example, believe in an unchanging idea of God, and if you say that God is something that changes throughout generations, isn't that a contradiction?

ARMSTRONG: It's not a contradiction. Fundamentalism has evolved in all the major world religions in the late twentieth century as particularly one of these changes that we are talking about to meet the particular tensions of our own time. Fundamentalists today in all faiths do insist on what they call the "inerrancy of Scripture," that Scripture cannot err. But indeed, the whole idea of equating faith with belief, that is, with submission to a set of intellectual propositions or religious opinions about God, is a rather new development, again, one of these developments that we have been talking about. Faith has only been conceived of as religious knowledge in this way, in the Enlightenment, since the Enlightenment in the eighteenth century, and is especially a product of the West. Up until then, faith was more a sense of commitment, of virtue, rather than a set of correct orthodox opinions. It was a conviction that, despite the tragedy and the flawed conditions of our life, there was an ultimate meaning. You might not be able to explain that meaning, but you went on living in the conviction that there was an ultimate purpose. That is certainly the way in which faith is spoken of in the Bible, for example, by people like Saint Paul.

HANSEN: So *faith* and *belief* are not two interchangeable words.

ARMSTRONG: They are not. Indeed, our word, belief, comes from the old English *bileven*, which means "to love." When early Christians said the word *credo*, I believe the word *credo* comes from *cor dare*, "to give your heart." So it's only since the eighteenth century in the West, particularly, that we have begun to equate faith with accepting a set of religious opinions, and in fact, traditionally Jews, Muslims, and Greek Orthodox Christians have not held much faith in doctrine. Our doctrinal obsession is one of the peculiar preoccupations of Western Christianity.

HANSEN: By doctrinal, do you essentially mean, say, a code

of conduct? Hasn't one thing remained unchanged — that the experience of the mystery, that God is achieved through a code of conduct, that is, how we live, not necessarily what we believe?

ARMSTRONG: That is precisely the difference. You define it between orthodoxy, which is correct teaching, which is what the Western Christians have put such emphasis on, and orthopraxy, which is precisely, as you say, a code of conduct, which, if you live your life in a certain way according to the Torah, according to the Koran and the shariah, you will experience this sense of ineffable meaning. So most of the religions see faith more as a response, an imperative to action rather than an imperative to accept certain religious views.

HANSEN: The God of your childhood you have described as a harsh taskmaster. You left the convent in 1969. You said it was a very painful experience for you. You were depressed with grief for quite a long time. For a while, you defined yourself as an atheist, but it wasn't that you didn't believe in God; you just didn't believe in the Western anthropomorphic idea of God. What is your understanding, personally, of God today?

ARMSTRONG: I would say that since researching this book, and it took me five years to research and to write it, I have developed a much more positive idea of God and I have begun to see how inadequate my previous conceptions of God were, despite the intense religious background I came from. I spent a great deal of time studying theology. I think in the West we have developed a notion of God which is highly personal. We tend to talk about "him," difficult pronoun, as though "he" were a male personality out there. We talk about God as a Supreme Being, somebody whose existence can be proved and whose activity can be discerned in the world. Someone who created the world, rather as you or I "make" something, and who "runs" the world rather as you or I would organize an event. But I realized when I studied the whole history of monotheism, especially in the Jewish, Eastern Orthodox, and Muslim history, how very limited that conception was. Jews, Christians, and Muslims have, over the centuries, adhered to a much more agnostic approach to God. Some have said that God is nothing, others have said that God does not exist, because it's nonsense to say that God exists in the same way as you or I do. So that gradually I began to see that the limited idea of God, which had begun to seem incredible and unsympathetic to me and to many people in northern Europe, was very much just one of those products — an inadequate notion of God which is losing its valence, at least over here in Western Europe, and is being discarded in favor of the larger conceptions of the Divine.

HANSEN: In spite of the fact that you have written ten books about this, do you find it hard to approach the idea of God through words?

ARMSTRONG: Indeed, God-talk is always impossible. And one of the things that I discovered while researching my book was how endlessly monotheists remind us that we cannot talk about God in simplistic terms. Indeed, that it can be dangerous to do so. If we start talking about God as though we know exactly what "he" thinks and approves of, and what "he" forbids and condemns, it's all too easy to simply make God a projection of our own prejudices and get him to give a divine stamp of approval to our own limited conceptions. Some of the worst excesses of history have been performed in the name of a God who is created in our own image and likeness. The crusaders went into battle to kill Jews and Muslims with the cry "*Deus le vult*, God wills it," on their lips. So we have got to be very careful about the way we ascribe our human opinions to God.

RAY VALDEZ, a plumbing contractor, describes to
Linda Wertheimer the annual Easter pilgrimage to the
tiny adobe church of El Santuario de Chimayo in
northern New Mexico. He attempted the fifty-mile
journey on foot from his home in Santa Fe on
Good Friday. April 9, 1993

VALDEZ: I started out about five o'clock in the afternoon. It
was a beautiful day yesterday. The sun has been great and the
weather had changed for the better and the moon didn't come
out until, I would say, eleven o'clock, and when it did come out,
the path was a little more well lit. As you walk along the highway and it's dark, the only light you have to go by is the passing
cars in the night. With about fifteen miles to go, I couldn't go
any further. I had a big blister and I was in great pain and I was
full of energy, and I was willing to do the walk, but with this
injury there was no way.

WERTHEIMER: But you did go on to the *santuario*, to the
little church?

VALDEZ: I made it with a ride that picked up me and some
friends that I was walking with. So I was there about eight
o'clock, finally.

WERTHEIMER: Were there many other people making the
walk to be there on Good Friday?

VALDEZ: There was a pretty good steady crowd coming from
Santa Fe and coming from Espanola, which is north of the *santuario,* or actually west, northwest, but the atmosphere there
this morning apparently was that there was not as many people
as usually come to the *santuario* at that time of day.

WERTHEIMER: I wonder why?

VALDEZ: There has been some story going on here with our
archbishop. Archbishop had to resign and he was subsequently

replaced by the Pope just this week and in talking to some other people, I found out that they thought the same thing and that's why there wasn't such a big turnout.

WERTHEIMER: When you got to the *santuario* in Chimayo at, what, you said about eight o'clock this morning, what was that like?

VALDEZ: Between eight and nine. One thing I did find that was interesting was the news media was out in force. Two of the local networks had their helicopters and their cameras and I guess they had made some people angry. Some of the people that do the pilgrimage, as they get to the church and they go in and they are kneeling and they are doing their prayers silently, some of these cameras were kind of getting in their faces. I guess there was an incident. There were some villagers talking about it, how they were angry that had occurred.

WERTHEIMER: So it's a very old church, though?

VALDEZ: It dates back to the 1500s, as I understand it, and it's in dilapidated shape, and a lot of the local people had their wares out for sale, chili and Chimayo crosses. Interestingly enough, I saw Chimayo walking sticks for sale today. I hadn't seen that. A little vendor on the side of the road had a spray-painted sign, CHIMAYO WALKING STICKS.

WERTHEIMER: Just for you?

VALDEZ: Yes. Another one of the big traditions here with the walkers is the carrying of crosses to enact Jesus Christ's perils as he walked with the cross through the city, and so you have a lot of these men carrying homemade crosses almost eight feet long, four to five feet in width, six-by-six lumber, six-inch-by-six-inch lumber, carrying them the whole way. It's an interesting picture, it really is, of a tradition born here just in New Mexico.

At the National Gallery of Art, the Muslim theologian Dr. Seyyed Hossein Nasr talks with Robert Siegel about the dilemmas facing Muslims who come to study in America, the subject of his recent book, *A Young Muslim's Guide to the Modern World.* Dr. Nasr was a university president in Teheran until the rise of the Ayatollah Khomeini. He is currently a professor of theology at George Washington University in Washington, D.C. December 13, 1993

NASR: The Muslim thinks that everything that people do in the West is related to their religion in the same way that everything he was doing back in the Islamic world was related to his religion. Even if he didn't do it, it was related to his religion. He cannot understand that there are many people here for whom the basis of their action, the criteria which determine the value of their action, the morality or lack thereof, in fact, has very little to do with the religion even if they hold on to a religion. Many of them do not hold on to that. He cannot understand that. That's very difficult for a Muslim to understand, the category of a secular mind.

SIEGEL: What is it about the intellectual approach of an American university that would be unexpected or perhaps unsettling even for a Muslim student coming here?

NASR: The first thing that would be intellectually jarring is that there are so many voices which are contradictory in a certain sense, as you don't have any kind of principle of unity as far as the various voices are concerned. First of all, you have the voice of modern science, the voice, then, of sociology and social sciences, the voice of the humanities. I use the word *voice* here, of course, metaphorically. There is very little correlation between them. Then within those contexts, putting the sciences aside, there are so many different theories and points of view presented within the fields of the humanities and the social sciences, that the student finds it very difficult to orient himself intellectually.... I have always said that, paradoxically enough, there are two places in the world where Muslims meet, in Mecca and in American campuses. You will have a Moroccan and an Algerian here meeting with a Malaysian and Indonesian. Where else would they meet? In the Islamic world there are those who go to the Hajj. They meet from all over the world. But otherwise this community created in America, this open, relaxed social atmosphere that it has, even if the students do not take advantage of the great works of Japanese art or Chinese art, nevertheless, they meet a large number of Chinese, Korean, Indian, and so forth, students from all over the world. And that itself is gradually beginning to have its own dynamic, you might say. Here, [*looking at an altarpiece that depicts the Virgin Mary and the infant Jesus*] you don't have God himself. That would be the greatest shock, the Sistine Chapel, something like that — to have God painted. But here is not God, but nevertheless it is sacred history. A Muslim student would know very well the Virgin Mary. Her name, Sayyidatuna Maryam, was always very deeply revered in all the Islamic world. We say, *"Allah as-Salam,"* peace be upon her, like you do upon the prophets. And one of the chapters of the Koran is named after her. So the figure is very well known, but this student had never experienced a purely human form representing her. If the Muslim student were to imagine Mary, what she would look like, she would look like an Arab woman, or a Palestinian woman, which she was in that part of the world. So this would be a great shock: "Oh, my God, is that what Mary looked like?"

SIEGEL: Yes.

NASR: Parallel with that, as important is the image of Christ, here. Again it is a blond little child. Christ is a very important figure in the history of Islam and in the religious world of Islam to this day. After the prophet of Islam, he is the most important prophet, and therefore this would be a great blasphemy to his eyes. Mary, he could sort of live with, perhaps a little bit, but Christ would be very difficult for him to conceive it in these forms. Most of all, he would think, Well, what does this have to do with religion? Why do they need this kind of painting? It would be very hard for him to understand.

SIEGEL: What is it doing here in this room? Why a painting?

NASR: Why a painting? Why do you have to have the Divinity anthropomorphized like this? Because Islam, like Judaism, insists upon the refusal to have the graven image made. That is applied not only to God, but even to the prophets and sacred history, especially as far as a place of worship is concerned. It is true that in Islamic art in miniatures, among the Persians and the Turks and the Indians, not among the Arabs, there are depictions of the life of the prophets, of prophet of Islam, of Christ, and so forth. But they are always highly stylized. They are not anthropomorphic. Their faces do not look like human beings. They are not part of religious art objects. They are not in a mosque. The aggrandizement of the human being as the central subject is precisely what a person of Muslim mind sees as a kind of rebellion against God, as a kind of reassertion, or assertion, of the human as the center of reality, rather than of God as the center of reality and therefore against a very basic Islamic idea that there should not be a kind of titanic or Promethean aspect to the human being, that man finds his grandeur through submission to God and not by asserting his humanness. [looking at Van Dyck's life-size portrait of the seventeenth-century Marquessa Bolbi] These big, very large canvases in which dignitaries, kings, queens, various nobility, have their painting done, especially in such dimensions, is totally alien to the Islamic worldview. That is, the whole idea of a kind of titanic civilization, which is one of the characteristics of the Renaissance, really never took root in the Islamic world, which is one of the very mysteries of history, because Islam had a science which was much more elaborate than that of the West up to the Renaissance. They had this marvelous civilization, with its technology, its poetry, its philosophy, and so forth. But it never took that step of making man so central as it happened in the Renaissance with Petrarch and others leading finally to this kind of humanism, which places humanity as the absolute at the center of things, rather than God.

SIEGEL: So when you speak of the tradition of miniatures in the Muslim world, for example, you always remark that first they are stylized representations, but also the very fact that they are miniature, that's important.

NASR: Very important. Islam did develop, especially non-Arabic Islam and especially Persian art, some of the greatest art in the world in the form of the Persian miniature, but it was always related to the art of the book, to the great art of calligraphy and of writing, and it was never taken out of context and made very large so it would be a reality by itself. It always was bookish, part of the art of the book.

SIEGEL: Even though I could say that the grand, full-standing portrait of that lady done by Van Dyck across the room — actually she is life-size. That is to say, it's the miniature that would reduce her dramatically and make her very small. We think she is huge, but the picture is probably all of five feet tall.

NASR: This is precisely the point. The famous debate that was carried out on Muslim theologians: Why try to replicate God's creation? What is the purpose of creating a life-size portrait if we are created by God? The painter, by doing that, is trying to play the role of God. What is the purpose of that? Since we cannot breathe life into this, in a sense we have mistaken ourselves, therefore, for a Creator without really being Creator. And it's this dichotomy which Islam always criticized. Whereas the miniature would be always part of an illustration of a text, although very beautiful, a great work of art performed a function, a utility. Not in the material sense, but in the deeper sense of corresponding to some kind of purpose. Islam believes that all art should be related to some function of life.

SIEGEL: Is it realistic to say that one, without being a particularly brilliant intellectual, can come to appreciate all these other aspects of Western civilization that are on display and that are part of daily life and that are going every which way in the West; understand them; learn the rationale behind them; and then return to Saudi Arabia or Pakistan still a believing, observant Muslim?

NASR: It is not possible for everyone. But it is possible for the few who then have the responsibility of helping and guiding those who do not have such an intellectual outlook. And that second possibility certainly exists. When Islamic thought was a great challenge to the West, it challenged its whole existence. Not every Westerner was able to read Avicenna and other philosophical texts or scientific works that were coming and Europeanize and Christianize them and make it their own. It was a few great intellectual leaders who did it, but they provided, then, the map which made it possible for the rest of society to follow and this is precisely what the Islamic world must do today, the other way around.

The biblical scholars BRUCE METZGER and MICHAEL COOGAN discuss with Bob Edwards the veracity and the interpretations of the accounts of Jesus' life according to the Gospels. Metzger is the Collord Professor Emeritus of New Testament Language and Literature at the Princeton Theological Seminary. Coogan is a professor of religious studies at Stonehill College. They are co-editors of *The Oxford Companion to the Bible.* December 24, 1993

METZGER: Both the Gospel of Matthew and Luke fit together as correlative. Religion involves both the head and the heart of an individual, and the symbolism, with regard to the wise men coming to the infant child Jesus: they follow the star. They are wise men, intellectual people. They follow the leading of the star, whereas, on the other hand in the Gospel according to Luke, it is the song of the angels, the cheer. There is joy among the shepherds that heard this. I think these two, the intellect and the emotions, focus at the time of Christmas, still today.

EDWARDS: Jesus was born in Bethlehem, according to the Bible.

COOGAN: According to Matthew and Luke, he was born in Bethlehem. Historians are not quite sure whether we should take that as actually true. Certainly, there are other sources which might be taken to imply that he was from Nazareth. There is an interesting passage in John's Gospel where the claim is made that Jesus is the Messiah, and people say, "But the Messiah is supposed to be from Bethlehem, and he is from Nazareth." It seems to me that would be a perfectly appropriate point for the author of the Gospel to say, "But he was born in Bethlehem." The author of John's Gospel doesn't say it at that point. So some historians recently have been arguing that he may have been from Nazareth from the beginning.

EDWARDS: He was born in a manger. There was no room at the inn.

METZGER: He was laid in a manger.

COOGAN: He was laid in a manger. A manger is a feeding trough for animals. In all of these narratives about the birth of Jesus, there is an extraordinarily extensive use of earlier Jewish Scriptures. I think that the story of the manger and stable implies that is an allusion to the beginning of Isaiah. The ox knows its owner and the donkey knows its master's manger. The early Christians were convinced that Jesus was the fulfillment of everything that had been written in the Jewish Scriptures, and so they often elaborated their stories of the life of Jesus by using what Christians now call the Old Testament as a kind of source.

EDWARDS: Was it a stable? Was it a cave?

METZGER: The Greek word, there, suggests perhaps an out-of-door camping place, where people with animals would forage.

COOGAN: There is another possibility and known from archaeological investigation of houses in those days, where people would actually, especially in the winter, bring their animals into the first floor of the house to keep warm and they would sleep on the second floor, and the body heat from the animals would actually warm the second story so that it may have been a small house in which the few animals that a family might have were actually stabled in the winter as part of the dwelling space. Sort of like living in the barn.

METZGER: But actually, we don't know the time of the year that Jesus was born.

EDWARDS: I was going to ask you about that. What about the date?

METZGER: In general, we think that it was wintertime, but it is only rather rarely, I am told, that in Palestine shepherds would be out of doors in late December. Perhaps that year it was warmer than usual and that was true, but we have no record in the New Testament, itself, as to the month or day of the month. We are not even told that it was that cold. But these are elaborations that later traditions have used to embellish —

COOGAN: It really wasn't until several centuries later that the date of December 25 was settled on and some Eastern churches, Eastern Orthodox churches, still celebrate the birth of Jesus on January 6.

METZGER: Exactly.

COOGAN: So even in Christianity today, there isn't agreement exactly on what the date was. In the West, we always think of December 25.

EDWARDS: Jesus disappears after his birth. We don't hear about Jesus for quite a while.

METZGER: The evangelists, the authors of the Four Gospels, are not really interested to write what we would call today a complete biographical account. But they pick out those elements — birth, ministry, death, resurrection — that in the early church naturally did receive the primary attention. Now, there are perhaps twenty apocryphal Gospels that were written in the succeeding centuries that elaborate this kind of thing and fill in what was imagined had taken place when Jesus was a child, when he was taken by the parents to Egypt, and so on; when in Nazareth he, with other children on the Sabbath day, was making mud pies, playing as a child, and an elder comes out and reprimands Jesus for desecrating the Sabbath. Jesus had formed, we are told in this apocryphal Gospel of the infancy, some little clay pigeons. Jesus claps his hands and they fly away. That means the evidence that he was breaking the Sabbath vanishes.

COOGAN: I should add to what Professor Metzger said, that it is clear that these are not intended to be comprehensive biographies as we would understand the term. We have no description of Jesus in the Gospels. As I would like to tell my students sometimes, for all we know, he could have been short and fat and bald. We simply don't know. So it is important, I think, to look at the Gospels and the narratives of the birth of

Jesus and, indeed, the Bible as a whole, not from the perspective of what we think is there, but at what the authors were actually intending to write. And they were not wanting to give us a full biography, but their understanding of the importance of Jesus for them and their cobelievers.

STEPHEN JONES and JIM JONES, JR., talk with Scott
Simon about the painful memories of their father
and the mass suicide of nine hundred followers of the
People's Temple in Jonestown in 1978.
November 20, 1993

SIMON: Jim, if I might turn to you first, you bear that name.
What is that like?

JIM: For many years I contemplated changing it to my real
name, Larry Allan Knox, but the realization is that I am Jim
Jones, Jr., as a very strong part of my past and I came to a point
in my life to where I'm proud of being the son of Jim Jones in a
sense of what he has provided me in my life. Even though he did
maintain a dysfunctional family unit, there is still a positive
aspect to Jim Jones.

SIMON: We should explain. You were adopted, right?

JIM: Yes, I was adopted when I was ten weeks old.

STEPHEN: I thought back on what he was to me as a young
boy, and there was compassion and love. Unfortunately, he
talked a good game. He lived a very different one, and I think it's
important for all of us to recognize that human beings are won-
derfully complex.

SIMON: I gather you both feel that there is something in that
man whose voice we heard, that man who was roundly remem-
bered as a murderer, a fool, a crank. There was something worth
remembering for you as children.

STEPHEN: He was not a well man for much of the time that
I knew him, but before he reached insanity there was much
about him that was really unique and special and it is what
he presented to the unsuspecting when they first came to the
temple.

SIMON: When you gentlemen were watching the scenes this
past spring and summer of the standoff in Waco around the

Branch Davidian compound, what are some of the things you noticed that maybe went past the rest of us?

JIM: Personally, it was a real denial of the association. My coworkers and friends and family were repeatedly asking me if I was OK, and I didn't want to make the association. I think that was kind of a denial piece. And finally, until my four-year-old child asked my wife, Erin, after seeing a runner on the news about Jonestown and their association with Waco, and he made a comment: "Oh, Mommy, it's named Jonestown. Can we go there?" i.e., representing that the town was named after us. That hit home. I think we have looked at the horrors of Jonestown, the horrors of Waco, as if these people are lepers and not victims.

STEPHEN: In addition to that, I think that as long as you can dehumanize and just write people off as kooks, and clearly this was an exclusionary group. This was a group that felt like they could not find their dreams or their solutions operating within society, and they had separated themselves, only to magnify the lines that were drawn by them certainly was not a solution to the problem there.

SIMON: Among a hundred other different things that those of us who just read about it over the years can't make sense of is how is it that so many people would walk into their own death?

STEPHEN: I don't know that it went down that way. I don't know that they walked into their own death.

SIMON: You mean, people didn't know what they were doing when they swallowed the grape juice?

STEPHEN: No, they knew what was happening. First of all, what happened at the very beginning was that the children died and we all know that these children didn't walk up and voluntarily take their lives. It was squirted down their throats. For example, the stories that I have heard from people who actually fled, and I have even been able to pick up from the last tapes, is that my mother resisted until the last baby died. There was a scene even then where a young gentleman named Gary Johnson, we called him Poncho, stood up because my mother was being restrained. And he stood up and protected her because of his love for her. Because of that, he was ordered to take the poison and turned, out of devotion to his belief, considering himself a soldier in whatever army fighting for whatever cause, took that poison on that instruction. But that in itself is a paradox. Once that ball started rolling, it became not only to a loyalty to Jim Jones. It was very little of that. It was more loyalty to the people around you that you called your brethren and to a community and a world that was all you knew.

SIMON: Jim, your wife died there.

JIM: Yes, she did.

SIMON: And she was carrying a child.

JIM: Yes. At that point there was a loss when I found out that my wife had died. I think I have just recently made peace with the loss of my wife and the fact that I felt that personally I had sent her to Jonestown to her death.

SIMON: I'm wondering if the two of you have asked yourselves as mature men, if, when you were teenagers, if you had been there that day, what you would have done. If, in fact, you might have been the only two of three people in that community that might have been capable of taking your father's head in your hands, and saying, "Dad, this isn't good. Don't do this."

STEPHEN: Gosh, if anybody was capable of stopping it, I think that we were, but what I have always said is that when I look at the people that died in Jonestown, and I have described my mother already, and there were many other people who hated my father that were still a part of that dream, and I know that they lost their lives there. I can hardly justify saying that had I been there I could have made the difference. It may very well be true that we would have interrupted some part of the process early in the game that would have stopped the domino effect. But that, in my mind, does a great disservice to the people that lost their lives there. For me to say that had I been there, I would have stopped it, I don't know.

SIMON: There is an annual remembrance, which amounts to a reunion for many of the families of people who died there at

Jonestown. And, Stephen, I know last year you met Patricia Ryan, the daughter of Leo Ryan, the congressman from California who was killed in Jonestown.

STEPHEN: Yes. What I do remember is a real need to apologize to her and being grateful that I had the opportunity, not so much for myself, but for my father. So it's ironic that on the one hand I can separate myself very easily from him, and on the other hand I can feel the responsibility for what happened, and I didn't feel any animosity or anger from her, and she was very forgiving of all that had happened and was content to move on with her life.

SIMON: Now, she indicated that at least she can revere her father's memory and you, Stephen and Jim, can't do that with your father.

JIM: I think that's some of the reason why after fifteen years we have finally made the decision to say something, but life does go on and we have separated Jim Jones the monster or the madman, as people will call him, to Jim Jones the father. Looking at Jonestown for what it was in the sense that there was a humanity there. There was a statement of civil rights and what it meant to us, personally.

STEPHEN: I don't know that I need to revere my father's memory. There is much in my past and many people in my past and in my life now that I can revere, and I can love him and I can forgive him, and that's what is most important to me.

THE STORY OF THE YEAR: BOSNIA

As 1993 began, the Bosnian capital, Sarajevo, was under
siege. The city had long been home to Catholics,
Orthodox Christians, Muslims, and Jews. When Yugoslavia broke apart, Bosnia declared independence —
a move favored by the republic's Muslims and Catholic
Croats, but opposed by its Orthodox Serbs. The Bosnian
Serbs left the government and went to war against it.
The capital was one of several Bosnian cities besieged
and denied food and medical supplies. SYLVANA FOA,
on the staff of the United Nations High Commission
for Refugees, describes to Linda Wertheimer the
deprivation facing residents of the city.
January 6, 1993

FOA: I never saw such misery in my whole life. There is
something about people being hungry and homeless, but when
it's fifteen degrees below freezing and people have no electricity, no heat, no water, they have to walk miles just to pick up
one can of water. It's horrible misery. They can't wash. They
have lice. These are proud people.

WERTHEIMER: You went into Sarajevo just to look it over
and to see what?

FOA: I went in because they needed some help in there for a
few days over the holidays. I went in to give some help and to
take a look myself because it had been a couple of months since
I had been in there. Things had changed so badly. People are
demoralized. People are separated from their families. They
don't know if their husbands are alive or dead. Many people
haven't seen their wives or children for a year. They don't know
if they're alive or dead. They are totally cut off and isolated from
the rest of the world, and they are beginning to feel abandoned.
I saw old people walking in the street, lugging these cans of

water, with blood coming out of their hands because their hands were so frostbitten. They cracked and they were bleeding. It was awful. I have never been so cold in my whole life.

WERTHEIMER: And there is just no relief from it?

FOA: We are trying to get as much fuel as we can into the city now. People have cut down all the trees in the city. The hillsides have been totally denuded. I saw them cutting down the trees in the cemeteries.

WERTHEIMER: It sounds like the accounts of the siege of Moscow in the Napoleonic Wars. It just does not sound like a twentieth-century event.

FOA: It is getting to be like that, too, because one of the problems we are having now is the ice and snow on these mountain roads. We were using a fairly good highway into Sarajevo from the port of Ploce. We can't go up that highway anymore because they have blown up one of the bridges. Now we have to go on a back mountain road that's just a sheet of ice, and our trucks are spinning around and blocking the road for hours. In many ways, right now, we are able to get more trucks into the city, but what we worry about is for how long we will be allowed to do that.

WERTHEIMER: How does that work? You say you are permitted to get trucks into the city.

FOA: We negotiate it with the people who run the checkpoints on the roads into the city. We have to negotiate how many trucks we are allowed to bring in, what can be inside the trucks, whether or not we can bring in fuel or fuel wood or whether it can only be food and medicine. They check.

WERTHEIMER: So every day is a renegotiated arrangement?

FOA: We try to do it by the week, and on some items we do it by the month. But every day, it's iffy. If, for instance, we got a convoy into a town called Srebrenica — this is a town that is very badly cut off. The next day, the people of Srebrenica attacked a Serb-held town and killed quite a few people. We aren't going to get another convoy into that town of Srebrenica because they blamed us for giving the people of Srebrenica the strength by giving them food to attack this other town.

WERTHEIMER: Sarajevo's principal source of fuel, in happy times, was electricity, isn't that right?

FOA: It seems that most houses had electrical-powered boilers, or whatever they called them.

WERTHEIMER: If you could get the electricity turned on tomorrow somehow, would that save the situation?

FOA: It would make a major difference. If we had the electricity, we would also have water. Living in a place for weeks on end without water is a big problem. You have to walk a mile to get a little container of water so you can wash your face or drink. But these crews go out to try and repair the power lines, and they are sniped at, and even if they do manage to repair them, the next day, somebody comes and cuts them.

WERTHEIMER: Are Sarajevans losing their resolve in this terrible situation?

FOA: I think some of them are, especially those who have been separated from their families for months and months. They evacuated their families in June or July, and they have not seen them since then. They have had no contact. One doctor at the hospital told me that he had had enough. He needed to see his wife and kids. He could not stand it anymore. He could not stand doing an operation and having the electricity from the generator go off because the generator kept breaking down. He could not stand seeing the electricity to the incubators go off and these kids being in these incubators. He said, "I've had enough. I can't do it anymore." But we were talking about most of the people not getting a full ration of food, and there was some discussion about whether any of this food was being diverted. They said, "If it's being diverted to the boys fighting, that is OK with us because we want them to be well fed. They deserve it." So there is this kind of fighting spirit out there. I think you see that on all the sides actually, that everybody wants to make sure their soldiers and their sons and their fathers get the food first. But the cold is something that really drains you. When you're freezing cold all the time, it is very hard to keep your morale up.

The Muslim-led government was at war with the militia of the Bosnian Serbs. It was sometimes allied with, sometimes at war with, the militia of the Bosnian Croats. An arms embargo imposed by the United Nations ostensibly applied to all the combatants, but in practice it worked to the unique detriment of the Bosnians.

ELVIR KARIC, a wounded Bosnian soldier and a Muslim, was evacuated for surgery to the United States. In an interview with Katie Davis, Karic describes defending his hometown of Kotorosko against better-armed Serb forces. He speaks to Davis through an interpreter. February 28, 1993

KARIC: When the fighting started, almost immediately, they cut off the power line and the water to our city. At this point, all the women and children were evacuated. Only the men were left behind to defend the city. To know how it is when only men are left, we had to cook for ourselves, we had to do everything for ourselves. There was no electricity, no water. But we were determined to defend our city. We had some guns. There were people who were buying guns, and we used different channels to get guns. Of course, there were people who made guns. We used plenty of handmade guns and hunting guns sawed off that we used to protect ourselves. There were also people who couldn't fight, but they were buying guns and they were trying to supply us with guns so we could fight. You have to understand that we mostly fought with handguns. We had some grenades, but we didn't have any of the heavy equipment. We didn't have tanks. We didn't have machine guns and heavy armament like the Serbians did.

DAVIS: What was the strategy that you used to try to defend your town?

KARIC: Strategy? No strategy. You dig yourself into the ground and you wait. They were coming. They were coming at us with everything they had, and we had guns and we were trying to stop them. We waited for them. The Serbians were coming and they had guns. They had big tanks. Worse than that, they had the airplanes. They had the planes, and they were throwing bombs at us and they were throwing grenades. The tanks were shelling us constantly. Most of the people that died and most of the people that were wounded were not wounded by bullets, they were wounded by grenades. They were wounded by bombs thrown by the planes. You cannot fight planes with guns. You can't shoot the plane down with a hunting gun. That is why we lost.

DAVIS: When you dig yourself in like that and you're waiting, what are you thinking about?

KARIC: I was just waiting, and asking myself, Why are they coming? Why are they doing that? I couldn't understand, I couldn't comprehend why the Serbians are doing that. It was something I couldn't answer myself. I had friends who were Serbians, and they never protested the policies nor the actions of Belgrade. I don't understand that, I really don't. Even if a Serbian fights on our side, I don't think that I can be a friend with him. I just don't trust him. Even if he is fighting for our cause, I just lost my faith in the Serbians.

DAVIS: Do you think that could ever change again? Can Muslims and Serbians live as neighbors near to each other and live in peace?

KARIC: No, I don't think that we will ever be able to live with them the way we used to. What do you think? Would you be able to live with somebody who raped your daughter or raped your sister? Do you think you will be able to live with this person like a friend? No, I don't think we will ever be able to live the way like we did before with the people who tried to destroy our spirit, tried to destroy our culture and our beliefs. No, I don't think so.

DAVIS: Often, when the charges are made by Muslims or Croatians that the Serbians have committed atrocities, the countercharges come back that the Muslims also are guilty of committing atrocities, like putting people in concentration camps. It's also often said that the hatred between the groups is so strong that the charges are exaggerated.

KARIC: No, there is no common ground at all. How can you say that we did the same thing? We were just defending ourselves. We never went into Serbia. We never attacked Serbians in their homes. We never invaded cities. We never raped women. Even when we capture somebody, some Serbian soldiers, we treat them with respect. We put them in jail. We never had camps. We keep them in jail until agreement for exchange was reached. Then we will let them go in exchange for our soldiers. But we never raped their women. There is no common ground for even talking about us doing the same things like the Serbians.

....

Reports of atrocities streamed out of Bosnia and
neighboring Croatia, where many survivors took refuge.
From Zagreb, the Croatian capital, an American nurse,
JUDY DARNELLE, speaks with Alex Chadwick about
the rapes alleged to have been committed by Serb
militiamen against Muslim women. Darnelle says she
had heard that hundreds of Bosnian women had been
raped, but finding women who would talk about
it was difficult. January 12, 1993

CHADWICK: Tell me what have you found in trying to search
out these women?

DARNELLE: It's pretty much the same story over and over
again. One woman I interviewed was a twenty-two-year-old
virgin who had been raped by twenty Chetniks. She was held
captive for seventeen days in a concentration camp in Trnop-
olje, which is an area in Bosnia. And she was just repeatedly
raped by Serbians every night, every night. They would come in
and ask who the virgins were. I also interviewed a sixty-year-old
woman who had been raped, and she said that they inserted a
knife. She asked them, "Please, please, don't touch me. Don't
touch me, I just had a hysterectomy." She thought they would
back off, but they said, "Well, we'll show you a hysterectomy."
She said they were trying to pull out her ovaries and her uterus,
and she was just covered in blood. Finally she and some other
women that night were able to escape from their town. She was
not in a concentration camp. This happened to be in her home.

CHADWICK: Tell me what is happening to these women
now?

DARNELLE: It seems to me to be systematic. From hearing
their stories, I am absolutely one hundred percent convinced
that this is all a part of ethnic cleansing, to humiliate these

people into submission and to drive them away so they never ever want to come back to Bosnia. The Croatian government is trying to help them as much as they can, as well as the Bosnian government.

CHADWICK: What is being done for them now?

DARNELLE: Well, they are getting psychiatric care. There is medical treatment. Some of them are kept under sedation part of the time and they get a lot of counseling through the international rescue committee, Red Cross, various outside organizations, and feminist groups here. I went to a meeting in Zagreb of the Croatian Victimology Society and spoke with the minister of health. He says they are trying to set up counseling centers for these women. Of course, it will all have to be on a voluntary basis, so they are not singling them out as rape victims. Many of them, I am finding, are not speaking to physicians and not speaking to government but are going to churches and mosques.

CHADWICK: Many of the women are not speaking to the government or to physicians?

DARNELLE: No, because they're afraid of reporters. They are afraid of the stigma. I know of a pregnant woman. She does not want her husband to find out or her mother-in-law. They are still in Bosnia. Her husband is a Bosnian soldier, and she does not want him to find out. She feels she's just going to be able to give birth to this baby and then go back to a normal life. She has a psychiatrist trying to take care of her in the hospital, but she is in shock. She can't even look at her stomach, because to her, in her mind, it's not a baby inside of her. It's a result of an evil. It's easier for her mind to look at it as a tumor. She is nine months pregnant, and she can't understand why she can't have an abortion.

CHADWICK: You are an American nurse and a professional medical person. What are conditions like there for these women?

DARNELLE: In the hospitals, they are very good. The refugee camps are nice. It's just that the conditions are very crowded at the moment. They get clothes and food and various other presents for the children from international organizations, but you can find a family of fifteen living in a very small room.

CHADWICK: I think a lot of Americans are perhaps a little confused about the geography there. You say these women are removed from immediate danger now? There is no fighting going on around there?

DARNELLE: Right.

CHADWICK: Where they are being kept?

DARNELLE: Right now in Croatia, per se, there is not very much fighting going on. Along the borders of Slavonski Brod, there are still some snipers. The other day was Serbian Christmas. They sent us a grenade, and an eighteen-year-old boy was injured. But there is really no active fighting. Many of them are kept either in the capital, Zagreb, or various other parts of Croatia, near the Slovenian border, or maybe near the Adriatic coast, where there is no fighting and it's peaceful.

CHADWICK: I wonder, Ms. Darnelle, if there is anything that can be done or anything that you can say as a nurse to these women about healing?

DARNELLE: As far as healing psychologically, it's going to take time, but nothing can really be concrete until the war is over or until they are able to defend themselves. They still need the arms embargo lifted. That is all these women ask for because they're concerned for family and friends that are still in Bosnia that are being killed. Once there is peace and this war is over with, then the healing can begin. Because psychologically, they can't calm down, they can't think about anything else except family and friends who are still in Bosnia, in occupied territories, who are still fighting and still dying.

....

Refugees belonging to all of Bosnia's religious factions
told of brutal campaigns of ethnic cleansing carried out
against them. A Serbian couple, SUSANNA and MLADIN
BASARIC, fled Mostar, the capital of Hercegovina.
In 1992, Susanna went to America while Mladin, a
Yugoslav army helicopter pilot and technician, stayed
behind. When a group of men stopped him and put
a gun in his mouth, he decided to leave the town, too.
In Washington, D.C., they tell Katie Davis about
the war, and what it had destroyed in their hometown:
the peaceful coexistence that Mostar's different
communities had long known. Mladin Basaric speaks
through an interpreter. March 21, 1993

SUSANNA: We all lived together. No one cared who was who
in that time. We all lived together. We went to school together.
We were in love with each other. We married each other.

MLADIN: The biggest group, the largest portion of the population of Mostar, are the Muslims. In second place come the
Serbians, and then the smallest part, the Croatians. I also want
to say that in Mostar right now there are only about three hundred Serbians. Before that, we had about thirty-five thousand.

DAVIS: What happened?

MLADIN: Some left, some wanted to leave, and some were
killed.

SUSANNA: One of those three hundred Serbs are my parents.
They didn't leave. They didn't want to leave because they be-
lieved that they could stay together and live together with
Croatians and Muslims, and that was true.

DAVIS: Was there any one thing that made you decide to
leave?

SUSANNA: My husband, he wanted me to leave. He wanted

me to leave, and I decided to come here. In that time, I didn't realize that I was going to stay here for this long because everything was OK when I left. I mean, there was a lot of tension. If I say everything was OK, it wasn't OK.

DAVIS: Your husband is shaking his head no.

SUSANNA: Yes.

DAVIS: Mladin, what was going on that disturbed you, that made you want your wife and your two daughters to leave?

MLADIN: At that time, I was working for the army and everything started falling apart. The army, the government, started falling apart. I couldn't place my family on either side. Everything was dividing into three different groups and I couldn't identify my family with either one of those groups. I knew that a real hardship is awaiting us.

DAVIS: What do you mean, you "couldn't identify your family"? You are Serbian.

MLADIN: I am Serbian, but I am not a militant Serb. I don't want to kill anybody. I would like to save somebody but not to kill anybody. I don't want to go to war for no reason at all, not for such stupid reasons.

DAVIS: Do you think the war that happened in your city, in Mostar, was a stupid war?

MLADIN: I think so, and not only in Mostar, but for the whole country the war started for no reason. The politicians are the ones responsible for the war, not the common people. Politicians had the chance to prevent it and they didn't do it. The common people have nothing to do with the war.

SUSANNA: I am so sad when I think about it now, because my father, who lived in Mostar, was arrested by three uniformed men at the evening of March 1, 1993. I don't know where is he now, if he is still alive or not. We don't know where is he now. We are trying to find him now, and it's such a difficult time for me and for my mom because she is alone. She is scared to stay in her apartment now.

DAVIS: Do you know who took him?

SUSANNA: I don't know exactly who took him because there

are a lot of irregular groups over there now. We have contacted the Croatian army and the Croatian government in Mostar. They said they didn't take him because they didn't have any reason to take him. He was not politically active. He's sixty-six. They didn't have any reason to take him. The only reason I can think of is ethnic cleansing. Ethnic cleansing, because all those groups have irregular groups to do those dirty things for them.

DAVIS: Ethnic cleansing, I think that is a term many Americans associate with Serbians going into a town and cleansing it. Are you suggesting that Serbs have also been the victims of ethnic cleansing?

SUSANNA: I am a witness. My father is a witness.

MLADIN: I would like to say that in my opinion he was taken by right-wing Croatian soldiers who go by the name Ustasha. As far as ethnic cleansing is concerned, I would like to say that it's more popular than people believe. It's done by Croats, as well as Muslims, even though maybe the Serbians are the ones who do most of the damage. The other two groups also participate, and that is something that started and it's still enforced by the politicians on the top. They are the ones who provoke it.

DAVIS: Now that you are here and you're in the United States and you are able to listen or read the news about what's going on, what do you think of it? Do you think that the situation is portrayed fairly? The Serbs get much of the blame for this war and they are, of course, the principal aggressor in Bosnia, but what is your feeling looking at the war from afar?

MLADIN: I am getting sick to my stomach and I really can't believe that the United States, which I regarded as the most objective country in the world, would present the situation so one-sidedly and will always speak only from one point of view.

DAVIS: What point of view is that?

MLADIN: I would have to admit that Serbians started this and are responsible for many really ugly things that were done during that time. But on the other hand, people that lived in other parts were innocent. I would like to see those people — those Serbs who did criminal acts, and I regard them as war criminals — I would like to see them punished. I am so disappointed, not only by what happened in Mostar but by what happened in Yugoslavia, that I don't think I will ever have the right to go back there. I would also like to say that my grandfather was born in Minnesota. So I don't want to repeat his mistake and go back to this part of the world.

SUSANNA: I wish to go back one day, not now, because it's impossible to go now, but I wish to go there one day, because there is a little hope still in my heart that maybe we can live together again one day. But it's still a little hope. I am a musician, I am an artist, and I see all these things in my way and maybe it's not a good way, but my husband said he has another opinion for that. And maybe, I don't know, maybe I was blind all of those years in my life. I couldn't see any difference between Muslims and Croatians and Serbs. I feel now that, how do you call that sickness, when you —

DAVIS: Amnesia?

SUSANNA: Amnesia. Sometimes I want to have that sickness, to forget everything before, to start over again. It is so painful for me.

DOBROMIR ELEZOVIC, a Croat who taught high school Latin and history, lived in the Bosnian town of Prijedor. In April 1992, the local government was taken over by Serbs, and a population that had previously ignored religious differences became segregated. The events Elezovic related to freelance reporter Neenah Ellis (his cousin) led him to join his brother in Chicago: Nearby villages had been shelled. The Serbs had burned mosques and homes. Twenty-five thousand people were displaced, he said. Women and children were taken to concentration camps. People he knew were shot in the street in front of his apartment building. Dobromir's cousin John Elezovic interprets. March 7, 1993

ELEZOVIC: One night, around two o'clock, they had a list of the Serbian population in that building. They were only giving the weapons to the Serbians. So when the conflict started, all the Serbian population came out with rifles on their shoulders, and I couldn't believe it. I asked, "Where is my weapon? Who is going to defend my family?" I am entitled because I paid taxes, same as everybody else. I had to defend my family. We understood the people needed weapons, that the people all together, we were going to defend ourselves from the foreign enemy. And then the tragedy started.

ELLIS: What happened to you?

ELEZOVIC: The first time they took me, the police came and took me away June 1 (1992) at two in afternoon. They took me to the police station. They wanted to talk to me. I was there until evening, just like the Jews during the Second World War. That's how I felt. I was accused by the police of belonging to the Croatian organization, so-called Ustasha Croatian Democratic Union. I was never member of any political organization. I was just a Croatian intellectual, that is all. Then, after this interrogation, they let me go. They give me a release and write in the release that they are not going to bother me anymore. I just continued to work at my job in my own school. The second time they came after me and took me away on June 17, at five thirty-five A.M. That time they came, four policemen after me, in a police car. They took me to the concentration camp in the city. In that camp, there was a thousand people already there.

ELLIS: What did they tell you? Did they say anything to you about why they were taking you there?

ELEZOVIC: They didn't tell me anything. I show them the release paper, which they give me before, that they are not supposed to touch me. They didn't bother with this, and they just took me away. They just put me in a police car, which I couldn't see where I am going. Even my wife, she didn't know where I am going, where they take me. When they let me out from the police car, then I saw where I was. Then I did have something to see. Blood. They were washing blood with water . . . they took the people during the night, and they would just crucify them. They were beating them, killing them, doing anything they wanted. They did not beat me up, but all around me, guys were all beaten up. There was a young boy who was fourteen years old, and the oldest man was seventy-five years old. This little boy, they beat his head in. He was a Muslim. I have to give thanks to my son-in-law. He was there in Prijedor. I think that was my luck because, if he wouldn't be there, I would never be alive today. He is Serbian by nationality, and he helped me through his friends. They took me from that concentration camp, and they put me in a hospital. The floor where they put were all the people that needed medical attention from all these concentration camps. At night it was worse in the hospital than it was in the concentration camp. On the second floor there were all the Serbian wounded soldiers, and they were coming every night to mistreat all of us. . . . Me and my wife, we are sure we are never going to go back there. I don't know about my daughter and my son-in-law. I have to go, sometime, to see the grave of my little grandson. He was only fifteen months old when he died. That was everything to me in this war. The kids, they kept me there. Everything to me, my life, my work, were those kids. I am a pacifist and a humanist because of my nature and my belief. I can't hate anybody. Just because of my tragedy, I don't accuse the Serbian people. I just accuse the individuals who are the war criminals. I want this world to know what is true. There is very little known about these atrocities which were done around this region where I was. It's very sad that nobody knows about it, because where I lived there was no war, there was no fighting. And just because there was not a war, there was very big genocide. I am asking myself, "Why?" I am going to ask myself as long as I am alive, "Why?"

The war in Bosnia presented the new administration in
the United States with hard choices. The U.N. mediator
Cyrus Vance and Lord DAVID OWEN, representing
the European Union, had proposed a decentralization
of Bosnia into ten autonomous provinces. The Bosnians
and the Croats signed the Vance-Owen plan, but
the Serbs declined, preferring instead to pursue gains
on the battlefield. The Bosnian government hoped that
the Clinton administration would come to its aid,
either with airstrikes or by lifting the arms embargo.
Lord Owen, a former British foreign secretary, urges
the United States to back the peace plan in this
interview with Katie Davis. January 30, 1993

OWEN: There is a belief in the Bosnian-Hercegovinian government, the Muslim delegation, effectively, that all they have
to do is to go on appealing to President Clinton, and the United
States cavalry are going to run in and help them and save them
and intervene. Since, in my judgment, President Clinton isn't
going to make that decision, and certainly isn't going to put
American forces in a fighting role on the ground without a
peace, that illusion will have to be shattered. And, hopefully, it
will be done fairly soon.

DAVIS: How do you think the U.S. can be most effective in
helping to end the war, to achieve peace?

OWEN: Make up its mind and support the peace process and
accept the plan that we've presented as most other countries are
doing.

DAVIS: The administration has raised the possibility of asking the United Nations to lift the arms embargo to the Muslims.
What do think about that idea?

OWEN: Quite crazy, in my view. At this juncture, when you

have got a negotiation almost at the point of agreement, to even talk about lifting the arms embargo only encourages those people who want to go on fighting in the Muslim fighting force. There are hopefully not too many of those.

DAVIS: Mr. Owen, you sat down with the leaders of the three sides in this war for months. I wonder if the discussion that you observed, and watching their interactions, gave you any insight into why this war has been so brutal, so intractable?

OWEN: It's rooted in history. It's rooted in attitudes of mind. They all come from actually the same ethnic stock. Why did some choose the Muslim religion under the Ottoman Empire? Why did others stay with their Catholicism or with Orthodoxy? It's hard to say. The dispute is not entirely religious by any means. It's also historical. But there are long and deep roots in it. In the period of autocratic rule under Tito, many of these people developed almost as a reaction against Communism an intense nationalism. They built up in their resistance to Communism their sort of commitment to the idea of the Croatian nation or the Serbian nation. When Yugoslavia broke up in the aftermath of the breakup of the Soviet Union, this nationalism became very strong. There was a heavy mix of nationalism and racism, and that is a very nasty mixture. It's such a maze and mixture. Yet when you most expect them to be bitter and difficult, which is when they eventually managed to get all the politicians around the table, they actually talked constructively and without too much emotion and bitterness. It was there, but it was controlled, which gives me some grounds for thinking that they can work together. And you are seeing now some people beginning to build a relationship, which I think, in the interim government, we could manage to get nine people who could work together.

Throughout 1993, Americans read and heard accounts of the war in Bosnia, a war in which civilians were frequently the targets. On *All Things Considered,* nine Americans offered their thoughts on whether the United States should become involved militarily. May 10, 1993

BARRY GOLDWATER: In my opinion, no troops or any forces at all should be sent to Bosnia. It's the one country that Germany nearly got beat by in World War II. They are far better fighters than any country I know of, and we should stay home.

ROBERT DRINAN: I am a Jesuit who teaches at Georgetown University Law Center. I was a Democratic member of Congress from Massachusetts from 1971 to 1981. I and everyone in the religious community have great difficulty in justifying the several conditions for a just war as applied to Bosnia. Essentially, the just-war theory requires, above all, that every less-violent means be exhausted before war can be justified, and I don't think that has been done. Secondly, the just-war theory clearly requires that the good to be achieved outweighs the harm that is to be done. In my judgment and the judgment of many people in the entire religious community, that has not yet been justified. Likewise, the just-war theory requires that there be provisions made for innocent civilians, and in all of the projections of warfare by the allies of the United States in Serbia, there has not been even a thought for the thousands of innocent civilians that will be bombed. On balance, therefore, I don't think, at least at this time, that there can be a justified, moral, ethical intervention by the United States in the Balkans.

PAUL WARNKE: I am a Washington lawyer. I was chief arms-control negotiator and the head of the Arms Control Disarmament Agency during the Carter administration. With regard to

U.S. intervention in Bosnia, the United States ought to go to NATO, and say, "If you're going to have any use in the post–cold war world, this is your opportunity to prove it." We ought to get authorization from the United Nations for NATO to act as an arm of the United Nations to put an end to the slaughter in Bosnia.

FRANCES FITZGERALD: I am a journalist. I write for *The New Yorker* magazine, and I am the author of *Fire in the Lake*. I believe the U.S. military has had the absolute right to ask all the questions they have been asking all along. However, I believe that morally it is extremely important to do something, and politically as well. The possibility of a wider Serbian aggression, the possibility of involvement of the whole Balkans in war, is too great to leave unnoticed. Of course, the European countries ought to be doing this themselves, but there is, unfortunately, no leadership in Western Europe, and they will not do it without us. So I think we are going to have to put their feet to the fire. It's not clear, also, politically, how the various communities in Bosnia-Hercegovina are going to be able to get along in the end. There is no clear solution. However, I think that in this new post–cold war period, we as a nation are going to have to get along with the notion that there are not any perfect solutions anywhere in the world. It seems to me that it's important to increase the price to the Serbs, to make them pay a severe penalty for doing what they are doing, even if it doesn't work and doesn't produce a complete solution. We have to give the Bosnian Muslims a fighting chance.

RAMSEY CLARK: I am a former attorney general of the United States, and I was in Bosnia and Serbia just the week before last. The U.S. military action in the area would be an absolute disaster for everyone involved. There are real problems there that you can't bomb away. It's very doubtful that Bosnia-Hercegovina is viable economically or politically. We have balkanized the Balkans, and now we're atomizing Bosnia into ten separated armed or guarded camps. What is required is comprehensive U.N. leadership and action, and that is what President

Clinton ought to seek. It's imperative that we have moral leadership on this issue and not simply continue trying to bomb people into compliance.

ELAINE DONNELLY: I am president of the Center for Military Readiness and a former member of the Presidential Commission on the Assignment of Women in the Armed Forces, commonly known as the Women in Combat Commission. I don't think the president of the United States, Bill Clinton, understands the needs of the military. I don't think he respects the military, and I would have great fears for our men and women in uniform if they are deployed to that part of the world by a president who has said in the past that he agrees with those who loathe the military. I think that this president has been using this institution as a political punching bag, a public relations gimmick, to promote his first hundred days of dubious accomplishments. I see a lack of vertical cohesion, that is vertical respect between the president and the military and vice versa, which could have dangerous consequences if these troops are deployed to a very dangerous part of the world.

BOBBY MULLE: I am executive director of the Vietnam Veterans of America Foundation. The president will get an expression of congressional support for what he wants to do. No president has ever not gotten congressional and public support once the American flag has effectively been committed to battle. What he will not get is a clear declaration of war, although war is what we are about to get involved in. When the question is framed in terms of a limited engagement — no ground troops, only airstrikes — we are not being honest in our debate about what we are getting involved in. We are talking about joining an ongoing, all-out, bloody, civil and religious war. The point is, let's not engage in the politics of deception for the reasons of immediate political pressure and expediency. While some kind of hurried resolution of congressional support, along with all the other prerequisites of some form of collective action with our allies, vague United Nations cover, and at least some initial public support can all be achieved. We need more. We need to approach the question of intervention so as to gain a full appreciation of what the possible consequences may be. That is something that will only be done through something as dramatic and sobering as what the framers of our Constitution had in mind when they made it a requirement in our democracy, namely, a congressional declaration to go to war. When the seriousness of purpose involved in going to war is stated, it helps to galvanize and engage the attention of the people and thereby inform the debate. Will people be shocked when you frame the issue in this way? Sure. Will they be more frightened and hesitant? Of course they will. That is precisely the point. We must not gradually slip into this fighting, slowly escalating the price paid and to be paid. It may well turn out that, with a full appreciation of what's been going on in the former Yugoslavia and what it means for us as Americans and as fellow human beings, that we will determine that our involvement is warranted. But let's be clear about what we are doing, why we are doing it, and what price we may be called upon to pay.

CECIL L. MURRAY: I am senior minister of First African Methodist Episcopal Church in Los Angeles. There seem to be two prime considerations. One, that the United States as much as possible makes this a United Nations action. The blanket approval of the world society is better than to have the approval of a single cell of that society. Even if the majority of the resources must come through the United States, the sanction should come from the entire world. If we cannot get the sanctions, of course, then we have another decision to make. Secondly, the question of whether we use armed might to save lives has a prior question: Have we exhausted every effort to be peaceful and amicable? We don't have any choice about helping people who are being victims of genocide. We have no question there. The only question is, Have we exhausted every alternative? If we have, we go and we don't look back. We don't do hand-wringing.

LEONARD ZAKIM: I am the New England regional director of the Anti-Defamation League in Boston. The fact that this conflict in Bosnia is complicated and also centuries old can't be allowed to keep the United States from exercising the strongest leadership in moving to stop the violence, the atrocities, and hatred. I think it is the responsibility of the United States to bring Europe into the mix, to try to find a solution to these problems. If the solutions include some military intervention, then I think our responsibilities must be to the lives of those young children and others whose lives will be lost if we allow this conflict to work out its own deadly way. I am certainly supportive of limited military intervention. I believe that unlike the days of the Holocaust when many claimed they did not know, the rest of the world cannot say now that they did not know. I think, in particular in the Jewish community, the memories of the Holocaust are sharp. Our nerves are so exposed by all of what we understood in terms of the lack of the world's response, the silence that greeted the news of the Holocaust. We in America and, I think, we in the Jewish community have a special responsibility to mobilize people to take the kind of efforts and the kind of actions necessary to save the lives of those innocent people in Bosnia.

The photographer MARTIN SUGARMAN talks with Noah Adams about his book of photographs *God Be with You: War in Croatia and Bosnia-Hercegovina.* His work shows young soldiers on patrol, the shattered towns, desperate victims in hospitals, bodies exhumed from a mass grave. The pictures are all black and white, and there's one image that could come from a post-nuclear nightmare: passenger-train cars, abandoned, burned, and twisted. March 23, 1993

SUGARMAN: That's the train station in Sarajevo. When the war started, the Serbs blew up the bus station. They tried to destroy all means of transportation in and out of the city. They destroyed all the trams and the buses. They blew up the train station.

ADAMS: It looks as if it's been abandoned for about half a century, in fact.

SUGARMAN: One year ago, those trains were running. The city is pretty much demolished and destroyed.

ADAMS: You have a photograph of the last bear, the last animal in the Sarajevo zoo.

SUGARMAN: That is an interesting story. There were a hundred animals alive in the zoo, and the bear was the last remaining animal. I thought this photograph would be very important because it more or less acts as a metaphor for the entire city being more or less caged in, no one permitted to leave, also the whole city starving to death. I went out there with a very brave guide. We ran through the fields. We were shot at. When we got to the door, it was locked, and the guide forgot to bring the keys. So he left me out there, exposed, and he ran back and got the keys and let me in, and I took pictures of this grizzly bear. All the other animals in the cages nearby were dead. Some animals resorted to eating their mates. A week later, the grizzly bear finally succumbed to starvation.

ADAMS: Photographers in this situation, over the years, have been concerned about the predatory nature of what it is they do, taking these images away and coming back to, in this case, a comfortable home, getting out of it, to Europe and then to the United States. Did you have any misgivings along those lines at all?

SUGARMAN: I did. One day, in Travnik, which is outside of Sarajevo, it's about a hundred miles north, three Serbian MIGs flew over the city and launched three or four missiles. It blew up a factory. The factory was on fire, and people were running out. People were pulling the dead out. I went with my interpreter and started taking pictures of this unfortunate event. This woman who had just seen her fellow worker blown to bits came up to me and slapped me in the face and told me how dare I take pictures of people here dying. That really set me back. What we did is I put my camera down, and we started taking people to the hospital in the car.

ADAMS: Near the end of the book, you have a long series of photographs of children in Sarajevo. Some of them do have guns, albeit toy guns and wooden guns, and seem to be quite proud of that. Every child that I can see lined up is smiling. Was it a natural temptation to end this book with pictures of happy children in Sarajevo, and is it disingenuous to do that, do you think?

SUGARMAN: No, because it's real. These kids are optimistic and, in fact, they give hope and psychological comfort to the older people. These kids are very resilient. Unfortunately, they are living in hell. There is the one of the two girls standing in Sarajevo with their mother, and their faces are scarred with shrapnel wounds.

ADAMS: This particular photograph does not show the mother's face. It shows her hand and her scarf and the two children, who look to be five or six years old, and both their faces are, as you mentioned, scarred.

SUGARMAN: What happened here was these children were sleeping one night, and a shell slammed into their bedroom. Fortunately, they were not seriously injured, but they did succumb to superficial wounds. You look into these kids' eyes, you see that they have matured way beyond their age. However, on the whole, these children are very happy to be alive.

NPR's TOM GJELTEN covered the war in Bosnia, as well as the fighting in Croatia the year before. His work earned him the George Polk Award for Radio Reporting. Susan Stamberg asked him about his personal views and experiences as a war reporter in the former Yugoslavia. March 27, 1993

STAMBERG: It's good to see you. I want to take advantage of you being here a little bit to ask you to do a reporter's notebook with us, some behind-the-scenes sense of what it's been like covering this war. All of us in this business are paid to be impartial, but you certainly get the sense that in an experience like this, you may be impartial but you certainly cannot go unaffected.

GJELTEN: This war has probably brought together the most hardened war correspondents in the world and international aid workers, who have been in the most terrible places on the planet. I don't think any journalist, or any aid worker, has been unaffected by this. In my own case, I covered the wars in Central America for several years, and it was nothing like this. The scale of the suffering is so much greater, and the brutality is so much more horrifying. The amount of civilian casualties really leaves you weakened and numbed sometimes.

STAMBERG: Do you not ever have the feeling that you just have to get away, that you can't take it anymore?

GJELTEN: Of course I have that feeling. I think probably I have now become used to traveling a lot as a foreign correspondent. I don't have a family, so I don't have a sense of needing to rush back to a more familiar life. The fact that this war has affected me as much as it has makes it harder in some ways for me to pull out. When I am in Sarajevo, for example, I have a lot of friends in Sarajevo, and every time I leave, I feel a certain guilt that I am leaving them behind because you can see it in their faces, they feel so trapped. To come in and out of their lives in a quick way like that is often really painful.

STAMBERG: Do you get the feeling that you are, in some ways, a lifeline there, as far as getting their story out, and also keeping them within our attention?

GJELTEN: I have never before felt, as a journalist, that what I do matters as much as it does in this war. So many places in Bosnia, for example, are inaccessible to everybody, and so little is known about what goes on. I remember when the U.S. State Department put out a report on human rights abuses in Bosnia. They basically just reported what had come out in the press because no one else, including even U.N. workers, is often as close to what is really happening as the international press has been. So I think that journalism in this case is finally a profession that is really a calling.

STAMBERG: Tom, what are some of the experiences you have had that have made the deepest impression on you? I remember a report that you did not long ago for this program, in which you were riding in a car crossing a bridge, and hearing everyone breathe a sigh of relief when you had crossed that danger point.

GJELTEN: That was the suburb of Dobrinja, just outside Sarajevo. Everybody in the van was lying on the floor, and we crossed this bridge that is the scene of sniper fire all the time. I also saw people walking, and as they got to that bridge, old women would get down on their hands and knees and crawl across it in order to make themselves smaller targets. This is their daily lives. It's one of those moments when you are glad that you can get in and out of there in one day. But these people cross that bridge every day of their lives. Just this past week, in eastern Bosnia, I came through several villages where Muslims had just been expelled. In some, the clothes were still hanging on the clotheslines and people had come into their houses and loaded up trailers with TV sets, and washers and dryers, and so forth, and were carrying off their possessions. The people had gone. I am just now reading the book *Bridge on the Drina*, by Ivo Andric, which describes, over a period of three or four hundred years, the intermingling of cultures in the Drina valley in those very villages that I was driving through. And to realize that the commingling of cultures that has taken place in the Drina valley over hundreds of years, right before your eyes, is over. The Muslims have been pushed out. There is not a single one left in any of these villages, and being a witness to that is really quite an experience.

STAMBERG: Tom, I have noticed a change in your language as your reporting has gone on. You are making it clear that it is the Serbs, again and again, who are the perpetrators here, and that is something in your reporting, I think, that has evolved over time, the reporting of responsibility.

GJELTEN: I think that it is important to assign responsibility if you know for certain who is responsible. I, as a journalist, cannot be a party to something that I know is untrue. There was just an example this week, when the town of Srebrenica was being shelled and the Serb forces claimed that the U.N. forces had themselves dropped bombs on the soccer field in order to frame the Serbs. It was so ridiculous, so inconceivable, and so obviously untrue that, in that case, I am not going to say that the soccer field was shelled, and sort of leave unsaid who did it. It was the Serb forces who did it, and I am going to say it.

STAMBERG: I cannot begin to imagine, Tom, what it is like to try to do the professional work of reporting in the midst of situations like this, and keep your head clear to do it. How do you do that?

GJELTEN: It is very important to keep your patience and to keep anger under control. Let me just give you an example. This past week, the drivers of the aid trucks who were going into eastern Bosnia were forced by Serb police to park in a city dump for nine days. Several times they got authorizations to leave, and they started off. They would get one kilometer down the road, and would be turned back with all kinds of insults and humiliating things. It's the same thing being a journalist. You are constantly being insulted. It would be easy just to get angry and let that affect your reporting. But it's important in those cases just to keep a cool head.

The Bosnian newsman ZLATKO DIZDAREVIC talks with
Noah Adams about the proposal by the Bosnian Serbs
that Sarajevo be divided along ethnic lines. He also talks
about the spirit of Sarajevo. Dizdarevic is editor of the
newspaper *Oslobodenje*. A collection of his newspaper
columns has been compiled in the book *Sarajevo:
A War Journal.* December 3, 1993

DIZDAREVIC: I think it is not possible to make two Sara-
jevos. It is not acceptable for anybody in the town. But it is very
difficult to say today for anything it's not possible, because in
Bosnia-Hercegovina everything is possible. After all this time,
after two years, it's clear that everything is possible and it's
clear the international community is ready to accept everything. They said that the changing of the border by force is not
possible, but it's possible. They said the ethnic cleansing is not
possible, but it's possible. They said that the killing of the children just like that is not possible, but all that is possible. I would
have said just that for the citizens of Sarajevo, it is not possible
to have another Berlin Wall in Sarajevo. But I think that the
international community is ready to do everything except to do
something real and something concrete.

ADAMS: Have you had this thought since the war began in
Bosnia, that it is in many ways a coward's war? Two hundred
thousand people either dead or presumed to be dead in all of
Bosnia. That it's not a military battle?

DIZDAREVIC: Ninety-five percent of all victims in Bosnia-
Hercegovina are civilians. It's not the war. The Second World
War, including the last bombarding of civilian targets in Germany, including old concentration camps, et cetera, it was fifty-
fifty, the civilians and the soldiers. In Bosnia-Hercegovina,

ninety-five percent of all victims are civilians. This means it's not the war.

ADAMS: What questions will people ask you, when you go back, about your visits to Europe and to the United States?

DIZDAREVIC: The first time I prepared to leave, my friends and family prepared long lists of many different small things to buy and to bring back with me to Sarajevo. The second time that list was very short. This time I asked, "What do you want? What do you need from abroad?" Everybody said, "Nothing." This is like the news on the radio. Today, nobody cares about the news on the radio. I think that even the situation in Geneva now, nobody cares about the conference. Nobody speaks about it.

ADAMS: You wrote earlier, "Why should we take an interest in politics when it was politics that led us into this disaster?"

DIZDAREVIC: We don't believe that it is possible to do something with politicians, especially in Yugoslavia. I think that for us, I said, "This is the end of politics. This is the end of illusions."

THE WORLD

The Nobel Peace Prize recipient Archbishop DESMOND TUTU speaks with Katie Davis about the state of world peace at the start of 1993. He talks about civil wars, from Somalia to Bosnia, and what should be done about them. In the case of the former Yugoslavia, Archbishop Tutu believes forceful intervention is now a moral obligation. January 2, 1993

TUTU: I do actually believe that there are times when the world community must step in, and say, "This far and no further." We cannot tolerate this kind of conflict because it poses a very real threat to the world community. We cannot sit by and see what is happening in the former Yugoslavia and say this is something that is being contained within the boundaries of that particular country because, for one thing, there are Muslims in other parts of the world who are going to be incensed by what they see happening to their fellow adherents of faith.

DAVIS: What happens if the world does just sit by and watch that situation develop?

TUTU: For one thing, our own humanity is affected very deeply. You can't watch people behaving in a debased and dehumanized way and not, in fact, be affected. If we don't recognize that we have a common humanity, we are all going to be losers. The fact that it is one section of the world community away in the distance which is suffering and we sit by and do nothing doesn't mean that does not have repercussions on our own humanity. We are hardened by seeing cruelty happen and we pass by on the other side. We are affected very profoundly, even when we don't at the time note that this is actually happening to us.

DAVIS: I wanted to ask you about what you think of the military intervention in Somalia.

TUTU: I believe that, ultimately, there is a justification for the world to see. We can't be looking on and seeing children walking around like walking skeletons with gaunt eyes and all skin and bones when there is food available. They can't reach that food because some people have guns. We have got to say, "Why did they get the guns in the first place? Where did they get the guns?" Again, you see morality is so crucial to continued human community. There was a time when people were arming certain groups because of so-called geopolitics. Now the chickens, as it were, are coming home to roost in a horrendous kind of way. But I would say that it is justifiable now to say we can't let these children die just as much as we would not let Hitler continue to throw children into gas chambers. So we cannot sit by and let those warlords in Somalia allow children who have done nothing and who are guilty of no fault to expire just because they want to be able to rule the roost as to who controls the food.

DAVIS: Did you have any misgivings at all about this intervention? Did it raise any specter for you of colonialism, even if it is being done for humanitarian reasons?

TUTU: There are a lot of problems about it. One of the problems is why should it happen there and not elsewhere? Why is it not happening in Sri Lanka, for instance? But I would say that the situation is so desperate that it may be a paradigm. The world may be saying that although we do this with very great reluctance, it is, in fact, a moral universe. Your goodness matters, compassion matters, injustice matters, and we cannot pretend that we aren't moral creatures, that God actually has put us on this earth and made us people who can make choices, and that is what makes us persons and that is why a person has to be reverenced and treated with awe. We are able to choose to say yes to God or no.

DAVIS: Archbishop Tutu, what do you see in the coming year around the world and in your country?

TUTU: I must say that I am thrilled with ordinary human beings, that even when people have been oppressed and down-trodden for a long time they do not lose the sense that they are made for something different, that they are made for freedom. You don't have to teach people that repression is wrong. No matter how illiterate they may be, they know that they are not meant to be treated as a downtrodden bunch, that they are meant to be free. It's almost the rash of free countries in Africa, countries that are making the transition from totalitarianism to multiparty democracy. That gives one very considerable hope. In South Africa, although we certainly have been deeply distressed by the mindless violence that has taken place and has continued to take place in our country, the fact of the matter is that most people know that we have nowhere else to go but forward to a negotiated resolution of the crisis of our country. I think that is penetrating the skulls of the politicians and that they jolly well have got to get on with this business. There is a far greater sense in the world of human rights and of justice to all people and justice to women and to groups that in the past have been marginalized. This is very exhilarating, and the sense that you have from young people, who obviously are always more idealistic than others, that this world can become a better world, a world without war, a world of greater justice, of greater compassion, a world that says all of us are made for greater things than just merely material possessions. We were made to enjoy music, to enjoy beautiful sunsets, to enjoy look-ing at the billows of the sea and to be thrilled with a rose that is bedecked with dew. There are incredible things that God has given us that you wouldn't be able to buy with money, and many people are aware of this. What Saint Augustine said is actually quite true, that we are an incredible kind of paradox. We are finite human beings who are created for the infinite. He said, "God, thou has created us for thyself, and we are restless until we find our rest in thee." Human beings are actually created for the transcendent, for the sublime, for the beautiful, for the truthful, and you don't teach people these things. It comes with the package of being human, and all of us are given the task of trying to make this world a little more hospitable to these beautiful things — to love, to compassion, to caring, to sharing, just to being human.

....

The diplomat, historian, and political adviser GEORGE
KENNAN discusses with Liane Hansen the cold war,
Communism, and the delicate balance the Clinton
administration must maintain between domestic
and foreign policy. Kennan's book *Around the Cragged
Hill* is an accumulation of eighty-eight years' worth of
personal and political philosophy. February 7, 1993

HANSEN: With regard to the cold war, do you think one
person deserves credit for "winning it"?

KENNAN: No, and no country. In fact, I think all of us lost by
it. It involved enormous expenses on the defense establish-
ments, both in the Soviet Union and here, much of which could
have been avoided if it hadn't been for the whole cold war situation and the psychology that surrounded it.

HANSEN: So we actually lost more than we gained by winning it?

KENNAN: I think we all did, and I am glad it's over. I think
some of it was necessary, but not all of it.

HANSEN: What do you think was necessary?

KENNAN: The Russians came out of World War II, the Soviet
leaders I should say, with unrealistic ideas about their great
military success in Europe and what it was going to mean. I
think they thought that they were going to have greater influence over the entire continent than we thought was permissi-
ble, and that had to be corrected. They did, of course, retain very
large forces numerically in Europe at the time when we had
demobilized most of ours. I think those forces were actually not
as formidable as we saw them as being at that time, but that
they were much larger than ours and that meant there did indeed have to be a certain effort of remilitarization in this country, but I don't think it needed to be presented to the public here

in the way that it was or that the necessity needed to be interpreted in the way that it was. There was much too much militarized cold war. If it had been a political one, it would have been more understandable and better, and we wouldn't have spent so much money and had so much tension.

HANSEN: You don't agree with those who say that, perhaps, Ronald Reagan's policy and the whole policy of deterrence is what actually ended it?

KENNAN: Not really. I don't think there was any time when the Soviet leadership thought or intended or wanted to invade Western Europe. What was needed was really not military deterrence. What was needed was to stabilize the political situation in Europe, which was largely done with the Marshall Plan, and then to talk with them when the opportunity presented itself about the future of the continent. But we would never do that. On the two occasions when I pressed very strongly for this, once in 1949 when I was still in government and on another occasion on the Reith Lectures on the BBC in 1956, the government just would no longer talk with the Russians. They had more or less stabilized the situation, and one should have talked with them then about what has happened in the last three or four years, about the possibilities of their withdrawal, about the demilitarization of the conflict, but we wouldn't do it. That was one of the great disappointments of my life.

HANSEN: Do you see the atmosphere inside this country at the time, in 1947, in 1949, and the witch hunts, as directly related?

KENNAN: Yes, I do. Of course, some of this took off from the shameful and still unexplained phenomenon of McCarthyism in those immediate postwar years. They were built up again much to a sensational and exaggerated picture of the danger and the hostility presented by the Soviet government. People forgot that these were people who had gone through incredible sufferings and exertions to win World War II, and the last thing that anybody was thinking of was trying to go launch another military invasion. There was a limited degree of penetration of the American government and of American organizations by people in the Communist Party, but this was vastly overrated and misstated by the McCarthyites to the point of complete absurdity. When you had General Marshall being accused of being a traitor by Senator McCarthy, you get an idea of how extreme this was. This led right on to the overstatements and the overreactions that constituted the cold war. It wasn't that there was no reason for any of these things. It was that they were all expanded out of all relationship to reality.

HANSEN: In April of 1951 you wrote an article in *Foreign Affairs* about America and the Russian future. Given where we are today, I would like to pose a question to you that you actually posed in that article. What kind of Russia may we reasonably and justly look forward to?

KENNAN: I tried to answer that question in the article. I think I pointed out that it was not a country which would be run in the way that we run ours. There would not be a Russian democracy absolutely conforming with our own here. It would take time to rearrange the country. After all, there was a very slight democratic or parliamentary tradition even before the revolution so that the people were unaccustomed to anything of that sort. Of course, it's coming now, but it's not exactly what we expected. The whole breakdown of Communist authority came more suddenly than we thought it was going to come. I say "we," meaning those of us who were serving in Moscow during the wartime period. We knew it would have to come someday, but it all broke down much too suddenly. It is causing great strains on everyone today in Russia. On the other hand, I am not as pessimistic as some of the others are who are writing about the Russian question. I think they have greater reserves of resilience, of imagination, of energy, and really, with many of the youth, of a certain idealism, than we have given them credit for.

HANSEN: If not a democratic society as a mirror image of our own, what is it that you think will now emerge?

KENNAN: That is very difficult to say because the country is also partly in a process of geographic disintegration. There is a great difference between the mentality of common people, particularly in the countryside and among the lowest elements of the industrial proletariat, on the one hand, and the intellectuals in the main cities on the other. It's very hard to see how or where the balance is going to come here. I think they will need a certain amount of what I might call "benevolent authoritarianism" in this early period. I don't see how they can get along without it, but I would hope that it would be a humane authoritarianism without the tinges of totalitarianism, which we have known in the party before that, without the terror, without the horror, and without the exaggerated police persecutions of people. I see some reason to hope, because if we look at what happened after the putsch a year and a half ago in Moscow, where you had tens of thousands of young Russians out in the streets trying to prevent this. It was explosive in the highest degree, and yet these young people did not beat up a single person. They didn't lynch anybody. There was no violence. They did it their own way. They climbed up on the tanks and argued with the tank commanders. The whole thing was surprisingly nonviolent. There was no precedent for that in earlier Russian history. So I think we have reason to see some hope.

HANSEN: You said the United States had to think about what we wanted, and one of the things you wanted from Russia was a more open society, one in which there is no subterfuge, there's no lying, and there is no concealment. That, indeed, has happened too.

KENNAN: That has completely happened, and the Russian press, over these last two or three years, has been marvelous. It's quite exciting to realize they have a very good press. The Russians are a literary people. They write well. They have a good sense of humor. They have a certain tough sense of humor now, and it makes very good reading. It's, as you say, completely open. There seem to be no limits on criticism.

HANSEN: And this is healthy?

KENNAN: It's enormously healthy. It's so healthy that I don't think there is any going back. I don't think you could put this genie back in the bottle again.

HANSEN: Are there lessons that the United States should have learned from history about our relationship now with Russia and the other republics?

KENNAN: I don't know of a more difficult question than that. I think there is a lesson that we should learn and that is that our own political system is intimately connected with and derived from our own national experiences. I say experiences because there are lots of different people in this country today. We must not expect people who have had different historical experiences to see problems of political organization and political structure exactly the way that we do.

HANSEN: Do we actually do damage, then, to paraphrase your 1951 article, applying a daily litmus test?

KENNAN: I think we are much too much inclined to do this, and this explains something that's going to be very controversial in the book, that is, the doubts I have had about some of our policies with regard to human rights, because I think they imply a certain talking down to other people on our part, saying you are wrong because you're not like us.

HANSEN: You have said that the United States, indeed, our society, does on the one hand serve as an example for the rest of the world, but this is not a messianic concept?

KENNAN: There is a difference between an example and a precept, trying to preach to other people. It's one thing when we show other people what can be done in a democracy. Nothing is more useful than that. It's another thing when we go and talk to them in a manner which brings the inference that we consider ourselves superior and they ought to learn to be like us.

HANSEN: Do you think we still act like the stern schoolmasters?

KENNAN: I think we often do. Not just the government, but the press and even public communication. There are limits to what we can do. We cannot run the whole world. Other modern powers have to pick up a much greater share of the burden and carry it, and that applies particularly, in my mind, to the major Western European countries. In the first instance, there are the people who should be trying to do what can be done about this situation in the Balkans. I would be glad to see us help if they took the leadership in doing it, but I don't think we should pick up the entire burden. We just can't do it, we're not that great, and we have our problems here in this country. It's going to take a long time to put things into proper shape here, and that is what we should be thinking of. I think we have to recognize the limits on our own capabilities. That's the part of a decent modesty on the part of any people. But I do think this situation in the Balkans is the most terrible and the most baffling situation I can recall ever seeing in foreign affairs in this century. I can't say that there would be clean and good and promising solutions to it even if the Europeans wanted to do all that they could. But I do say that this is their responsibility in the first order.

HANSEN: You say we have problems in our own country. One of the problems you bring up is our own approach to foreign policy. You say there are two voices in foreign policy; one, the interest of the entire country as the regime perceives them and to the extent it chooses to defer to them, and the second one is the voice of the single, political faction, deeply concerned to serve its own fortunes in the face of whatever domestic, political competition that confronts and threatens it. You say in your book that we tend to hear more of the second voice than the first voice now in foreign policy. Do you think it's a matter of achieving a balance between the two voices or does a third voice need to be created?

KENNAN: Of course it is a matter of achieving the balance. There is the internal political competition in this country. It's bound to intrude on foreign policy. But I think the greatest of the weaknesses that we have shown in the conduct of foreign policy, not just in the recent years but in recent decades and way back perhaps to the beginning of the Republic, is that we have permitted domestic political considerations to run away with the formulation of foreign policy. We all know that there are highly organized and powerful minority interests. Many of them of a commercial nature, but not all. Some are of ideological persuasion in this country. The nature of our political system is such that they are capable of bringing tremendously intensive pressure on the people in Washington, and they would argue that the things that they want are in the interest of the country as a whole, but I think that is obviously specious. They are in the interest of the people who are bringing these pressures to bear, but that's not identical with the country. I have seen many mistakes made in American foreign policy simply owing to the undue power of special interests on our government, and I think that it is up to the executive power to show greater resistance to that, and to say to these people, "Look here. You feel this way, but we have a duty to the country as a whole, and not just to the present of this country but to the future of it, and that is a duty to all the American people. You must excuse us, but we are not going to yield to your pressures when we think those are contrary to the real national interests." That's been my life for twenty-six years in the foreign service. We were supposed to be acting in the national interests and to inform our government as to where the national interest was with relation to given countries, and for that reason it's been very hard for many of us who were in the service to forgive our government for its flaccidity and its weakness in the face of special political interests.

HANSEN: You suggested the president actually have a deputy, someone who would function almost like a prime minister without any political or partisan affiliation?

KENNAN: For foreign affairs. And I think that should be the secretary of state.

HANSEN: You think that the secretary of state, that position, has not been used to its greatest advantage?

KENNAN: It couldn't be today, because foreign policy is farmed out all over the Washington pasture to a number of other departments of the government. Each one has its finger in the pie, and the secretary of state simply does not have the authority to pull things together. First of all, there is the military voice, and that has now been institutionalized through the president's security adviser. That's an institution that didn't exist before World War II, and I am a little afraid of this. Not that I think that the military are bad people, and I think they try to have the national interests in mind much more than do other influential elements. But there are dangers in that because the president, as commander in chief, can give orders in the military field, as we all see and know, whereas in the domestic, political field, he has to accommodate a thousand other interests. I don't think that our political system was meant to work that way and to give to the president the power that he has just exhibited, for example, in sending American armed forces to Somalia for tasks which may involve the use of armed force, and doing this, as far as I could see, without any prior formal consultation with the Congress or with the people. I think these are innovations in the way our government works, which I find somewhat troublesome and not to be reconciled with the original concepts that underlay our government.

HANSEN: How do you think we should redesign our military posture?

KENNAN: The world has so many problems today, such dangerous problems — economic problems, problems of overpopulation, problems of environmental deterioration. Those are the problems that ought to preoccupy us more than the political ones. One can say, "Well, they can't be solved unless you get the political background." True, but we can't do all that solving ourselves, as I said before, and, for the moment, I think we should concentrate on our own country and put that in order. Then, when we have got that straightened out, when we're not living on borrowed money, when we have a strong economic and political system here, then we can see where we can contribute.

HANSEN: One of your proposals for doing just that, for basically cleaning our own house, is that of a council of state. Tell us how that would work and what its primary purpose would be.

KENNAN: We are the country that makes the worst use of its experience in government. We let people serve in government and then go on and we never consult them again. My feeling is that we could perfectly well mobilize in an institutional way a body of people here who could speak only in an advisory capacity. They could not replace anybody in their constitutional powers. They could only say what ought to be done in the long-term interests of the country. If you want an example of that, you can take it in the fact that we have never had any real energy policy in this country. We ought to have one. An advisory group could tell you what that policy might look like. It would be up to the government either to adopt it or not to adopt it, but I do think that we ought to have near the government an authoritative voice, an independent and thoughtful voice capable of looking at the long-term problems of this country, which the elected political system doesn't do, and of telling us which way we ought to be heading. After all, the practical vision of the elected political establishment of the country is, at the most, limited to about six months into the future and that's probably an exaggeration. There are problems which are going to take years to correct. It has taken years to produce them, and these are the problems which an advisory body of this sort, which could be heard in the country above all the cacophony of our press and opinion, which would be a very useful thing to have.

HANSEN: Are you optimistic about the future of our country?

KENNAN: I am old, and like many older people, I am skeptical. I live here in the East and read what goes on in Washington and New York, and what is decided in these places, I am not very optimistic. When I go to my native Midwest, I find a much more cheerful atmosphere, and I have more confidence in the country. If they are able to make their energies, their honesty, their courage, felt in the government, then I am not pessimistic. But I do think there is a great deal of very troublesome cynicism and corruption both of government and of understanding and deterioration of strong moral habits throughout this country which has to be corrected. I can't get used to what seem to me to be these sick manifestations of pornography, of petty suspicion, all sorts of things that we see around us, and of cynicism on the part of the youth, bewilderment.

HANSEN: Looking back at your decades as both a political insider and outsider and as a critic of the government, what do you think you have contributed?

KENNAN: I have only been a sort of pestiferous insect on the hide of the Washington political establishment, and occasionally I would bite them. They would have to scratch. That's about all I have been able to do. I think I am moved by the following I have had among a great many people in the country, but not in the seats of power. I can't tell you how many wonderful letters I have had from quiet people around the country and people who don't expect to exercise any power, but I am also very much moved that I seem to have much more support among this youth than I ever expected to have. The youth understand much of what I am writing much better than do their fathers and mothers.

The former National Security Agency Director General WILLIAM ODOM talks with Robert Siegel about the danger of a possible rise in Russian imperialism. He discusses the interventionist behavior of the Russian military in former member republics of the Soviet Union and the popularity of such behavior among Russians of many political stripes. December 7, 1993

ODOM: Russians across the board, liberal and radical reactionaries, are undergoing a psychological shock at losing the empire, and that is not an easy thing for a political elite to experience. Look at the French, look at the British. Other empires behave the same way. Even though, quite remarkably and very positively, some of the liberals around Yeltsin favored the breakup of the Soviet Union because they saw the empire was impeding serious progress toward democracy and marketization. But within six months after that, most of them had begun to shift back to this pro-imperial view. There are two other factors. You have a huge Russian military establishment whose mission was taken away from it through the revision of the ideology. What is the purpose of a military big enough to take the whole capitalist world? There is no justification for it. Given the size of the threats they face today, there is no justification for more than a very small military. Therefore, the military elites are madly looking for a job. A third factor are the old Communist elite in the other CIS [Commonwealth of Independent States] states who make alliances through bilateral treaties, through informal arrangements with their reactionary counterparts in the Ministry of Security, the Ministry of Internal Affairs, and the military within Moscow.

SIEGEL: Some examples would be in Azerbaijan, where a

pro-Turkish government went out and in came an old Abkhazian Communist who had formerly been on the Politburo.

ODOM: Exactly. It's probably the case that this Major Guseinov, whose military unit actually defected from the forces and then went over and created sort of a military coup, took power in Baku. He then allowed Geidar Aliev to install himself. That was probably arranged and managed with Russian agent support. It was an effort to kind of teach the Turks a lesson.

SIEGEL: These republics may be nominally independent and formerly part of a Soviet Union, but that doesn't mean that they're there for other countries to come in and wield that influence.

ODOM: A next-door example, of course, has been Eduard Shevardnadze, a man who fought to keep Georgia independent and found the Russian military collaborating with Abkhazian separatists. They essentially together lopped off that piece of Georgia, and then poor Shevardnadze was sort of at their mercy. To get them to get off his back, he agreed to join the CIS. He also signed a treaty allowing a more or less indefinite stationing of Russian forces in Georgia on the Turkish border.

SIEGEL: What is the doctrinal explanation of Russian military presence, say in that case, the Trans-Caucasus, that is the three republics south of the Caucasus Mountains, or in other former Soviet republics?

ODOM: Recently, I think on November 2, the Russian Security Council approved, with Yeltsin present, the so-called New Russian Military Doctrine. While it talked about the remote possibility of a global war, it talked about an even greater possibility of local wars and internal violence, particularly within the old CIS states. It said that Russia has a very strong interest in stopping those wars and having peace in that area. It also set, as a threat to Russian interests, any violation of Russian rights in the former Soviet republics that are now non-Russian republics.

SIEGEL: You mean the rights of Russian individuals or the rights of Russia as a country?

ODOM: The rights of Russian individuals, but then this is interpreted as a legitimacy for using Russian military capabilities to ensure those things. It furthermore talked about the potential danger of military alliances and arrangements by these other sovereign countries outside of the CIS, and those are not to be allowed.

SIEGEL: Were the neo-imperialists in Moscow in the military greatly strengthened by the reliance of President Yeltsin on the Russian military to get him through the coup this past summer?

ODOM: I began to notice a shift in Yeltsin's own actions on this policy line in the spring after his failure to bring the parliament to heel in April.

SIEGEL: But some say he didn't have sufficient military support behind him.

ODOM: I think that is probably the case that he didn't. At that time he began to raise military pay, more than he had previously. He began to visit military units. In July he let Pavel Grachev and the military more or less have their way in Abkhazia.

SIEGEL: Grachev, we should say, is?

ODOM: He is the Russian minister of defense. Yeltsin sort of stood aside for that. He could have stopped that, but he didn't. Then we see in the course of the summer and fall Yeltsin becoming the aggressive leader in Russian involvement in Tajikistan, even being chided by members of the parliament, who said, "This could be another Afghanistan. We do not need to be bogged down in Tajikistan." Yeltsin essentially said that Tajikistan's borders are Russia's borders. Now that was a rather major reversal for Yeltsin, who had been ambiguous at best on this policy and probably had tilted rather strongly to the kind of liberal view that I just described earlier. We saw that manifestly when he want to Prague and

Warsaw and actually told those leaders that if they wanted to join NATO it was their sovereign choice. Then only to return to Moscow and reverse that position, probably under the pressure of the kinds of people I have just been mentioning, who are interested in Tajikistan.

The Israeli novelist AMOS OZ talks with Robert Siegel about reactions to the Israeli-PLO accord among Israelis and Palestinians. In late September, Oz and the Palestinian-American historian Hisham Sharabi traveled around Israel and the occupied territories, working on a BBC documentary about those reactions. He also talks about his book *Fima*, which touches on the stereotypes of both Palestinians and Israelis. November 12, 1993

OZ: My impressions from traveling around the country on the whole are positive. Namely, deep down below everybody knows that this is leading to a two-state solution. But no one knows exactly how this is going to materialize.

SIEGEL: Professor Sharabi returned and wrote an article for the *Washington Post* in which he declared himself less hopeful than he had been before, in part because of Israeli negotiating positions that he mentioned. But more so, what he wrote about was his fear of the administrative, managerial incompetence and the deep corruption of the PLO.

OZ: I find this very remarkable. I haven't read the column, but every criticism of the PLO from within the Palestinian intelligentsia and by a Palestinian is a symptom of a good change. For too many years, peace-oriented Israeli intellectuals and Palestinian intellectuals were unified by criticizing together the Israeli government. There was a taboo on criticizing the PLO. The PLO was regarded as being either above or below criticism.

SIEGEL: You have run often into the suggestion that if only Israelis and Palestinians could get to know one another better that might improve chances for peace, and you have offered a very interesting rebuttal to that proposition.

OZ: I find this a little sentimental. There are many peace-oriented people in the West who tend to think that essentially all conflicts are really misunderstandings. The Israeli-Palestinian conflict is a very real one. They love the land because they regard it as their own, and we feel exactly the same way. There is no misunderstanding. There is a real conflict, which can be resolved through a compromise, not through having coffee together. That is not enough.

SIEGEL: The opposite of making war is not making love, you say, it's making peace.

OZ: I get sick and tired with certain Western well-meaning sentimentality about peace and love and brotherhood and compassion and sacrifice being synonymous. Actually, they are not. The opposite of war is not love. The opposite of war is peace. Hence my attitude toward the Palestinian nation and movement: make peace, not love.

SIEGEL: What about the Israeli outlook? What have these past couple of months been like? And are Israelis ready for what many people see as the inevitable result of all this, namely a Palestinian state, sandwiched in or making a sandwich of, perhaps, Israel?

OZ: I would prefer the metaphor of a semidetached house. We cannot live together happily under the same roof, we will have to build a partition inside this beloved homeland. I think in their heart of hearts most Israelis realize that this is going to happen. They are not happy about it. Even the peace-oriented Israelis are nervous about the provisions. Are we really going to get security in the bargain? Can the Palestinians and the other Arab nations deliver peace?

SIEGEL: There is a passage in your new novel, or new in English at least, called *Fima,* that I wanted you to read, but I only have it in English.

OZ: I would rather you read it. Your English seems to be better than mine.

SIEGEL: This is a conversation between Fima, the main character of the novel, and his father, Baruch, who is a very European gentleman.

oz: And a flamboyant right-winger to boot.

siegel: Fima, who is an adult, reproaches him:

"Baruch, you are blind and deaf. We're the Cossacks now, and the Arabs are victims of the pogroms, yes, every day, every hour."

"The Cossacks," his father remarked with amused indifference. "Nu? What of it? So what's wrong with us being the Cossacks for a change? Where does it say in Holy Scripture that Jew and gentile are forbidden to swap jobs for a little while? Just once in a millennium or so? If only you yourself, my dear, were more of a Cossack and less of a shlemazel. Your child takes after you: a sheep in sheep's clothing."

Having forgotten the beginning of their conversation, he explained all over again, while Fima furiously crushed matchsticks one after another, the difference between shlemiel and shlemazel and how they constituted an immortal pair, wandering hand in hand through the world. Then he reminded Fima that the Arabs have forty huge countries, from India to Abyssinia, whereas we have only one tiny country no bigger than a man's hand. He began telling off the names of the Arab states on his bony fingers. When he enumerated Iran and India among them, Fima could no longer endure in silence. He interrupted his father with a plaintive, self-righteous howl, stamped his foot, and exclaimed petulantly that Iran and India are not Arab states.

"Nu, so what? What difference does it make to you?" the old man intoned in a ritualistic singsong, with a sly, good-natured chortle. "Have we managed at last to find a satisfactory solution to the tragic question of who is a Jew, that we need to start breaking our heads over the question of who is an Arab?"

An argument that Israelis have had? A dialogue between different types of citizens of your country?

oz: And how! Israel is a very argumentative country. Everybody argues with everyone. But *Fima* is meant as a comedy. Although I have very strong and clear positions on Israeli politics, when I write a novel, I am on everybody's side, and this particular bit that you have just read had been written with more or less an equal degree of sympathy, with both conflicting points of view, the father's and the son's.

SIEGEL: When you say Israel is a very argumentative society, you remind me of something. A Palestinian journalist in Gaza remarked to me two months ago, in a sentiment not unknown to people who sympathize with Hamas or the more militant groups, that, "You know, once there is peace, Israel is going to fall apart. There will be nothing left for them to unite about once the Palestinians are no longer at war with them." I wondered whether that perception of Israel, which strikes me as quite inaccurate, is fueled by the disputatiousness of Israeli society and the public arguments.

OZ: Poor Palestinians. If this is what they are hoping for, they'll have to wait for ten thousand years. We Israelis are in the civilized habit of conducting our internal civil wars by inflicting ulcers and heart attacks on each other, calling each other terrible names. We don't normally shoot at each other. It's an extremely verbal society. It's very pluralistic. Every line by a bus stop is likely to catch a spark and turn into a fiery street seminar on God, on politics, on Jewish history, on who is a Jew and what is an Arab and where is India. But this doesn't mean that Israel will disintegrate once we have peace with the Arabs. It will become one of the most magnificent, pluralistic, culturally rich societies, with nobody agreeing with anyone on anything.

....

Ambassador EDWARD ROWNEY has gone to the table
as a senior negotiator and special adviser for five
presidents. He talks with Liane Hansen about his
book *It Takes One to Tango,* in which he describes
the fancy footwork of arms control. January 3, 1993

ROWNEY: The title *It Takes One to Tango* is designed to
point out that people think differently than we do. When I
talked to my Russian counterpart and complained that he was
not talking back to me, that I was doing the talking and doing
the compromising, I said, "Come on, you know it takes two to
tango." He said, "No, no, you're thinking like an American."
He said, "It only takes one to tango." Then he told me that
when he was a young officer in Ukraine, he went to a Sunday-
night dance and all the women were on one side of the hall and
he just picked up a chair and danced with it. When one of the
women smiled and nodded approvingly, he said, "I knew I had
her on the hook." He said, "We do the same thing with you.
When we see that you nod approvingly, we know we have you
on the hook. It only takes one to tango."

HANSEN: In the heat of negotiations, you have had to tango
not only with a full range of hardened cold war Soviets, but also
had to deal with the personalities of your own bosses.

ROWNEY: Personalities do make a difference. I will give you
two extremes. President Carter, a well-meaning man, a nice
Christian gentleman, telegraphed the fact that he was willing to
compromise. As a matter of fact, he instructed Cyrus Vance, his
first negotiator, the secretary of state, to not only put down our
position, but before Andrei Gromyko could answer, to put down
our fallback position. That was one type of personality. The
other type of personality, of course, was President Reagan, who
knew how to keep secrets. He knew his other person's mental-

ity, and he also knew how to break the tension at a critical point
with some story and turn off even a man like Mikhail Gorbachev, who came in originally described as a man that had a
nice smile, but teeth of iron. He did. This man was a very easy-
going type of person in a large group, but across a negotiating table was just tough as nails. Reagan knew how to handle
that. And when things came to an impasse, Reagan could tell a
story and then it made even Gorbachev laugh. It even got to a
point where Gorbachev tried to imitate him by telling stories of
his own. Two different styles.

HANSEN: How much a part did alcohol play in all of this?

ROWNEY: Alcohol played a very strong role off the scenes in
our negotiation. Before my time, they had bottles of whiskey on
the negotiating table. The theory was that it would loosen up
tongues and everybody would be a little easier to deal with. It
would break the tension. The Soviets, of course, liked Jack
Daniel's only and disdained their own vodka. We took the
vodka. They could handle their liquor, and we couldn't handle
our liquor, so we tended to talk too much. So when I came to the
negotiating table and took over, I talked to some people, and
they said, "Look, let's keep up that same thing so that we have
this informal atmosphere." I said, "Look at the record. It was the
Americans whose tongues got twisted and who gave so many
secrets away." The Soviets can handle their liquor, and we can't.
I said, "I have to handle myself and limit myself to two drinks."
Whereas Anatoly Karpov could have five or six and then I'd just
get one. So we cut it out except at social engagements.

HANSEN: It's interesting to think that what you were doing
was negotiating these weapons of mass destruction at the same
time. It's such a delicate balance between dealing with little
idiosyncrasies, as well as trying to keep the big picture in focus.

ROWNEY: That's right, and we didn't have to remind ourselves. We knew that we were dealing with very serious matters
and that deterrence was all-important. The Soviets had to realize that we would take care of our own strength and would
retaliate if struck, and that was the impression we had to leave

with them. But it was more than impression. We had to have the wherewithal. That's why Reagan was so good, and when he came into office, at a difficult time, we had double-digit inflation, double-digit unemployment. The cabinet members were saying, "Mr. President, you just can't spend money for defensive purposes when we have all these social programs." He said, "Look, I am the commander in chief of our armed forces and these social programs are important; but the most important social program is our security. If we lose that, we have lost everything."

HANSEN: We have made a lot of progress over the years on arms negotiation. Some would venture to say the world is much safer now than it was before. But you write that we are entering a new phase and we need to avoid the mistakes of the past.

ROWNEY: I think that's a point we have to recognize, particularly today, when President-elect Clinton has concentrated on the economy almost to the exclusion of foreign policy. I was in Europe two weeks ago, and people were asking me, "Does he know that we exist? Does he know about the rest of the world?" The fact that the world is safer because the lid is off from the superpower relationship has just opened up the lid to all this boiling caldron of ethnic and nationalist problems. We have Bosnia-Hercegovina today. We are going to have Macedonia tomorrow. We are going to have Kosovo the day after that. We have religious groups coming to the fore again with the Hindus and Muslims in Pakistan and India. It's very scary. So we have to learn to negotiate with a larger number of countries on a larger number of problems because there are some real problems out there.

HANAN ASHRAWI talks with Liane Hansen about her decision to resign as the Palestinian peace delegation's spokesperson to set up a watchdog commission to help guide the new Palestinian government. She says her decision was not meant as a protest against Yasir Arafat and the current Palestinian leadership, but instead it was a response to the needs and concerns of Palestinian society. December 12, 1993

ASHRAWI: The commission that I am working on setting up is an independent commission that is legally constituted and therefore has legal status and has the mandate to review the legislation and to monitor the activities of the new government or the Palestinian national authority. This I have done because I felt that there are concerns, there are doubts, and people are expressing a need. I felt that it would be much better to move into civil society and to respond to this need and to these concerns. In order to do that, one has to do it completely and specifically, not by being part of an authority but by providing a watchdog, so to speak, a system of accountability.

HANSEN: Do you think the Palestinian authority, particularly under the leadership of Chairman Yasir Arafat, needs to be watched?

ASHRAWI: I think any authority needs accountability and needs to be watched, frankly speaking. It can be done through public opinion, it can be done through the force of moral pressures, through the force of civil society and generating a discourse on awareness of democracy, and also through institutions that can hold this authority accountable.

HANSEN: What problems do you think the integration of the people who have lived under the occupation over the past four decades and the people who have lived in exile during that time is going to create?

ASHRAWI: There is a complexity, a variety of problems, that one can anticipate. All along a leadership in exile was living outside its territory and therefore has not been used to direct accountability and has not been used to running specific institutions of the state or institutions of civil society. Therefore, at the legal level, at the legislative level, as well as at the executive level, these institutions have to be set up and protected. Number two, I think the Palestinian people under occupation themselves have to have a whole change of attitude and mindset to think of the authority as representative of the people and their interests, i.e., authority in the service of the people rather than to oppress the people.

HANSEN: What about in the short term, though? Violence has been a problem certainly over the past few months and because of that the deadline Monday might be pushed back. What do you think can be done in the short term to perhaps stem the violence?

ASHRAWI: Actually it's very hard to stem the violence, frankly. That does not come by edict or decree because violence is generated by situations. First of all, you have a situation of settler violence, and the settlers consider themselves above the law and they are trying to undermine the agreement and they are trying to impose their own will. On the other hand, we also have an opposition that is resorting to acts of violence in order to show that a negotiated settlement is not going to work and that the only way is the military solution. We feel that both these have to be faced, not by escalating military presence, but by showing that peace can work and by showing that peace can pay dividends, and by transforming realities of people even in the short term.

HANSEN: When did you realize that your own role as a Palestinian peace negotiator was over?

ASHRAWI: This wasn't an epiphany or a sudden decision or

an overnight decision. I have been thinking about this for a long time. Basically, I entered the public political arena several years back in order to accomplish something concrete for the Palestinian people, but to present the Palestinian narrative honestly and directly and the reality of the Palestinian human substance and dimension. Now I feel that my work has to be diverted towards more internal issues that deal with the quality of the Palestinian society and Palestinian institutions and Palestinian system of government. That should be the prime responsibility of Palestinian people as a whole. I took that decision gradually. Since the signing of the Declaration of Principles, I have been thinking about it and I felt a moral conscience, and as something that would be more amenable to my nature and my preference, as well as for the collective good. This is something perhaps that I can do that maybe few others can do but not many.

HANSEN: So you don't feel that you were undercut by the fact that a lot of the agreements were made in back channels?

ASHRAWI: Not at all. Actually, the back channels are channels that I personally have worked to set up, including the channel that worked out in Oslo. And I don't have any ego problems attaining that at all.

HANSEN: You have said that there is no shortage of people who would like power. Are you concerned at all that perhaps the more radical elements in Palestinian society could become powerful? Are you concerned that there are indeed many power struggles going on within the Palestinian leadership now?

ASHRAWI: There is an active and intense dialogue and internal debate on this within the PLO and outside the PLO. The radicals gain strength only in converse proportion to our achievements. If through democratic means, they are able to persuade our public opinion or to gain a constituency, then certainly it's legitimate. But I certainly don't want to see resorting, see them or anybody resorting to violence to impose opinions.

HANSEN: Has it been difficult for you as a woman, and perhaps as a Christian, to be a Palestinian leader?

ASHRAWI: It hasn't been easy. To be a Palestinian is always a difficult task. As they say, if you're born a Palestinian, you're born with a risk and a responsibility. But add to that the additional descriptions of being a woman and a Christian, which perhaps may make life more difficult, primarily as a woman, because our society, on the whole, is more traditional. Women's issues and the role of women are crucial to my perspective and I do not think that women are going to come into their own just by sitting back and waiting or demanding, but by creating facts, by being part of this process of transformation and building, by challenging the given and the traditional male-dominated attitudes and factions and institutions, particularly in politics, where women have always been, on the whole, excluded.

HANSEN: I don't suppose you're going to consider running for office in the elections next year?

ASHRAWI: Although I am a strong supporter and an advocate of women running for election, as things stand now, I would much rather work with establishing this independent commission. But should I feel that there is a need, I certainly will reconsider.

HANSEN: You come from a political family. Your father was a founder of the PLO. You have been the official representative of the Palestinian people. What are your hopes for your daughters' future?

ASHRAWI: My hopes for my daughters are that they will, first of all, live in freedom with the dignity that they deserve and with the security and safety that they deserve. Part of my main motivation to work is the fact that I just could see our children's childhood being destroyed. There are children robbed of their childhood and the right to live as other children. I felt that what we could do is promise them a better future than what we have inherited, that the legacy of the past and the pain of the past be replaced by hope for the future.

JANE KRAMER talks with Alex Chadwick about the
rise of violent racism and neo-Nazism in Germany and
various theories propounded to explain it. Kramer
wrote "Neo-Nazis: A Chaos in the Head" for
The New Yorker. June 12, 1993

CHADWICK: You begin your article in the city of Ludwigs-
hafen in western Germany, with an attack on a young Turkish
man by some of these young skinheads. Tell us about the
"skins," as you call them. Who are they and how many of them
are there?

KRAMER: There are about sixty-five hundred skins in Germany, East and West. Proportionately, the majority are in East
Germany, but lately, the most violent crimes have been in West
Germany, something that has terrified everyone. People could
plot the trouble coming in East Germany because of unemployment because of the traumas of unification. All of these anal-
yses seem to fall apart when you look at the rise in skinhead
violence in West Germany.

CHADWICK: What is it, do you think, that motivates them?
You report a kind of frightening sense of nihilism about them,
and an inability to explain why these attacks are going on.

KRAMER: One of the problems facing people in Germany,
now especially with world consciousness of German history
being replayed in the West, is, are they really a kind of sociopath
you would find in any country on the fringes, or is there something specifically German about their violence? Is there something specifically ideological about their violence? There is a lot
of argument about this. It has been very hard for me to figure
it out. Though you can say that these are basically working-
class kids in the West, you do not find many skinheads out
of a bourgeois environment. You find them often out of back-

grounds that the Germans call *"Schlüsselkinder,"* latchkey children, kids who have grown up to parents who they never see, parents who work in factories all day. The important thing to think about is what is the connection between these kids and the people trying to recruit them, the clandestine parties of the far right, like the neo-Nazi parties that get raided and banned all the time, or the so-called legitimate parties of the new right.

CHADWICK: Because of the asylum laws in Germany, there are an extraordinary number of foreigners. You said 450,000 people just in the last year coming in, looking for work, and really putting stresses on the society.

KRAMER: That is true. What is not reported much is that half of those people have already left and only four percent of them actually have qualified for asylum.

CHADWICK: These people really cannot become citizens, can they? You write about the concept of blood citizenship.

KRAMER: Germany is one of the only countries on earth that practices what is called *"jus sanguinis,"* law of blood. A Turkish child born in Germany, third generation in Germany, has basically no rights to German citizenship, whereas a German child born in Russia or in South America or anywhere, whose family left Germany two hundred years ago, is considered by birth German.

CHADWICK: Is it German blood that these young skinheads are feeling and celebrating in some way?

KRAMER: They are definitely celebrating German blood, and one of the ironies of their violence is that many of their attacks are against people called *"Ansiedler,"* meaning Germans who are coming from abroad. The term comes from *settler*, so German-by-blood people from other countries coming back are often perceived of as foreigners by the skinheads and are themselves attacked.

CHADWICK: One of the conclusions of your article is that the middle class doesn't understand these kids at all. The police don't understand them. You report a sort of bafflement about what to do, and I wonder, as you left Germany this last time, what did you think the prospects were?

KRAMER: I thought the prospects were very dim because as crazy or as pathological or whatever you would like to call them, they're still choosing targets that reflect the mood around them. The skins attacked two weeks ago in Solingen. Two or three days after, German politicians, people who considered themselves liberal Germans, dismantled what had been the most liberal asylum laws in Europe, if not the world. These laws were dismantled by the respectable German population under a lot of pressure from the right.

CHADWICK: Ms. Kramer, may I ask, are you personally frightened to be in Germany?

KRAMER: Not really. I have spent a lot of time in Germany in the past three or four years. This is the first time I have sensed fear around me. But was I glad to leave? Yes, I was very glad to leave. This is the first time I have been glad to leave Germany. In my last several visits and projects, I have always wanted to stay a little longer and do more work. This is the first time I thought, Phew! Get me home!

HELEN SUZMAN was a member of the South African Parliament from 1953 to 1989 and is a long-time opponent of apartheid. She talks with Liane Hansen about her autobiography *In No Uncertain Terms: A South African Memoir,* in which she recounts her experiences in the fight against apartheid.
November 14, 1993

HANSEN: Describe your district of Houghton. It sometimes has been referred to as the Silk Stocking District?

SUZMAN: It was a constituency which consisted mainly of sort of middle-class and upper-middle-class people, professional people, enlightened, and well-educated people, who were not in competition with black people for jobs. That was very important. We never had a hope of winning a seat in the blue-collar area or in one of the rural seats, which are always very reactionary. There was also quite a large number of Jewish constituents, and I think that helped me.

HANSEN: You are Jewish.

SUZMAN: Yes, I am.

HANSEN: Because the race classification act had gone into effect in 1950 and you ran in 1953, did you run on an anti-apartheid platform?

SUZMAN: I originally ran as a member of the United Party, which was General Jan Smuts's opposition party, and I was there for six years in that capacity. But in 1959, a number of us in the United Party decided that the party was not fighting apartheid unequivocally. We finally left and formed our own party, which we called the Progressive Party. In 1961, there was an unexpectedly early election called by Dr. Hendrik Verwoerd, then prime minister and, of course, the great architect of apartheid. Having taken South Africa out of the commonwealth and having made it an independent republic, he went to the country, and, alas, all my colleagues lost their seats, except myself.

HANSEN: You describe Hendrik Verwoerd as an evil genius, someone who scared you stiff.

SUZMAN: He was like that, I am afraid. It was because he really felt he had a divine mission, and you cannot argue with people like that.

HANSEN: What happened after he was assassinated? A story you tell in your book is that P. W. Botha, when Verwoerd was assassinated, basically turned to you, and said, "Now, we will get you."

SUZMAN: He did. He came out in a rage down the aisle of Parliament and stopped opposite my bench and waved his finger at me, and shouted at me in Afrikaans, "Yes, it's you liberals. You have done this. You incite people. Now we'll get all of you!" He blundered out of the house, and of course I was absolutely astonished. Though I have to admit that in the past years, as I watched Verwoerd introducing one appalling measure after the other in Parliament, the thought had crossed my mind. But, in fact, I didn't arrange the assassination, and I reported him to the speaker and he was made to apologize.

HANSEN: Have you spoken to P. W. Botha since?

SUZMAN: No. I only, of course, had to speak to him in Parliament when I was arguing debates and so on. But on a personal level, I never said good day to him, I never gave him a greeting. In fact, it was mutual. He didn't greet me either.

HANSEN: Your voice was sometimes like a clanging bell in Parliament all those years, making people sit up and pay attention to what you had to say about the policies of apartheid and your country. Very often the lone voice, you were attacked for being a woman. You were attacked for being Jewish. You were attacked for being loud. But the fact that you were re-elected, term after term, is that something that gave you the strength to continue to challenge what was then the majority view?

SUZMAN: I was re-elected over and over again because I was very lucky in having the absolutely enthusiastic support of the

English media in South Africa. They gave me marvelous coverage of all the speeches I made, and I think I was saying the things they wanted to hear said in Parliament and that nobody else was saying.

HANSEN: Your proposals at the time were considered unacceptable and would have been catastrophic at the time. Do you think they would have been really?

SUZMAN: Oh, no. I think that what's happening now should have happened thirty years ago. Trying to maintain segregation in an integrated economy was absolutely hopeless and it meant terrible disaster to the lives of millions of people. Naturally bitterness builds up over the years and black resistance escalated, and that is why the government over and over again had to introduce states of emergency and introduce measures which abrogated due process and the rule of law. In other words, people could be detained without trial. None of that would have happened had the government abandoned this hopeless policy and allowed development of people, training and skills for black people. The economy expanding all the time, we would not have had this terrible situation. They are late in their changes, but at least they've come.

HANSEN: Economics is what got you into politics in the first place. Do you think conditions have improved, for example, in the homelands since the time when you first visited them?

SUZMAN: Oh, no. They have deteriorated because the government's policy was to shove more and more people back into those rural homelands. They are poverty-stricken and they don't have adequate resources, loans from the land bank and so on. They deteriorated constantly. That is why so many people just drifted into the towns illegally because of the pass laws and what was known as "influx control," which tried to keep the women and families out of the urban areas while allowing men to come in on contract as migratory workers. The thing just got worse and worse because you had a population explosion. The men obviously took up with women in the urban areas, fathered children there, didn't have much responsibility towards them, and when they went back on holidays to the Baantenstans their wives became pregnant again. So that in itself has contributed to the problem.

HANSEN: You objected to the imposition of sanctions, which put you in bed with some mighty strange companions, not the least of which was Britain's prime minister, Margaret Thatcher. What were your objections to the imposition of sanctions?

SUZMAN: Because I felt the economic effects would be appalling. I knew that they would mean the loss of export markets. Our labor-intensive industries, such as mining and agriculture, lost their markets, sugar, fruit, wine, metals, except the ones America wanted. I noticed that in the antiapartheid act, America excluded the metals that she wanted badly. It wasn't only just moral outrage. There was also little expediency in this whole business. But I knew it would cause unemployment among masses and masses of black people, which is what happened. We don't have a proper welfare support system in South Africa. We have old-age pensions, disability pensions, but there is no dole and there are no food stamps. Unless you are in an occupation where you contributed to an unemployment fund, and that means really the skilled and semiskilled jobs, which were not largely the jobs that blacks had, then you were really in dire straits when you lost your job.

HANSEN: Sanctions have been lifted, but you don't agree that sanctions being lifted brought about the political change in South Africa.

SUZMAN: I am not denying that they certainly had an effect in expediting it, there's no question. I believe that apartheid would have gone anyway, and, in fact, a lot of the laws actually were repealed before sanctions were imposed. I talk about, for instance, the Job Reservation Law, which reserved all skilled jobs for whites. That went at the end of the 1970s. The legal recognition of black trade unions, which was very important for blacks. It gave them the weapon of the strike. I think empowerment of the black trade unions would have led to the breakdown of apartheid, albeit later perhaps than did the sanctions because economic empowerment almost invariably leads to political empowerment, and it would have not had that dire effect on the economy. But there were other things, of course, that led to the breakdown. There was the escalation of black resistance and the isolation. Sporting isolation was a terrible punitive action against South Africa. And of course, the whole feeling that South Africa had become a pariah nation all played its part.

HANSEN: Now that the sanctions have been lifted, now that the political process is under way, where do the seeds of economic recovery need to be sowed?

SUZMAN: What we need desperately is to kick-start our stalled economy with foreign investment, and inside South Africa investment from entrepreneurs there as well because everybody is sort of holding fire at the present time, but that is what we desperately need. The new government will have to be pretty resolute in putting down the violence in the townships and the criminal violence. When we have security forces that have some legitimacy, then I think they can act fairly firmly in that regard. Presently it is not happening.

HANSEN: There is so much good news and bad news in all of this. On the one hand, IBM is negotiating to go back into South Africa; but, on the other hand, you have the statistic that one out of every one hundred people who graduate from college is going to find a job in South Africa now.

SUZMAN: I don't know how many people who graduate are going to find jobs in America or Britain or Australia or Canada at this present time with this sort of worldwide recession. But if we have people coming in and investing in proper projects . . . I don't mean just putting up a building; that is a one-off thing, and it provides employment while the building is going up, but I want factories, I want exports. I want South Africa to become the workshop of the continent of Africa.

HANSEN: To try and deal with issues of self-determination, boundaries, citizenship, taxation, is there any democratic model being followed?

SUZMAN: No, you would be amazed at all the people who

come out for conferences weekend after weekend in South Africa, seeking to teach us the culture of democracy, which I must say we badly need since we have not had it. But some of them come from very strange countries that do not seem to have had much democracy themselves. We are all trying. They are trying to frame a bill of rights for South Africa which will entrench the basic human rights of freedom of speech, of association, of movement, et cetera. I think everybody will accept that. Of course, having accepted it does not mean necessarily that it's going to be implemented. The U.S.S.R. had a bill of rights in its constitution, and I do not think that helped you much when you were sitting in the Gulag. Equally, most of the African states have signed the People's Charter of Human Rights, and I do not think you will find much there in the way of human rights being implemented if you will rather go through some of the countries in Africa. I am hoping because we have at least got and have had an independent judiciary. We have experience of a parliamentary system that will be able to enforce a bill of rights. That is very important.

HANSEN: Elections are set for April 27, 1994. Are you involved in the campaign at all? I know you are not running, but are you involved?

SUZMAN: I am not running. I am not even standing. I am sort of peripheral. When I go back home, I may serve on one of the committees that have been set up to monitor the election and see that it will be declared free and fair. It is no good having an election, as they have had in Angola, if at the end it is declared not to be free and fair by the losing party and ends up in civil war. We do not want anything like that. So it is possible that I will be involved. I do not see how I can totally keep out of it. On the other hand, I rather look forward to sitting in the rocking chair in the sun.

HANSEN: Would you say that you are optimistic about the future of democracy in South Africa?

SUZMAN: It is going to be a long haul because people are inexperienced in democracy, particularly the new voting public. We are going to have twenty-two million people eligible to vote, it is estimated. Sixteen million of them are black, and they have no experience really of voting in a major election. They have voted in local government elections, but most of those they boycotted anyway. You have got to teach people the elements of democracy, such as hearing the other side, allowing political parties to campaign freely in the areas even if the majority of people there don't agree with them. We have got a long, hard haul ahead of us. I am not a starry-eyed optimist that this is going to be an easy task. But because of the plus factors, like the infrastructure, the material resources, the human resources in South Africa, I am hopeful that we are going to emerge, if not as a full-fledged nonracial democracy, at least on the way to becoming one.

HANSEN: One must try democracy to find out whether it actually works.

SUZMAN: That is right. We have tried apartheid, and we find it didn't work. Now we've got to try democracy to show that it will work.

WASHINGTON

....

At age eighty-five, HARRY BLACKMUN was in his last
term as justice of the United States Supreme Court when
he gave a joint interview to NPR and the ABC television
program *Nightline*. He was also both the oldest and
longest-sitting justice on the Court. Nina Totenberg
and Ted Koppel asked Justice Blackmun about his
experiences on the Court, his writing of the argument
in *Roe* v. *Wade*, and his view of capital punishment.
In early 1994, before announcing that he would retire,
Blackmun wrote that the death penalty cannot be fairly
administered and is, thus, unconstitutional, a position
that he signaled but was not yet prepared to state in
this extensive interview. December 27 and 28, 1993

BLACKMUN: I am personally opposed to the death penalty,
and were I a legislator in a state or in Congress or something, I
would not vote for the death penalty. In part that is because I am
convinced that there is no element of deterrence in the death
penalty. I come from a state that does not have it, that has not
had it for seventy years or so. And the crime statistics there are
no different from what they are in states that have a death
penalty. On the other hand, the public wants it, apparently,
because it exists in two-thirds of our states today, and there are
certain federal provisions for it. But I did not reach the point
that Justice Brennan and Justice Marshall reached, that the
death penalty is contrary to the Eighth Amendment's proscrip-
tion of cruel and unusual punishments. I have difficulty with
that notion because the Fifth Amendment, among other things,
speaks of a capital crime and it speaks of one being subjected to
a danger of loss of life or limb, so that it recognizes the death
penalty. But it always bothers me. These cases are wretched.

They hit us at the last minute usually. Executions are scheduled in most states in the wee hours of the morning, and the application for stays gets in here sometimes not too far in advance of the time set. And of course there is the problem also of the execution of a person who is possibly innocent, even though he has been convicted in a fair trial. There is a fairly responsible study recently made by people in the academic world to the effect that during the twentieth century, an alarming number of innocent people have been put to death. Of course, that depends on whether you believe the arguments that are advanced. But, as I say, the American people are in favor of it. Every time there is a striking, vicious killing of some kind, there is always the move for the death penalty. I can understand this, but I think we should accept it as pure, sheer retribution, and that there is no deterrent effect to it at all. If people want to be retributive in their approach, they have that privilege.

I'm not sure the death penalty as administered is fairly administered. I think it comes close to violating the equal protection clause of the Constitution. And I'm not certain at all that the death penalty can be constitutionally imposed. I haven't taken that position yet, but I am getting close to it.

TOTENBERG: You're getting to it? I remember when you were first on this Court, and the Court was struggling with the death penalty issue and, in fact, wavered very significantly, at one point virtually striking it down and then a few years later upholding it. And at that time, I think it's fair to say that you felt as long as the public wanted it and expressed that through legislation adopted by majority vote in state and federal legislatures, that should be abided by. I hear in your words that you are close to changing that view.

BLACKMUN: I have seen us struggle with these capital punishment cases through a series of decisions. And I think a question can be raised as to whether we have been consistent and as to whether it squares with other provisions of the Constitution of the United States and the Bill of Rights; namely, in particular, the equal protection clause. And of course cutting across all of it are the disturbing statistics that come in when one considers race.

TOTENBERG: Statistics that so many more, disproportionately, African Americans are executed?

BLACKMUN: Of course some people can rationalize that to their satisfaction. But there it stands, and I am bothered by it. I don't like death penalty cases. I cringe every time we get them, and in some states, particularly Texas, they are moving along so that in some weeks we have more than one.

TOTENBERG: Have you had times when you thought that possibly genuinely innocent people were executed? In the cases?

BLACKMUN: Yes.

TOTENBERG: Have you ever cried over them?

BLACKMUN: Figuratively, yes, but not actually.

TOTENBERG: Since you clearly care about them a great deal and have thought about them, and in some ways been haunted by them enough to be on the verge of changing your position to some extent, how do you keep going?

BLACKMUN: That is just part of the job, I suppose. I wonder myself at my age how I keep going and how long I should keep going. And you obviously are here because of my age and the fact I have just had a birthday. But I think if I'm kept busy, that keeps me going. If I weren't busy, I would probably fall apart.

TOTENBERG: Justice Blackmun, it is said that this is the only institution in government where the top dogs do their own work. What kind of hours do you keep? How many days a week do you work?

BLACKMUN: Some of us are dumber than others, and I think I put in hard work. For me, it's a seven-day-a-week job. Justice Douglas used to twit Chief Justice Burger by saying, "It's only a four-and-a-half-day-a-week job." But for me, there never is enough time. I get down here around seven-thirty A.M. and breakfast with my clerks every day, which for me is a distinct pleasure. It is the one time of the day that we can get together and discuss cases or yesterday's arguments, what they learned, and what they learned not to do. They keep me out of trouble and instruct me in many ways. And then we go through the day. I usually work until about ten-thirty P.M. or eleven P.M.

TOTENBERG: Do you work Saturdays?

BLACKMUN: Oh, always. And it's a rare Saturday I'm not down there. But that's a good time because the telephone doesn't ring very much. The secretaries don't bother me, and we can get some work done.

TOTENBERG: One of the seminal moments in making a decision in this place is the weekly conference that the justices have. Could you describe what happens in that conference? It used to be said in the Vinson Court era the fights were so loud that they could hear the justices screaming outside. The people outside the doors could hear them screaming some of the time. Does this ever happen?

BLACKMUN: It hasn't happened in my twenty-three years here. We haven't had anything like the alleged Black and Frankfurter controversy or as Justice McReynolds would not shake Justice Brandeis's hand, that sort of thing. We don't have that. Since I have been here, I think the court knows they have to get along together. We all come from different backgrounds, of course, but that is why there are nine. If we all thought alike, we might as well have the chief justice decide everything; the rest of us can go home and enjoy life. But at times opinions are expressed that are rather firm. There had been one or two occasions where we approached the flare point of discomfort, if I can call it that, but nothing like table pounding nor insulting remarks made to others. Once in a while, I think, in written opinions each of us has gone a little bit far, but they are ladies and gentlemen around the table. And most of the cases are close, of course, or they would not be here. Most of them perhaps have produced conflicts among the lower courts in the decision on the issue. But in this respect, it has been a happy occasion Friday after Friday. You asked how things go. We, of course, discuss the argued cases one by one, and each of us takes a temporary position. We are not bound by the position we take to affirm or to reverse or vacate or whatever it is in the first conference. One can change his mind right up to the last minute.

TOTENBERG: Justice Blackmun, what is it that you are doing during oral argument, that all of you are doing? Are you trying to get questions answered for yourself? Are you trying to get questions answered for your colleagues who you know are concerned about a particular subject and you want that justice's vote? What is it that's going on there? Or is it a game?

BLACKMUN: Usually I go in with two, or three, or four questions that I would like to ask in case counsel don't answer them on their own accord. And I have those listed, ready to go. I take notes, as you may have noticed, in part to keep myself awake in some cases. It gets pretty dull. Then just for sheer mischief, I put a lineup as to how I think the votes are going to fall. Usually I can tell from the questions that are asked how they are going to fall, but not always.

TOTENBERG: You're a better man than I, Charlie Brown. I can't always tell by any measure or means.

BLACKMUN: Yes, it's a good way to be misled. That's certainly true. One should remember, of course, that questions often are asked because the justice is troubled about a certain point. It may sound hostile, but it really might be completely uttered in a spirit of a search for information.

TOTENBERG: Do you remember the advice Justice Black gave you, when you first were on the bench, about oral argument?

BLACKMUN: He came in, and said, "Harry, I am senior here and you are junior. Never ask many questions from the bench because if you don't ask many questions, you won't ask many foolish questions." I think that is pretty good advice, and I have followed it ever since and don't say much. I think some of you in the media feel that I'm just sitting there like a bump on a log, but at least I'm a little more talkative than Justice Thomas is, who has yet to speak this term. I don't believe he has asked a single question in the two sessions we have had. He and I joke about it a little bit, as though we are the two silent members of the Court.

TOTENBERG: Of course, there are some members of the Court who are exactly the opposite.

BLACKMUN: Exactly.

TOTENBERG: Justices Scalia and Ginsburg probably ask a good deal more questions than anybody else.

BLACKMUN: Yes.

TOTENBERG: Do you think some of those are foolish?

BLACKMUN: Having practiced law for seventeen years, I'm a great believer in letting lawyers present their cases. There certainly have been instances where the Court has prevented this with multiple questions and multiple interruptions of the questioner. The other day a question was asked and before it was finished, somebody else interrupted and asked another one, then a third justice asked still another question and interrupted the second one. Well, poor counsel was in a bad way. But I think they should have the right to present their cases as they see them and not have them taken away from them in oral argument.

TOTENBERG: Have you ever changed your mind over the course of years about particular issues, or even in the course of writing an opinion? I'm talking about some justices who get an assignment to write an opinion, sit down to explain it and write it and commit it to paper, and can't do it. It doesn't work. It doesn't write, as they say. Has that ever happened to you?

BLACKMUN: No, it has not. But it has happened many times since I have been here where justices will send a note around and say, "I'm afraid I'm going to have to change my vote because it just doesn't write well." Of course, the opposite of that coin is that we often say, "These questions that we're discussing will come out in the writing," and that's a comforting thought. What it means is that whoever is assigned the opinion is given a little more leeway maybe than the conference vote would indicate. People often ask me if I had some of the old opinions of twenty years ago to rewrite, would I reach opposite conclusions. I think in all of them I would not reach opposite conclusions. I might write them a little differently. There is one instance where I joined Byron White in a concurrence that to-day I probably would have gone with the majority. But apart from that, I haven't equivocated.

TOTENBERG: Can I ask you about the other end of the spectrum? This Court has on it three relatively new members who have been added in the last few years. I wonder, as you reflect back on your own career, do you remember what your first conference was like, the first time you sat in with the brethren, as they call them, and what that kind of responsibility feels like in the very beginning?

BLACKMUN: I will never forget it. I remember when I was sworn in here on the ninth day of June, 1970, and walked into the conference room, and there were the others standing around in kind of a semicircle, robed. Just to mention the seniors, there was Hugo Black and William O. Douglas and William J. Brennan and John Marshall Harlan. I said to myself, What am I do-ing here? Plus being conscious of the fact that I was the presi-dent's third choice, not his first. I think probably that has been a good thing for me. It would be for anybody all of his lifetime to realize that he isn't good old number one, but is something else. What had happened, the vacancy after Justice Fortas's re-tirement had existed for a full year. So the Court sat with eight, I think for a full year. There were, as I recall, thirteen cases that had been marked by those eight for reargument. I was advised of this, and of course it was obvious that they were four to four. I would be the fifth vote one way or the other. So the first session in October 1970, I think consisted entirely of reargued cases. I remember John Harlan coming off the bench and put-ting his arm around Justice Brennan, and saying, "All the rest of us have been through these cases before. Why don't we let Harry go into conference with himself and the rest of us go back and relax." It meant that they were firm in their opinions. So Oc-tober and November of 1970 were not easy for me because of my imagination that those were the situations and that my vote was determinative. So when you ask, do I remember that first session, I do very distinctly, and it was most excruciating. I would have been happier had I stayed on the Eighth Circuit rather than coming down here in 1970.

TOTENBERG: Most of what you do at this Court is in writing. I think probably outside of the Court, people think that you sit down around a table and hash out the way the written word is going to be, but that is not true. Could you describe how an opinion is written and why there is so much writing?

BLACKMUN: Of course it would be a lot easier if we didn't have to write opinions and justify the results we reach. That would be almost a perfect world. Of course, that isn't what happens. It seems to me that our work divides almost everything into three parts. I am speaking only for myself. Other justices might disagree. A good one-third is deciding what cases to take. This is interesting, provocative, and sometimes it's a little bit defensive. The second is the preparation for the oral argument, the reading of briefs and trying to reach a tentative conclusion, perhaps. The third is writing opinions and justifying one's vote and hoping to get to court. By that I mean five on the opinion. It would be much easier if all we had to do would be to say affirm and let that go at that.

TOTENBERG: It's pretty hard getting five justices under one tent?

BLACKMUN: Every now and then it is, indeed. Every once in a while that comes rather readily. But most of the cases are close cases. Many times lower courts have differed on the issue. So they are not easy. You work at it and hope that you reach the right result and hope that you are not putting a damper on the development of the law as you think it ought to go in the long run.

TOTENBERG: How many drafts typically will an opinion go through?

BLACKMUN: That varies a lot. But it is rare when they go beyond seven or eight. Now and then, some textbooks will say there are twenty-three drafts. I have not seen that at all. Some revisions are made because the author wants to make them. Others are made because other justices say, "If you put in this kind of a paragraph or say this, I'll join your opinion." So you put it in. Many times the final result is a compromise. I think the public doesn't always appreciate this. But many times the final result is not what the author would originally have liked to have. Five votes are the answer and that is what the Court's judgment is. So you swallow your pride and go along with it, if you can.

TOTENBERG: You wrote *Roe* v. *Wade* when you were a relatively junior justice.

BLACKMUN: Yes, indeed.

TOTENBERG: You had been on the Court three years. I think you started work on it after less than two years, in fact. How did that feel? Did you know what a momentous decision it was?

BLACKMUN: It wasn't very easy and it was an emotional, highly divisive issue. I remember Justice Black coming in one day that first term, and I had circulated some opinion. He came in holding it this way above his head. He said, "Harry, I like it. You go for the jugular. Always go for the jugular. But there is something in it I don't like. You confess agonizing over the decision, that the decision was difficult. Never agonize," said Hugo Black. "Make it sound crystal clear and you'll be better off." I broke that advice in *Roe* v. *Wade* because, as you recall, two of the first three paragraphs are agonizing, describing the difficulty of the situation. But I am glad I did. I think it was true. Some of these cases are tough. The public doesn't realize that these cases come here and they have to be decided. Somebody has to write them. Frequently, not always, it is an unpopular position and the Court itself is criticized, but that is part of the job and all of us catch those undesired opinions to write every now and then.

TOTENBERG: I want to ask you about this being a collegial institution. Yet I have been in the courtroom when you on occasion, dissenting orally from the bench, have been almost engulfed in a kind of passion. You have accused your colleagues of carrying out something close to simple murder.

BLACKMUN: Not orally from the bench, but in writing, yes.

TOTENBERG: At the time of the 1989 abortion case, the *Webster* abortion case, you said you feared for the fate of a generation of American women. In the *Deshaney* case, involving a youngster who had been abandoned by the social welfare agencies and who had been beaten into a completely retarded, dysfunctional child, when the Court refused to hold the public welfare agency responsible, you lamented that. I remember you saying, "Poor Joshua." You said in your dissent that the Court was very much treating him in the same way that the Court had treated slaves in the 1800s. Those are pretty tough things to say about people that you are going to be serving with for the rest of your life. How does that work out?

BLACKMUN: They didn't complain too much about it, and they say things like that about me too, and I watch it when the crossfire is between other justices. I think most of it is in the written opinions, not very much in oral statements around the conference table. If one feels strongly, I suppose he speaks strongly. I did feel in the *Deshaney* case that nobody was taking care of that little kid. He was a child that got the bad side of life early and would endure it the rest of his life.

TOTENBERG: This Court is now accepting for review about half the number of cases that it did a decade ago. Why is that?

BLACKMUN: The strange thing about it is the docketing has increased.

TOTENBERG: More cases are coming here asking for review, but you are taking far fewer?

BLACKMUN: We're taking few. Oftentimes when we go into conference, a remark will be made, "Well, it's a long list, but it's very thin on substance." Of course, one would speculate as to why fewer cases are being taken. I think one fact for the increase in the docketing is due to the sentencing guidelines. Every defendant who is convicted and is sentenced feels that he should have had two years less in his sentence, or he is dissatisfied that the district judge lifted it out of the sentencing range for that particular crime. Every one of those comes up here, and we certainly do not give too much heed to those. But that is where the increase is. When I first came here, we had twenty-four cases each session, from October through April, and now we have had a couple of sessions where only twelve make it up here. We have more time to think about them and don't rush them out just to get them done. I have a feeling that we have bottomed out and that we will probably start taking more.

KOPPEL: Would you tell our audience, which rarely gets to hear from a Supreme Court justice, why you think this body is serving the American public so well or perhaps not so well in some instances?

BLACKMUN: I think by and large the Court does what it can. It is the third branch of government as we have structured it. And I think it is a necessary part of the balancing of governmental powers between the executive and the legislature and the judiciary. I never thought I would be here, and I certainly never thought I would be here for twenty-three years. An opportunity to serve on this Court comes to very few. It hasn't been easy, but it has been a fascinating experience. To use Byron White's phrase, "This has been a great ride." I'm indebted to the country for the privilege of being here. There are a lot of people who are of the opinion they wish I hadn't been here, but then, that is a part of the job, too.

Donna Shalala, former chancellor of the University of Wisconsin, Madison, talks with Susan Stamberg about her new job as secretary of Health and Human Services. January 9, 1993

STAMBERG: Is it true, as your friend Carol Bellamy, who used to be on the city council of New York, said, that you've been running for cabinet office since you were about five years old?

SHALALA: Absolutely not. I didn't know what a cabinet office was when I was five years old. I think I wanted to be a journalist when I was five years old.

STAMBERG: You may have made the right decision. But I love that notion that you were that kind of kid with that sort of drive, wanting to take on things, make changes, have some power.

SHALALA: Oh, yes. I used to read books about famous women, Jane (double *d*) Addams, Amelia Earhart. Those were my heroes as a kid. The stories of those women are stories of women working very hard to be successful.

STAMBERG: I wanted to talk to you some about women and drive because when women have it, it turns out to be something else. It's seen in unattractive ways. Ambition gets turned into bitchiness, that old story.

SHALALA: There are a set of code words about aggressive, ambitious, brittle, shrill women. There are a whole set of words. Self-promoters, that's my favorite one this week. If you network just the way men in power do, the new line on women is that you are a self-promoter. So they're a set of sexist terms. Most of which I am sure that have been said about me either behind the scenes or in the press anonymously at one point or another in my career.

STAMBERG: Looking forward now to this bigger campus and a lot more children and adults and old people you are going to have to manage in Health and Human Services, what are you anticipating your stickiest problem is going to be there?

SHALALA: Health care cost containment, obviously, is going to be a very serious issue. There is not consensus yet in this country. There is a lot of feeling, though, that we ought to have change, that we have to get these costs down so that they're reasonable and that we have to cover a lot more Americans. There are large numbers of Americans that are not covered. That's going to be a sticky political problem. The great issues, though, for Health and Human Services, have to do with children and families. I think that one of the reasons that President-elect Clinton wanted me to take the position was because I have spent much of my career worrying about poor children and about their access to health services, to other kinds of social services, to education, and to get that huge department to understand that the best investment we can make in our future is to make sure that our children grow up healthy and nurtured, and in the long run, that is what will keep the deficit out of trillion-dollar numbers.

STAMBERG: It's a capital expenditure if you really look at it.

SHALALA: It really is, and that is the way I think about it, and that is the way Americans are starting to think about it. Investing in kids is investing in the future.

STAMBERG: Of all the agencies, all the cabinet positions, I think Health and Human Services is the one that touches the most Americans on a day-to-day basis.

SHALALA: That's absolutely right. It's the largest department, of course. It's twice the size of the Defense Department. You will note that he had to put a woman in charge to really get into it. It touches the lives of every American, whether it's through the social security system or through the health issues, or, in some cases, through the family support issues, or research, which will determine whether we are going to solve problems like AIDS or cancer.

STAMBERG: What do you think your greatest strength is?

SHALALA: Gosh, I think it's probably my energy level. I obviously am a relatively secure person with administrative skills now. More than anything else, I think it's an energy level. There are lots of talented people, but if you don't have the energy level to get things done, if you are not persistent, if you can't keep working at the issue — it's never giving up and I never give up.

STAMBERG: I have to ask you this, and it's about marijuana. Everyone says that this generation that's moving in now — Hillary Clinton, a thoroughly professional woman to be wife of the president for the first time, people like you coming in to run things — you were the generation that came up with drugs. You came up against a war that was an extremely unpopular one and may have protested against it, and you, as a college kid, used marijuana.

SHALALA: I did. I smoked marijuana a few times. I did inhale. The student newspapers, my whole academic administration career, have asked me, and I have answered that question, so I don't mind answering it again. I am very much a child of my generation — the civil rights movement, the peace movement, the women's movement. I have very much been shaped by the great movements of at least my generation. I obviously outgrew some of the early excesses of my own youth and went on to sort of straighten myself out, but I am not afraid of saying that I was very much involved both in those movements and the things that young people were doing in those days. It was very special to grow up when we grew up because we did have these great movements. This generation of young people doesn't have those large issues which bond them and make them understand that they are, in fact, a generation. South Africa, a little bit, and they have a feel for that, and the environment, of course, and certainly, the continuation of racial issues, not only on college campuses, but around our country. But not those huge movements with extraordinary leaders. I hope it made me be a more sensitive, more responsive human being. I hope I go into a huge management job with a different set of values about how government ought to behave and what it ought to do, including a value that the government ought not do everything, that there are personal responsibilities, and that this is a compact between the government and people. I share Bill Clinton's view that the people on the recipient end are expected to do some things, too. Just because it's an entitlement doesn't mean that we don't expect people to work hard and either get an education or get off welfare.

STAMBERG: I wanted to ask you about your Peace Corps time. Where were you? Where did you serve?

SHALALA: I was in Iran. I was there in the early 1960s with the first Peace Corps group that went to Iran. I was stationed in an agricultural college in the South, actually a new agricultural college, which was just putting its curriculum together. I taught English and a little rural sociology and worked in community development a little bit. It was a wonderful experience.

STAMBERG: In those days with Peace Corps, it was the B.A. generalist. Go out, find out the problems in your community, and solve them, right?

SHALALA: That is exactly what we did, and we had very good training. We trained at Utah, at the Navajo Indian reservation. I have a great fondness for Native Americans because of my experience living in a Native American hogan, near Round Rock, Arizona. It really changed me in a couple of ways. Number one, it made me a citizen of the world, and I think that is what John Kennedy wanted. In fact, I mentioned that I had gone off to the Peace Corps exactly thirty years ago in my acceptance speech when President-elect Clinton introduced me. First, it made me a citizen of the world, and second, it made me understand what it was like to be a minority in this country because being a woman in the Middle East, people look through you. The emotional experience of not being taken seriously — more than not being taken seriously, having a male educational administrator go around the room and ask all the men their opinions and skip you. It was the taxicab drivers and the people on the street, when I asked them a question, basically they looked through me. I will never forget that. It made an emotional mark on me that gave me a kind of empathy. No white person can ever know what it's like to be black or Latino or Asian American in this country, but you can get a feel for it as a woman, not only by being discriminated against in this country, but being in a country in which women aren't fully human beings.

STAMBERG: That was really the golden age of the Peace Corps. It must have felt to you the way Bill Clinton did, at fourteen, meeting JFK, because you were in the first group to go out when the hopes were so high and so enormous.

SHALALA: I feel the same way now as I did thirty years ago. I feel the same sense of hope and sense of excitement. I never thought I would have that feeling again. I never thought that it would come back again, and it's here. I am all grown up and I got one of the big jobs.

DAVID GERGEN talks with Robert Siegel and Linda
Wertheimer about joining the Clinton administration as
counselor to the president. Gergen is a former adviser to
Republican presidents Nixon, Ford, and Reagan. After
leaving his last post at the White House, he worked as a
columnist, commentator, and journalist. June 2, 1993

WERTHEIMER: David, you come back to Washington after a
very short vacation and find that the *New York Times* is already
on your case.

GERGEN: I am surprised it didn't start earlier.

WERTHEIMER: It's in an editorial today, which, although it
does contain some personal compliments, points out that
you've been a defender of very different politics from President
Clinton's, and it says that your appointment, "points up a deterioration of political values and an erosion of journalistic standards," and goes on to talk about packaging becoming more
important than content, than philosophy. Do you think this
represents something new? Does this appointment represent
giving a great deal of importance to packaging and selling?

GERGEN: I didn't come in as a packager. That was not the job
that they brought to me, nor is it the job that I am particularly
interested in. Am I concerned about the president's message?
Of course. Am I concerned that he communicate more effectively? Of course. But what has concerned me the most is that
I think it's terribly important for this country to have a president who is successfully addressing our domestic needs. It
seems to me that we have not been addressing those needs as
effectively as we might in the last few years. It's critical to the
future of this country that this not be an unproductive time, and
to get the excessive partisanship that I think exists in this city.
There is a culture here which I think is unhealthy. I think that

the *Times* was right about that, but it seems to me to go to the issue not of who is in or who is out of government, but whether people of different views in this city can get together. I obviously bring to this administration some views that are not wholly consistent with what others in the administration have, but there's no secret about that. I salute Bill Clinton for reaching out. He said he wanted a bipartisan government. He said he wanted people of different backgrounds and views. He has brought a diversity to the government in terms of gender, of race, in terms of his appointments. Now he's bringing a diversity in terms of viewpoints, and I think that's healthy.

WERTHEIMER: This is beyond bipartisanship, in that you have defended an administration which the president was elected by attacking, saying that he was going to repair the wounds caused by, and so on.

GERGEN: We obviously may disagree on aspects of Reaganism. I am proud to have served for Ronald Reagan. I have no regrets about that whatsoever. I think Ronald Reagan did very important, fundamentally good things for this country. He broke the back of inflation, which was wrecking our economy, and frankly, destroying the lives of a lot of people on the lower end of the ladder. He also, I think, contributed in a very measurable way, to the defeat of Communism, which in my judgment was the single most important event of our adult lifetimes. But there's no question that there are some social needs in this country that I believe started before the 1980s, before Ronald Reagan came to office, that were left unaddressed and have been left unaddressed by people in Washington over the last several years, including the Reagan years, that I think desperately cry out to be addressed. It's not just a question of our schools. It's a question of the declining standards of our work force, the declining wages, and the growing racial and class divisions. I think all of us have to get together and deal with those.

SIEGEL: Can you honestly support the nomination of Lani Guinier for assistant attorney general for civil rights, given that the ideas that she stands for are quite at odds with the ideas you have stood for over the years?

GERGEN: It's fundamentally a decision the president has to make. I have some views on that. I may or may not be asked for my thoughts on it. Internally, I don't think it's appropriate to be free-lancing on something like that decision he has to make.

SIEGEL: You haven't offered your thoughts already on that subject.

GERGEN: I think there is no secret about where I am on civil rights, and that is that I basically am very pro–civil rights. I am not for quotas. I am not going to take issue with whether Ms. Guinier is or isn't, or what her views are, but I will tell you this: whatever decision the president makes in this regard or what-ever the outcome on that nomination, one of the things that attracted me to Bill Clinton, I have said in repeated speeches around the country over the past year, is, I greatly respect Bill Clinton because he is a progressive on civil rights. He is dedi-cated to civil rights. He came out of the South just as I did. I grew up in North Carolina. We're both white southern boys, if you will. We went through the 1960s at about the same age. The 1960s transformed both of us in terms of our views about civil rights, and I respect what he has done in that area, and whatever the outcome is on Lani Guinier, I think that won't change my impression of where he is.

WERTHEIMER: What about your title? Is this counselor to the president or mighty counselor?

GERGEN: My children have been sort of getting those same phrases from the *Messiah*, and they're poking fun at me. It is a grandiose title, but I guess we live in the age of not only grade inflation, but title inflation.

WERTHEIMER: But what does it mean?

GERGEN: When they came to me, and said, "We would like you to come in," — it's not a job I sought, it was something they came to me on. They said, "We would like you to be at the intersection of policy, of politics, and communications. We would like you, as a matter of fact, to serve as a senior adviser to the president in a counselor role that offers him advice on a wide range of things." I don't particularly want wide responsibility. I have agreed to take on the overall direction of the communications area. I am not expecting to spend a great deal of my time on that. Early on, I am going to have to get familiar with it, obviously, but I prefer to have a free-roaming role. I've been something called editor-at-large for the last few years at *U.S. News and World Report*, and I hope that I can be sort of adviser-at-large within the administration.

SIEGEL: The Reagan administration had a very understandable and clear message to Americans as to what it is about. This administration doesn't seem to have one yet. What is it? Can you express, for the Clinton administration, what it stands for, briefly, to people, so that they can feel good about it?

GERGEN: Obviously, during the campaign, he was the candidate of change, but he was also a New Democrat, as he called it. He said he wanted to draw from the best of the Democratic Party as well as the Republican Party, I might note. I think, somehow he has gotten off the message in that regard here in the first few months, and I think he wants to find his way back. How one expresses that, how one captures that, with the clarity of a Reagan, I am not so sure yet, but I think we have to work on it. I would like to talk to him more about it.

SIEGEL: Isn't that a big problem? Even if it is only a few months in, we're groping for an easy description of what this presidency is about?

GERGEN: Fundamentally, he is a progressive reformer. I think he is someone who is trying to come up with innovative ideas that get beyond the boxes of the 1980s, that get beyond whether Reagan was a good or wasn't a good president or all the rest of that, who defines solutions that will draw support and draw inspiration from both camps. We reek of privilege and power in this city. We have lots of it, but we refuse to get together and see if we can help define common ground and get some answers. I think people around the country are disgusted with that, and I think they have a right to be disgusted with it, and I think those of us who share in that power and privilege have some responsibility, it seems to me, to put aside some of our partisan differences, put aside some of our other differences, and see if we can't find those answers.

WERTHEIMER: Are you going to be able to help President Clinton with the problem that on some of his big votes he has had, what you might call, zero Republicans in the House and Senate?

GERGEN: Obviously, that's been a concern of mine. To be frank, I doubt I can deliver any votes for him. I don't think I have that kind of sway. What I would hope is over time we can change the atmosphere in this city so it's easier for Republicans to sit down with Democrats, and say, "Look, until the 1996 campaign comes around, we've got to govern this country. We only have one president at a time." In that context, I think maybe I can be modestly helpful. I must tell you, I will not feel comfortable. I don't want to take part in any Democratic campaigning, as a Republican. I simply don't want to do that. I don't think it's right. I don't think it's appropriate.

WERTHEIMER: The health care reform is one of this reforming president's biggest projects, and financing it is going to be anything but simple. Do you think that in your role as editor-at-large that you might like to edit that down into something simpler? Should he consider doing something like that?

GERGEN: I have been thinking about this, actually, in the last twenty-four hours. How does one present this to the country? How do you, first, come up with a plan that is understandable? I think it's going to be extremely difficult. A major part of whatever he does on health care has to be public education. He can't simply lay out a plan and expect everybody to understand it. It's so complex. We do not want to have happen in health care what happened with catastrophic reform back in 1988. The Congress passed something, and President Reagan signed it. The country didn't understand what it was getting. When people heard about it and learned what it was, they blew up. They had to reform. They had to repeal it. I think that would be a terrible mistake in health care reform.

SIEGEL: One quick question on defense, on a foreign policy issue. You criticized the administration for threatening force in Bosnia and then not delivering. Are you going to be a voice within the White House for redeeming the threat of deterrent force of the U.S. military? Do you feel they have to make up something because the Bosnian Serbs just took the measure of the White House in the threat to use military force?

GERGEN: I think the single most important issue there is that when the United States speaks, that it stick to what it says. What I have written about is that I happen to be in favor of a policy to come in and help the Bosnians. I think they are being slaughtered there. I think that genocide is awful, and I happen to be in favor of using military force. I have written about that in the past. But I think the critical lesson for this is that it's important when the president's advisers talk him into making commitments about quick and decisive action that that would happen, that you not march up the hill and march down again. I don't pose as a foreign policy authority. I am not that. I think I can help think through the consequences of policy and the announcement of policy.

Former Secretary of Defense DICK CHENEY reflects on his four years at the Defense Department. He talks with Katie Davis about the responsibility he turned over to incoming Secretary of Defense Les Aspin, from the continuing civil war in Bosnia to the ongoing conflict with Iraq. January 23, 1993

CHENEY: I tried to focus on the kinds of things that you don't really have a feel for until you go to the Defense Department and do it. An extremely important element of your responsibility has to do with military operations — when you commit the force, what you ask them to do, where you send them. Those are experiences no one can get except by serving in those senior Pentagon positions.

DAVIS: Do you think this was a particularly delicate transition because of the ongoing conflict with Iraq?

CHENEY: I am not sure *delicate* is the right word. It is different than other transitions that I am familiar with. This is my fifth transition.

DAVIS: During the Ford administration, you were chief of staff.

CHENEY: During the Ford administration, we took over when Nixon stepped down. There was almost no transition at all. One day there was a Nixon administration, the next day there was a Ford administration, almost without warning. So that was a very quick takeover, and we had some ongoing foreign problems at the time, especially a crisis in the Middle East, the aftermath of the 1973 Yom Kippur War. In the Reagan-Bush transition, there was more time. When we took over early in the Bush administration, the world was relatively stable. We still had a cold war. The focus, in terms of international problems, was in places like Nicaragua and Afghanistan, which were significant problems. But the fate of the world didn't rest on the outcome of the struggle between the Contras and the Sandinistas in Nicaragua. All of that has changed now. The cold war is over with. What used to be the Soviet Union is in a state of collapse and continuing to collapse. It's an ongoing revolution. There is war raging in Europe in the Balkans, significant problems in the aftermath of our successful effort to oust Saddam Hussein from Kuwait and to protect the Persian Gulf from his aggression. In some respects, it is a more dynamic world situation from the perspective of a U.S. policymaker.

DAVIS: President Clinton has said that he wants to focus on domestic issues, and yet he comes into office at a time of several crises. I wonder what you would say to him about being able to manage the foreign crises and focus on the domestic.

CHENEY: As president, sometimes you don't have a choice about what you're going to focus on. The United States is the world's leading trading power. Our economy is totally intertwined with the rest of the world. We will prosper and will live in peace if, in fact, societies based on values such as ours, democracy, freedom, and so forth, can prosper in the world, and that depends on a relative state of stability. If that state of affairs is going to exist, it will come about, I think, only if the United States provides the leadership to make it happen. The notion that an American president, whether he is Bill Clinton or George Bush, can ignore that and focus on domestic issues here, I just think is a fundamentally flawed concept. I think the campaign, to the extent that it was conducted this year, and I don't mean to limit my criticism just to the Democratic side, but the campaign was, in many respects, misguided, because we managed to conduct a presidential election and took a government that is going to rule for the next four years without any significant reference whatsoever to what's going on in the world around us. We just sort of had tunnel vision focused on what we thought was a serious set of problems here in our economy at home. That is not to say there aren't problems here in the

United States, but there is nothing as complicated or difficult as we have already overcome at times in our past. You cannot ignore what's going on around us in the world.

DAVIS: When you were secretary of defense, did you ever think of that as a burden? There was a problem in Somalia, and the only people that really can lead a mission there are the United States. And there is a problem in Bosnia. Did it ever seem like a burden?

CHENEY: I didn't see it that way. These were difficult problems. I think this generation of Americans has an opportunity that very few have ever had in any time in history, and that is the chance to shape the course of history, to shape the course of events, to take advantage of the end of the cold war, of the massive reduction in nuclear armaments that we have now gotten the Russians to sign up to, of the new birth of freedom and democracy in Eastern Europe, where Communist regimes used to be located, and of the growing prosperity not only in the United States but elsewhere in the world. We have got an opportunity to achieve levels of productivity and prosperity that never before have been seen in the history of the world.

DAVIS: Is it a relief not to carry the responsibility now as secretary of defense? Is there a part of you that is sighing and thinking, OK, I am not carrying all that weight on my shoulder for those decisions.

CHENEY: It's not really that, in that, in a personal sense, there are some attractive aspects of it. There is a greater sense of privacy now. I am a relatively private person. There is more time with my family and greater flexibility in terms of living a more orderly life. But I really enjoyed my time in the Defense Department. It's been an absolutely fascinating four years. I consider myself blessed to have been asked to serve, to have been there in the Bush administration, to follow the president's leadership, and to have the privilege of running what I think is the finest military force the world's ever seen, and to be associated with the men and women of the United States military.

They are a phenomenal group of people, better than anybody gave them credit for. I will look back on my four years with many fond memories. I don't have any sense of having had a burden lifted in that regard. I loved my job. It was a great job. It's one of the world's great jobs.

ROBERT MCNAMARA, secretary of defense in the
Kennedy and Johnson administrations and, later,
president of the World Bank, ends a thirty-year public
silence about the Vietnam War and tells Bob Edwards
about why he finally decided to write an autobiography.
He focuses on issues concerning U.S. intervention in
foreign crises. *In Retrospect* will be published by
Times Books, most likely in 1996. September 10, 1993

EDWARDS: Why would you say nothing for thirty years?

MCNAMARA: Let me remind you that I believe it was in the
fall of 1966 when it became clear to me that at a minimum we
were not going to achieve the U.S. objectives in Vietnam. It
became clear to me that at some point scholars should review
the history. It was really a history that went back even into the
Truman administration, certainly into the Eisenhower, but in
any event, scholars should review the history of U.S. involvement in Vietnam and draw lessons from it. To assist them in
that process in the latter part of 1966, I established what has
become known as the Pentagon Papers Project to try to bring
together the raw material and the documents that the scholars
would need for their studies. I did not plan then, and I have not
since believed it wise, for a participant in the decision-making
process to comment before the scholars did their work. Why
didn't I believe it wise? Because I have learned over time that we
participants tend to justify our actions and in a sense we color
history to achieve that objective. I would never do that consciously, but I have seen many people, many friends of mine, do
it unconsciously. I don't want to do that.

EDWARDS: Everyone else has spoken.

MCNAMARA: Not really, no. Presidents Kennedy and Johnson died. Robert Kennedy died. Several of my key assistants,

John McNaughton, for example, died. Dean Rusk spoke through his son. Mac Bundy hasn't written. There have been very few of the major participants in the decision-making process for the seven years I was involved in the Defense Department who have written. So my memoirs in that sense will be a first or a near first.

EDWARDS: Those who have written were members of Congress, ambassadors, and generals.

MCNAMARA: Those were not the people who in a sense participated in the decision-making process. Many of them didn't know what went on. In the limited period I have been researching the subject so far. Let me digress a moment to say I would never have started this project had I not had an understanding with the libraries, the Kennedy and Johnson libraries, with the Defense Department and the archivists, that I would have full access to written materials. I do not wish to depend on my memory. I must base what I write and conclude on written documents at the time. Moreover, I wouldn't have even done it then had I not had available to me the assistance of an extraordinary young man who is a professor, an assistant professor of history at the naval academy, whose field of expertise and scholarly interest is Vietnam. He has written one book on it. So I am coming at this with assets available now which I haven't had available to me in the past thirty years.

EDWARDS: Of what's been written, have you ever found something, and said, "That's it. He got it right"?

MCNAMARA: Number one, I stopped five or ten years ago trying to become an expert on literature. I will try to become one now. I have seen some books that I am very impressed by, Stanley Karnow's, for example, and a three-volume work to date by a professor named Gibbons, who has brought together the best documentary record that I have come across. There are documents out there. I am not going to duplicate those. I am going to pick ten or twelve definitive decisions, pivotal events, and describe what happened that led to the decisions that resulted from those events, and then trace through the results and try to draw lessons from them.

EDWARDS: Are you going to deal strictly with the public policy decision-making process or also the social consequences?

MCNAMARA: I have not written the book yet, but my intention is to deal with the public policy aspects of it. I will point to some of the consequences, which of course involved social actions.

EDWARDS: Very profound consequences of decisions you made or didn't make?

MCNAMARA: Very profound, no question about it. My purpose is not to dredge up painful decisions or events of the past, but rather to look to the future and to try to draw lessons from the past that we can apply in quite a different world. The U.S. participation in Vietnam in a very real sense was a function of the cold war. Does it mean that an event that was a function of the cold war can lead to lessons applicable to the post–cold war world? I think so . . . I do not believe that our post–cold war foreign policy in this country should be based solely on our decisions. We should take account of what other nations think and believe. We have not been given by God the right to determine the course of events in every nation in the world. We must take account of other nations. Moreover, I also believe that our defense program should be based on the assumption that when we intervene militarily, wherever it may be, we will do so in company with other nations. I don't believe that we should spend the money to develop a military force that will take care of every military problem in the world by ourselves. I am not entirely sure that belief of mine has as yet been accepted as a foundation for our defense program. I hope it will be.

EDWARDS: What about responsibility for the United States? It is the only superpower left in the world.

MCNAMARA: I would differentiate between the responsibility for our basic national security, the security of this continent and Alaska and Hawaii. I think we should be prepared to defend that unilaterally, and we should make decisions to move in defense of this basic security unilaterally. But when it's a question of intervening in Somalia, from my point of view, it should be in association with the Africans. Where is the Organization of African Unity in Somalia? So far as I know, it hasn't yet taken a position with respect to it. Where are the African troops in Somalia? I believe there is a small number of Nigerians, but the great bulk of the twenty thousand troops that are there today are not African. That to me does not appear proper.

EDWARDS: What do you do, though, if multinational organizations are reluctant to move for all the wrong reasons?

MCNAMARA: One could use Bosnia, for example, as an illustration. Certainly NATO, and to a greater degree, Western Europe, failed to act with respect to Bosnia. What do we do? I don't think we should move alone. For one reason, I don't think we could have been effective had we moved alone in Bosnia. So it's a difficult problem, it's a difficult world. We are left without the certainty. Larry Eagleburger, another friend of mine who was deputy secretary of state, was criticized because one of his statements was wrongly interpreted. He said we moved from a secure world, the world of the cold war, where we knew who our friends were and who our enemies were, to this post–cold war world, where in a sense we are adrift. This nation isn't adrift. We are a great power. We will be the greatest power in the world, but that doesn't mean that we should try to impose our will. It doesn't mean we should act as the policeman of the world. It doesn't mean that we should incur all of the costs that would be involved in setting up a worldwide police force that we paid for and was under our command. No way.

EDWARDS: The United States had allies with them in Vietnam.

MCNAMARA: We did, but it was primarily our decisions with respect to Vietnam and our force that was there. The casualties were largely ours. It's a good illustration of the point I am making, by the way. In the post–cold war world, let's not do things unilaterally.

EDWARDS: When you hear an analogy with Vietnam, as in the Persian Gulf War, you hear, "We have to be careful we're not getting involved in another Vietnam or Somalia."

MCNAMARA: I am going to write a book on the lessons of Vietnam because I believe that lessons can be drawn from it that will apply to the post–cold war world. But I haven't written the book yet, and therefore, I am not going to discuss those lessons today. Let me go back to the world we are living in today. I think Bosnia, which the president discussed a day or two ago, is a very important illustration of the problem, what to do in Bosnia. It's almost too late to intervene militarily. We should not do it alone, that is for sure. There are some problems, and it's difficult for me to say this, but I spent my life believing all problems had solutions. There are some problems that don't have solutions, at least not military solutions. I think today Bosnia may be one of those. But that doesn't mean that at some stage, the world, NATO, Western Europe, could not have applied military force with benefit to Bosnia. I would suggest that today, instead of thinking about military force in Bosnia, we should be thinking about the danger of Bosnia as developing in Kosovo and Macedonia, two other republics in Yugoslavia that are on the verge of conflict, which would extend beyond their borders, involving Greece and Turkey, and inflame the entire region. What are we thinking about that? What are we going to do with respect to that? With whom are we going to do it? What is NATO's view? These are the questions that should be debated today.

EDWARDS: At what point did you determine that not everything had a solution?

MCNAMARA: Rather recently, I might say, and it's very hard for me to say it. I am a problem-solver, whether it be at Ford or the World Bank or Defense, but I am gradually learning some problems don't have solutions. Moreover, even if they do, I am not wise enough to know them. I want to suggest to you, I am going to start this book by quoting four lines from T. S. Eliot that my wife, who was one of God's loveliest creatures, brought to my attention about thirty years ago. Eliot wrote,

> We shall not cease from exploration
> And the end of all our exploring
> Will be to arrive where we started
> And know the place for the first time.

I haven't finished my exploration. I haven't returned to where I started. And I don't know the place yet, which simply means I am quite clear on my limitations. I don't have solutions for all the problems.

BENJAMIN HOOKS talks with Katie Davis about his lifelong battle for civil rights and his work as executive director of the NAACP. Dr. Hooks says that fighting for civil rights runs in his family and that his grandmother got involved with the NAACP after it was founded in 1909, in response to race riots in Springfield, Illinois. March 27, 1993

HOOKS: My grandmother, Julia Hooks, was a charter member of the Memphis branch in 1912. I remember the stories of her being arrested because she was born, apparently, free, and she was a student before the law was passed segregating schools. After the Civil War, she was a student at Berea College in Kentucky, and it's a very prominent school now. She didn't receive her degree because she got into a big dispute. As liberal as Berea was, they were not prepared to let black students and white students go to the dance together, and she protested. As a result, she left Berea because she was in a protest. That must have been the late 1860s or early 1870s. So that may be in my genes. I read about how in the 1890s when Jim Crow came back into existence, my grandmother refused to ride on the back of the streetcar, and she would go to the opera and sometimes be arrested. So whatever it was, when I went to the army, I could not help but reflect on the fact that I was taking basic infantry training at Fort Benning, Georgia. Thirteen blacks in that group of two hundred had to live in a separate hut, eat from a separate table, and form a separate squad. It left an indelible impression on me.

DAVIS: I also read that during World War II you served in Italy and that there were some experiences that you had there that also left a sharp impression on you.

HOOKS: When I was in Italy, I was in the Ninety-second Infantry Division, which was all black in terms of enlisted men with white officers. But, actually, Italy was where I experienced the least segregation.

DAVIS: I guess I was thinking about the story that I read about that you had to guard prisoners of war.

HOOKS: Oh, yes, but that was in the States. Down in Georgia. One day, our contingent of black soldiers was guarding Italian prisoners of war. It was either in Columbus or Macon, I have forgotten which right this minute. But we took a rest stop to eat. The prisoners went to the restaurant to eat and we couldn't guard them inside the restaurant. We had to stand outside. Imagine the incongruity and the bitterness that could well up in you, that you are guarding prisoners of war, people that picked up their weapons to destroy your way of life. You picked up your weapon to defend it. And yet, those prisoners of war went into that restaurant and ate. And we, the black guards, had to dispatch ourselves, some at the front door and some in the back. That did strike me as one of things that always stands out as one of the supreme ironies of my life.

DAVIS: What was the conversation like that night when you were outside that restaurant?

HOOKS: I can't recall even discussing it. It was the kind of thing that burned so deeply that you suffer in silence. There is nothing to talk about. Some experiences sear you, and you really don't have anything much to discuss.

DAVIS: After you got out of the service, you went to law school in Chicago. But when you were done, you went back to Tennessee to practice law and later on to become a judge. What was that like?

HOOKS: I made a decision that I was going back to Memphis because I had made up my mind at some point that I wanted to use my life to batter down the walls of segregation. So I went back to Memphis deliberately and to a segregated town, where the courthouse still had separate restroom facilities for blacks, where we could not use the law library, where the preamble to the constitution of the bar association said, "This bar association in Memphis and Shelby County shall be open to all white lawyers practicing in this vicinity." I had to read that and abide by it. I couldn't belong to a bar association. At that point, you couldn't be elected a judge unless you had been recommended by the bar association. So it was a deliberate decision to make a change.

DAVIS: Do you believe in the U.S. justice system? I ask you this because of the ongoing trial of the four police officers accused of beating Rodney King in Los Angeles and depriving him of his civil rights. There is also a parallel trial of some African American men accused of beating the truck driver Reginald Denny at the beginning of the riots. And there is a lot of talk, especially among African Americans, about the fact that the justice system does not work for black Americans.

HOOKS: It really doesn't matter. It's the only system we have. What are you going to do about it? All this idle talk is just stupidity as far as I am concerned. I just get so tired of people sitting around arguing and raising hell, talking. They aren't doing anything to make things different. I get really tired of public radio and other radio listeners, with a lot of stupidity. The point is, if it's not right, what are we going to do to fix it?

DAVIS: You have to point it out first, though.

HOOKS: All I am saying is it's obvious to me that anybody knows the American justice system is unfair, always has been, and will be for years to come. The Rodney King case is a classic example of an aberration. I cannot describe my loathing and revulsion at a system where we looked at a television beating of a person, and those lying officers get on the stand and claim that it took that many people to restrain one man. If they're that weak, they ought to be off the force. Surely, it was a terrible thing. The thing that is so pathetic about it is black people, like white people, listened to their television for a long time and watched the Rodney King beating. Nobody set fires, nobody started a riot, nobody had civil disobedience because we naively believed that finally the police have gone too far. We caught them with their pants down, to use an old expression. Now the American justice system can deliver for us as blacks what it delivers for whites. But when that justice system failed utterly and completely, and no explanation can ever suffice for it, it was downright, as far as I am concerned, prejudice and racism that brought in that verdict, and not justice. The blindfolded goddess of justice peeked under her blindfold and saw a black man and white officers. I think that is the only explanation. When that system failed, you treat people irresponsibly, and sometimes they react irresponsibly. Surely, the system is bad, but just saying that it is nothing. How do we work to correct the system?

DAVIS: There are a group of people, the critics that say the NAACP is out of touch with African Americans, who are the most dispossessed, and they say that the NAACP has become irrelevant and lost its edge and that they need to get down more in the trenches and really fight the fight for the underclass, the African American underclass, the people that don't have jobs, that are involved in drugs, that are really alienated from the society.

HOOKS: That's stupidity at its utter worst. I really get sick of that question. The reason is I think it's unfair. The Harris Poll, that's a public document, did a survey among five hundred blacks at random, as they do. And the results: "Do you think the NAACP is very effective?" fifty-four percent; "Somewhat effective?" thirty-four percent; "Not effective at all?" three per-cent. Why must I spend all my time answering questions about what three percent of fools and nincompoops ask me? You don't do white folk like that. To me it's absolute racism.

DAVIS: Even asking that question? But I've heard that ques-tion asked by African Americans too.

HOOKS: But it's the same little crowd of know-nothings, malcontents, do-nothings. It's elevated to an art form. What-ever interview I've done in the last six months, that's why I am so upset about it. It becomes the *pièce de résistance.* It's a new form of journalism. I understand point-counterpoint. All I am saying is, you say "critics." What critics are you talking about? Are you talking about fifty percent of American blacks? The *Detroit News* did that poll.

DAVIS: I am talking about the *Detroit News* poll in part.

HOOKS: That *Detroit News.* But do you know what the *Detroit News* poll said? The *Detroit News* poll said that we had eighty-seven percent approval.

DAVIS: But it also said that the African Americans felt that the civil rights groups should be doing more to work on crime and on housing and on jobs.

HOOKS: It did not say that. I dispute that entirely. I know I shouldn't do that in an interview, but I dispute that entirely. If I am ever going to get it straight, I am going to get it straight now. If you conduct a poll, you can get any answer you want, depending on how you put the question together. We have the opinion from some leading polling people that it was a poorly done poll. I called the fellow who put the poll together. He said, "Well, I don't care what you say about it, you came out very good. So you ought not to get hot and mad about it." Buried down in that mess that stupid, low-down *Detroit News* did was the fact that we had an eighty-seven-percent approval rate. If I spent all of my time answering critics, I would have no time to do my job.

DAVIS: But don't you think that some discussion of what the role of the NAACP should be in the 1990s is healthy? That there ought to be that?

HOOKS: If one understands what we are doing and what our mission is, yes, it's healthy.

DAVIS: Within the African American community too, not just journalists or white journalists?

HOOKS: A part of the problem, and I confess that very readily, is we have a very difficult time conveying what we are doing because I send out hundreds of press releases that hit the garbage cans of all of these news organizations. But if somebody sends in a story that says that Ben Hooks is down there doing something wrong, that doesn't hit the garbage can. "Uh-oh, we got it now. We had better go down there and do an investigation." Anything that's derogatory that throws out slime or dirt, doesn't get to the bottom of it, as it relates to the NAACP. I don't know what happens to all the news releases that I send to National Public Radio about things we have done. If I tell you today that some critics say that we are not doing anything about jobs and opportunities, and I ask them, What in the ding-dong devil are you talking about? For fifteen years since I've been here, we have beseeched Congress to do something to create jobs in America. We have talked to the government. We have got on the soapbox. We have talked about the loss of jobs in the economic sector. We have beseeched the Congress to pass specific legislation. We led the fight to get the minimum-wage law passed. We have that effort going on the one side. On the other side, we have our fair-share program, which is designed specifically to work with industry on a case-by-case basis to create jobs. We have sixty such agreements in the private sector and about fifteen in the public sector, put billions of dollars into the black community, provided tens of thousands of new jobs, and had hundreds of new entrepreneurs doing things. This is our thrust. I am not upset about the fellow out there in south-central Los Angeles who doesn't know it. The *Los Angeles Times* never carried the story. The radio stations don't carry it.

DAVIS: But don't you think you need to connect to those people, people in south-central Los Angeles, people in other cities who are alienated from a lot of American society, black and white? The idea that they could work to change things is alien to them.

HOOKS: I understand that. I make every effort to do it. But I am saying, I operate on a sixteen-million-dollar-a-year budget, a hundred-member staff. If I spent all of my time trying to convert the unconverted, I can do nothing to change conditions. So they talk about what we don't do for those poor people. If one-third of blacks live below the level of poverty, two-thirds live above. Are we supposed to neglect the two-thirds who have happened to make it and only concentrate on the one-third? The fact is we have programs for both.

DAVIS: Where do you think race relations are in this country right now in 1993? I have spoken to many people, African Americans and whites, that say that they have deteriorated badly, that whites and blacks have just started to live more segregated lives, and just say, "Let's just not deal with it."

HOOKS: I just guess I can't agree with it, from my background. I am sixty-eight years old. You must remember I was born and raised in a completely segregated city. I am going home tomorrow to a banquet that the Freedom Fund is having.

DAVIS: In Memphis, Tennessee?

HOOKS: To the Peabody Hotel in Memphis, Tennessee. There will be twenty-five hundred people, black and white together. I am going home to a city that has a black mayor. When I went to practice law, there wasn't a black clerk in the courthouse. I am going to a city that has a black chief federal judge. I am going to a city that has a black chief of police. I am going to Memphis, Tennessee, that has a black superintendent of the public school system. When I go to the Peabody Hotel for that dinner, it's a place where I couldn't have gone at all except as a cook or some kind of cleanup boy or busboy. If I went in otherwise, I would be beaten to death. Now I go back to Memphis tomorrow night. And before I go to the banquet, I can stop and have my Diet Pepsi or Diet Coke in the main floor. I can drink from the water fountain and go to the movie theater. If you're talking about whether people love me or not, I don't know of any law that is going to do that. I look over. I think, if I make no mistake, that I see people in Bosnia fighting about ethnic differences. I think I see it in the former Soviet Union, where folks say, "You ain't one of us."

DAVIS: In Somalia?

HOOKS: In Somalia. I see it in Liberia. I see it in Ethiopia. I see it all over the world. I see it between Palestine and Israel. I am just trying to wonder again when people ask this question, are we looking at it from a world viewpoint? Did America expect to solve the racial problem in ten years? Did we have in mind the NAACP is a failure because you have been out there for eighty years and you haven't solved it? I don't want to come through as some Pollyanna. That's not realistic. But I look at

America, with all of its pains. I look at the progress. And I think we have to look at both. I think that part of the problem of the alienation has been this constant bombardment. Things are worse than they ever were. How, in the name of God, can I inspire young people to do something if I tell them we've been working all these years and it's worse. Why should they do better? Why should they try?

DAVIS: But you don't believe that it's worse, obviously?

HOOKS: No, I don't believe it's worse.

DAVIS: But I guess I am talking about, in the atmosphere of the 1980s, that there seemed to be more resistance to civil rights. There seemed to be a kind of sentiment, especially among white Americans, that, "Oh, we're just sick of African Americans asking for change" and a kind of distancing between the races.

HOOKS: I have no way of measuring that because white Americans wouldn't tell me that. So you give me an insight I don't have. But let me just say this. I am not dumb. I am not naive. I know that when black folk move into a neighborhood, even today, white people, by and large, move out. I understand all the racial hatred. What I am simply trying to say is that maybe we have to pinpoint a certain time. It is a vast difference between white support for blacks being able to drink from a water fountain and blacks living next door to them. There is a vast difference between blacks being able to sit anywhere they wanted on a streetcar or bus and going to their private clubs. The difference between perception has to do with a misunderstanding of what we are dealing with. What Martin King specialized in and what the NAACP was adept at crystallizing was the fact that in this country, in Chicago and Detroit and Los Angeles, during the 1960s there was not the type of overt segregation that you had in the South. So when you show pictures of little black kids being pinned against the wall with fire hoses, some white man says, "What in the hell do they want down there? What are they looking for?" I say, "Well, Mr. White Man, they would like to drink from the water fountain." Is that all that hell is being raised for? Let them drink from the water fountain. He was drinking from the water fountain in Los Angeles and thought nothing of it. Now the fight is not over water fountains, it's not over riding the bus. It's over who's going to drive that bus. Once we start digging into these economic issues, resistance may grow. Martin King said something to me that is very profound. I may not quote it exactly correct: "The law may not make you love me, but the law can make you treat me right until you learn how to love me."

The syndicated cartoonist HERBERT BLOCK talks with
Linda Wertheimer about his autobiography, *Herblock:
A Cartoonist's Life*, which documents the political
scandals and conflicts Block has drawn for more than
sixty years. Noting that unwise affairs were President
Kennedy's weakness, he observes, "If there was an
unusual amount of lust, there was also a good deal of
luster." On President Bush's account of his role in the
Iran-Contra affair, he observes, "Saying is believing."
Block has never lacked for politicians to deflate or
hypocrisies to hold up. October 20, 1993

BLOCK: There is a lot to be outraged about. You pick up the
paper almost any day and see something that makes you think,
Come on, they can't do that.

WERTHEIMER: In your early cartoons in the 1930s, you did
a cartoon which I would think would strike a lot of people as
being totally modern, in which two people are asking each
other, "Who do you think you will vote against?"

BLOCK: I had this little tussle with an associate editor at the
time, and he was a stickler for correct English, and he said,
"Well it was a good idea, but," he said, "it ought to be 'Against
whom do you think you will vote.' " And I thought, That is not
the way people talk, at least not the way they talked in my
cartoons.

WERTHEIMER: Some of your earliest cartoons are about political money. The amount of money that is spent on campaigns
is one theme. There are themes which run throughout your
long life of cartooning.

BLOCK: Oh, the spending, the scandals. The first cartoon I
did for the *Chicago News* was in 1929. It was a bunch of tree

stumps, and it was called "This is the forest primeval." Here it is all these years later, and we are talking about timber mining, and saving the old trees, and some of those issues are still with us.

WERTHEIMER: What do you think is the most famous drawing?

BLOCK: I don't know. One of them that has been used a lot was one I did during the time of a kind of un-American hysteria, which showed a man climbing up a ladder toward the Statue of Liberty's torch. He's carrying a bucket, and he's yelling, "Fire!" He's going to put out this fire. I still get requests to reprint that.

WERTHEIMER: You say in this book that a good cartoon goes bang.

BLOCK: I think it does. At different times they have tried animating political cartoons for television, and they are all right. But I don't think they have replaced the single cartoon in the paper. You look at it, and you just see the one panel, and I think it should go bang. I don't know how to explain it, but I don't know that the animation leading up to it improves it any.

WERTHEIMER: Bill Baggs, who was the editor of the *Miami News*, communicated with you by rubber stamp. I gather this is the way he answered troublesome letters sometimes?

BLOCK: It is, but he told me about the rubber stamp he used, which said, "This is not a simple world, my friend, and there are no simple answers." I had a stamp made, a one-time-use-only stamp, which I used to send a letter back to him. My stamp said, "It is too, and there are so."

WERTHEIMER: I wonder if maybe there isn't something about your life, or about your work, that is in that answer, that it is possible to reduce some very important things to one panel of a cartoon. You can look at it, and you can say, "There it is."

BLOCK: Actually, the stamp is really kind of a gag, just to answer his stamp. But I think you're right that in the cartoon what you try to do, you hope you do, is to distill something into a single picture in a few words. The interesting thing about a cartoon is that while it's an exaggeration in the drawing — people know that a fellow doesn't have ears that big or whatever it is — it's recognized as an exaggeration, but through an exaggeration, you do try to get at a basic truth. That's what you try to do, anyhow.

America Talking

In April 1993, with President Clinton nearing one
hundred days in office, a common occasion for
measuring a president's progress, Linda Wertheimer
travels "the nation's Main Street," Route 50, to
hear what Americans there say about the new president's prospects and the country's. The first stop is
Chillicothe, Ohio, where she speaks with three people.
WARD SEYMOUR, a lifelong Republican and council-
man, has retired from the Meade paper plant.
TOM BURKE was born and raised in Chillicothe and
voted for Ross Perot. In 1992, his Crosskeys Tavern
served as an informal headquarters for Ross Perot's
presidential campaign. JEAN KEARNEY was a professor
of educational psychology at Otterbein College in
Westerville, Ohio, and a Democratic councilwoman who
had worked on the Clinton campaign. April 26, 1993

WERTHEIMER: Who are your heroes?

SEYMOUR: Rush Limbaugh and Ollie North, if that tells you
anything.

WERTHEIMER: I guess that tells us something. Mr. Burke?

BURKE: Yes, ma'am. I suppose the former lord mayor of Boston, James Michael Curley, was one of them, and late lord
mayor of Chicago, Richard Daley, was another. Those were
people who knew how to use the system. Presidential timber —
John Kennedy.

WERTHEIMER: There is a little bit of an Irish streak running
through this.

BURKE: It was genetic, yes. I climbed out of the same pool
with my father.

WERTHEIMER: Ms. Kearney?

KEARNEY: My definite hero was John F. Kennedy. John F.

Kennedy stands very high. The second person that has excited me, in terms of politics, really has been Clinton, as far as getting excited. I really hadn't been excited since John F. Kennedy. When Clinton came along I got excited. In terms of the potential, I think I would say Clinton would be my next hero.

WERTHEIMER: A lot of people had a lot of ideas about what they thought Bill Clinton might be able to do. Is he living up to any of those expectations?

SEYMOUR: I don't see where he has done anything. He has failed with Congress, he has backed off on his gays in the service. There are different things that he has backed off on and many promises he has broken, so I really can't see where Mr. Clinton has accomplished anything.

BURKE: I read an article a week after Mr. Clinton was in office, and it was in one of the major publications. I can't remember which one. It said, "Clinton: The Failed Presidency?" The guy had been in office a bloody week, and they were starting to put the nails into his palms. His first major thud in the Congress was when he tried to get an incentives bill or a job-increase bill going. Whether or not it's a good idea is immaterial. The point is that the Congress took this opportunity to slap him around, and say, "Welcome to Washington, rube."

WERTHEIMER: Now, Ross Perot was your man in this race, right?

BURKE: Right, he was.

WERTHEIMER: Not Bill Clinton?

BURKE: No.

WERTHEIMER: But you're prepared to give Clinton the benefit of the doubt, anyway?

BURKE: He is my president. I looked around, and he is the only one I got. So if you don't at least give the man nominal support during the early phases of his presidency, you have no right, three years later, to say, "Throw the bum out."

WERTHEIMER: Ms. Kearney?

KEARNEY: I'm a realist, first of all. This is not a race that Clinton is in. This is a journey. This is a journey that he's on, and this journey that he's on takes time, and you expect some failure because he is willing to take risks. That is why I'm so excited. He's willing to take risks.

WERTHEIMER: What does Bill Clinton need to do for you, right here, in this part of Ohio?

KEARNEY: I would like to see his economic stimulus get going because we have in this community a need for jobs. Whether that job comes through agriculture, or whether or not it comes through manufacture, or whether or not it comes through small services or what have you, or whether or not it comes through PIK [Payment in Kind] programs, where young people would have jobs this summer, we need jobs.

WERTHEIMER: What do you think, Mr. Burke?

BURKE: An economic future that is based on something less fragile than corporate agriculture, although we still have an enormously high percentage of individual-owned farms. Another leg of our economy was manufacturing, but it was heavy-industry manufacturing, aluminum finishing, and paper, these things. These are fading stars.

WERTHEIMER: So a whole new basis?

BURKE: We would hope. Although, any nation which allows its manufacturing's infrastructure to wither and die or move to Mexico, as in our case, cannot for very long claim status as a great nation.

WERTHEIMER: So two votes for jobs being what this area needs.

BURKE: Absolutely.

SEYMOUR: I agree that it needs jobs, but they don't need temporary jobs. We need permanent jobs. Where you get permanent jobs is with tax incentives and different promotions for manufacturers to locate here. You are not going to promote any jobs by giving kids, as well as we need them, three-month jobs. That doesn't cut the mustard. The four billion dollars, I think it was, that was earmarked for summer jobs could be well put into permanent tax credits, things that are really going to put people to work permanently.

WERTHEIMER: Mr. Burke, you mentioned that the newspapers started declaring the Clinton presidency over in the first month. Now it's a little bit past the third month. When you read about Washington, watch on television, listen to the radio, about what is going on there, how do you feel about what you are reading and looking at?

BURKE: In all deference to Mr. Clinton, I consider his to be the most beautiful set of political skills I've seen in a heck of a long time. He's a better politician than John Kennedy. I didn't think I would ever say that anybody could be. He is superb. But at the same time, there is a great difference between campaigning and running the government. That is why I say, if we don't lay back and let the guy have his head for a while, I think we're just absolutely setting him and us up for failure. Either we go with the cat and get the job done, and maybe in four years vote, screaming, "Vote Nazi, vote Republican, vote Independent, vote for Perot." Vote for whomever you want, but give the guy the chance to get the job done, and stop quibbling about the size of his bloody belt buckle.

KEARNEY: We know how politics work. We're not stupid. We all know that each party has things that they want to do. But we also know it's the time for them to pull together, both the Democrats and Republicans, and sit down, and say, "Where can we compromise?" This is not a race between two kids tugging. This is our life, and these are our children's lives that we are really totally losing.

SEYMOUR: You've got to understand who controlled Congress. He has a Democrat-controlled Congress. Reagan had a Democrat-controlled Congress, Bush had a Democratic-controlled Congress. Look back. If you say we are in terrible shape, who put us in terrible shape, economically-wise?

WERTHEIMER: Mr. Burke, I'm going to give you the last word.

BURKE: We have created a system of government where the needs of the nation and the interests of the nation are subordinated to the personal interests of the representatives and

senators in being re-elected. We have created that. I can't remember who the genius was who said a nation will always get
the government they deserve. We have. We are not a nation of
citizens anymore. We are a nation of special interests. As long
as that situation persists, we will have the kind of miserable,
groveling, disgusting government that we have now, which is
spending us into bankruptcy. Even my good buddy Ward, two
blocks away from the Baptist church, will say they're sending
us to hell in a hand basket. We are allowing it. That's a pretty
dismal last word, but I believe in the final analysis that is going
to be the last word. Either we shape up and start kicking some
serious butt up that way or we allow the thing to just trundle
right on down into the cesspool.

Next stop on Route 50: Bedford, Indiana. Linda Wertheimer samples the views of MAE FLORA, of the Broadview Beauty Salon, as well as her professional services. LEE JONES, a friend of Flora's, stops by during the interview. April 28, 1993

FLORA: I want to do everybody's hair I see. I really do. I want to cut their hair or something. I really like it. I work at it at least twelve hours a day, but it's fun and the people are fun. They've always got something to tell you. Not always good, but they've always got something.

WERTHEIMER: Do customers ever talk about health insurance or health care reform?

FLORA: Yes, we do hear a lot about that. Too many people are uninsured.

WERTHEIMER: What kinds of things do you hear?

FLORA: Oh, things like, "Work's not always covering it now" and "It's hard to get insurance." The premiums are so high that a lot of people just can't afford it. A lot of people are uninsured because they can't afford it.

WERTHEIMER: I wonder if you've run into any stories about people who make decisions about their lives that are based on whether or not they have insurance?

FLORA: Probably so. Sometimes I think people get married because they need insurance, serious.

LEE JONES: My daughter just got a divorce, so she is without any health benefits. The children are covered through their father's insurance. She has none.

WERTHEIMER: Do you have any confidence that Mr. Clinton, and Mrs. Clinton, come to that, will be able to come up with something?

JONES: No.

WERTHEIMER: Why not?

JONES: I don't have any trust in him on anything yet. He's not shown me that he's going to be able to do anything yet.

WERTHEIMER: Why do you feel that way?

JONES: I guess because I'm a Republican. It's going to cost somebody.

FLORA: I've never had insurance provided for me, and I've had to buy it all my life on my own, and, believe me, it's a big chunk. It's my biggest bill every month. And it doesn't look like they've done much yet. Although, myself, I think women can get a lot done. She might just pull it off.

WERTHEIMER: Mrs. Clinton, you mean?

FLORA: Yes.

WERTHEIMER: Oh, look at that. You're making me look very fancy. All fluffed up here.

FLORA: Yeah, you're probably not used to that.

Richland Memorial Hospital, in Olney, Illinois, serves people for thirty miles around, in seven counties. Linda Wertheimer interviews Drs. ROBERT EINHORN, a pediatrician, and DON HATTON, an obstetrician, as well as SHARI RUSSELL, a nurse. Dr. Einhorn said that in downstate Illinois he treasures personal relationships with his patients and hopes health care reform won't change that. April 28, 1993

EINHORN: For a rural region there are disincentives for the providers to come here, and the disincentives are that the payments aren't as much as they are anywhere else. We are competing and recruiting providers in this area with suburban areas that may offer a lifestyle that is much more controlled than what mine and Dr. Hatton's certainly is. There is a lot of things about our lifestyle and our hours about which we have no control over. It makes the recruiting more difficult.

WERTHEIMER: Shari Russell, your family has some serious medical problems. Do you feel you are well served in a small town with just a few doctors, where you can't necessarily take your child to a great big city hospital?

RUSSELL: Definitely. I have every confidence in Dr. Einhorn when we visit him about every week. We have had all the kids here. I have had every confidence in Dr. Hatton, and I wouldn't go anywhere else for that kind of health care. With our diabetes, we do travel to St. Louis for the actual diabetes care for both my husband and son, but we still have doctors here that help with that and oversee that. We are completely satisfied and feel like our care is very good here, yes.

WERTHEIMER: One of the big concerns that people have about health care reform is that it might mean that they wouldn't have their own family doctor. Would that be that important to you, in this situation that you're in, where you have to see the doctor quite a bit?

RUSSELL: I think that's extremely important because that is the American way, and we have the freedom to choose. One thing that, as far as I understand, with HMOs that I don't really care for, because if I cannot choose what doctor I am going to go to, I think that's wrong.

EINHORN: I hear a lot of people talking about managed care and managed competition. I will be honest with you. I am not exactly sure what that means. I am not sure what it means for everybody else. I know I am not sure what it means for me here in this situation.

WERTHEIMER: Dr. Hatton?

HATTON: It scares me to death. Any time you get the government and the bureaucracy fiddling around with the health care system, the educational system, the postal system, I don't care what it is, it means we are going downhill, and it scares the life out of me.

WERTHEIMER: One of the problems that health care reformers are trying to solve is the question of the unserved population, people that are uninsured and don't have access to health care. What about those people? Are there people like that in Olney, Illinois?

EINHORN: The access in our little area of the world, I think, is very good. You can walk into any number of physicians' offices, and, in our pediatric offices, anyway, if you have a sick child we will be glad to take care of you and take a look at you.

WERTHEIMER: Even if you can't pay? Even if you don't have insurance?

EINHORN: Even if you can't pay and even if you don't have insurance.

WERTHEIMER: How do you handle that?

EINHORN: We have to absorb those costs, and we pass it on to the people who do pay. It's called cost shifting. It's been going on for ten years, or longer, and that's the way the system has worked.

WERTHEIMER: So what would work best to solve that problem? If those people did have some form of insurance?

EINHORN: To supply insurance for everyone is going to take a few dollars, and that's the big question, isn't it? Where are the dollars going to come from?

....

Farther along Route 50, in Warrensburg, Missouri, several people counseled patience with a new president, as they gathered around MAURINE ACHAUER's kitchen table. In addition to Achauer, who is a psychologist, Linda Wertheimer meets SANDY RUSSELL, a real estate agent; WALTER GUNN, a retired pilot; BILL BERNIER, an executive in a college fraternity; NANCY MANN, who was visiting from Kansas City; and PATRICIA SCOTT, a lawyer, a stockbroker, and a real estate agent.
April 29, 1993

WERTHEIMER: The first one hundred days of the Clinton administration is a traditional time to think about the president and how he is doing, but what I would like to do is ask you all to kind of set a benchmark for me. When you think of presidential leadership, who is the president that comes into your mind as a person who set a standard, I guess I would say, for leadership? Why don't I just ask Sandy Russell to start.

RUSSELL: The first person I think of is Harry Truman because I was born and raised just fifteen, twenty miles from where he lived, and, even though I was child, he was a friend of my grandfather and of that era. I always think of the "Give 'em hell, Harry" style as the true Midwestern style, and I look for that. He is the leader that I recall. Even though I was little, I think of him. That's probably because I have been a lifelong Democrat, and maybe it's ingrained.

WERTHEIMER: Harry Truman, I suppose, would come to a lot of minds in the state of Missouri. Anybody else? Anybody different?

GUNN: I think I would be remiss if I didn't mention Eisenhower. I like President Eisenhower, General Eisenhower. President Eisenhower epitomized the type of leadership we need now. I am a Goldwater conservative, which is somewhat in conflict with a few things that I am looking at now. I strongly feel that we have to give President Clinton a good chance, and a hundred days doesn't do it.

WERTHEIMER: When you think of presidential leadership, what do you think about Bill Clinton?

BERNIER: I think that when he came to the White House he had a long domestic agenda and international problems. The foreign agenda has overtaken him. It sidetracked his focus, and it's a bigger challenge, I am sure, than any of us could imagine, and I am sure a bigger challenge than Bill Clinton imagined.

ACHAUER: To me, Arkansas is part of the Midwest, and to me, it's a phenomenon that we have another person from the Midwest in the White House, like Truman, as you mentioned earlier. I believe they are human people just like we are. I just think he has married a wonderful woman who has been involved in many issues. I am glad we are giving him an opportunity to show that they do care about America somehow. It will work. I am supportive.

MANN: I am supportive as well. I am a Republican. So that may shed a little light on this. I think he is a very focused person. I think he truly wants to do what he has promised to do. I think that he has lost sight of the fact that what he wanted to do and then what he promised to do didn't possibly have the priority that the nation is demanding. I really think that it's the prioritization of the issues that just need to be handled. But he is so focused. He said, "I promised, I'll do this," and he wants to do it.

WERTHEIMER: Patricia, what do you think?

SCOTT: My perception of him is one of a very honest individual. He has his agenda, whether or not it's necessarily mine or yours, and he is trying his best to accomplish that. Whether or not he is successful in doing that is another question, but at this point, I could not question anything he is doing.

WERTHEIMER: Dr. Gunn?

GUNN: He has been stigmatized with the label "Slick Willie." I think that he can rise above any and all of that. I did not vote for the man, but I certainly do want to give him every opportunity to make the best out of the problems as they come to him. He is the only game in town, and I am hoping that he can show some real leadership strength.

WERTHEIMER: We have all had presidents that we have loved. America has had an emotional relationship with its presidents. What do you think about this president? Is this a president this country can love? Is this a president you individually could like?

SCOTT: He has a wonderful little smile. You can't help but like him when you look at him, like him as a person, not necessarily what he is doing, but just as a plain, old Bill Clinton. Yes, I could like him very much.

WERTHEIMER: Bill Bernier?

BERNIER: He is likable enough, but I don't think we are going to hold him in the same regard as we held a Ronald Reagan or a Harry Truman or a John Kennedy or an Eisenhower. I hope we are not going to despise him like Dick Nixon, but I think we are going to be rather ambivalent like George Bush or Jerry Ford or Carter.

WERTHEIMER: Maurine Achauer, it's your house, your kitchen table that we are sitting around here, so you get the last word.

ACHAUER: I agree with what they're saying. I'm a little ashamed at the Republicans that they are not helping him.

WERTHEIMER: You are a little ashamed at the Republicans?

ACHAUER: We have Senator Dole and we have Kassebaum in the neighboring state of Kansas, which seems like it's a game in Washington to get in somebody's way rather than help them do their job as quickly as it can happen. They may have their reasons, but I don't know what they are.

On the last day of her drive down "America's Main Street," Linda Wertheimer stops at BOB BACON's farm in Hutchinson, Kansas. April 30, 1993

WERTHEIMER: What do you do?

BACON: My father and I farm twenty-three hundred acres of dry-land wheat, milo or grain sorghum and corn. In the winter, we do feeder calves that will go to the feed lot in the springtime.

WERTHEIMER: Have you been making a good living farming?

BACON: Well, I have got two nice kids and a nice wife and a nice family, but financially, I would say, "Don't go into agriculture if you want to make a lot of money."

WERTHEIMER: When you look back at Washington and the government in Washington from Kansas, which is the home of the leader of the opposition in the Senate, what do you think about that white marble city back there?

BACON: Oh, kind of like mosquitoes on a hot summer day. They can suck you dry or they can leave you alone. Sometimes I don't like Washington, D.C., at all, and there are other times they're providing a very valuable asset to us out here.

WERTHEIMER: Do you think much about what is going on back there?

BACON: Oh, I think of it all the time. Agriculture is a very global economy, and so what happens in Argentina, what happens in Russia, has a lot more to do with what happens in the next county over. If we don't help Russia, which is a current topic in Washington, I'm in deep trouble. So I'm very concerned about what happens in Washington, D.C.

WERTHEIMER: What do you think about what is happening in Washington, D.C.?

BACON: Oh, politics is a game, and it's a game that has to be played. I wish we would work together a little more than we do at times. If we would all work together, I think sometimes we could accomplish our goal a lot faster.

WERTHEIMER: What would you like to see people working together on? Where would you like to see people get to?

BACON: I think a lot of times we don't know where we want to go. There are so many special interests, and we all want our thing. I would say I am not exuberant, but I am optimistic that Bill Clinton will do the job that we want him to do.

WERTHEIMER: Did you vote for him?

BACON: Yes, but don't tell anybody. I am on the Republican Central Committee here in Reno County, but I was very disillusioned with what George Bush was doing, so I voted for Bill Clinton.

WERTHEIMER: You think you might make a habit of doing something like that?

BACON: It was the first time I ever voted Democrat, but if he does a good job and focuses on the long term, I would vote for Bill Clinton again.

In the great midwestern flood of 1993, a levee collapsed, and six to eight feet of water flowed along the streets of Lemay, Missouri, twenty miles south of St. Louis. FRANKLIN SMITH decided to wait out the flood in his home. He talks with Noah Adams about watching the water rise. July 12, 1993

SMITH: There is a lot of trash floating and a lot of dead worms. There is a city trash-can dumpster floating in front of the house right here, various big pieces of lumber from who-knows-where. We have some park rangers sitting here in a boat. The neighbors' houses are all under water, up to the first floor. Some of them have their windows open, some of them don't. Whatever they had in their yard is floating somewhere. We tried to tie on what we could catch to a fence or whatever we could tie it up to. That's basically it. It's a pretty big mess. We are the only ones left down in here, from what I understand.

ADAMS: So you have lost quite a bit of stuff already?

SMITH: I have put up what I could. It's not done with us yet. Whenever it crests, it may be in my second floor. I don't know. I've put what I could up, squirreled away. I don't even know where half my things are. I can't even find my wallet.

ADAMS: Are there people advising you to go ahead and evacuate to get out?

SMITH: They have been doing that for a good four days, but everything we own is right here. The last flood they had back in the seventies, I wasn't here. My wife was and her father, but people just looted this place pitifully. They were supposed to be patrolling it, and the lower end down here, they just got everything raped. They just took all their belongings and the insurance people didn't want to pay off. Everything I have worked for my whole life is sitting right over here in this house.

ADAMS: So you are there to protect it?

SMITH: To keep an eye on it. Yes, basically.

ADAMS: When the people come by and advise you to leave, do they say that your property will be protected?

SMITH: They haven't actually told me that yet. My father-in-law asked them the other day if they could guarantee that the property would be protected, we would get out, but no one can guarantee that. Nothing. My father-in-law and his brother were here watching the place, four or five guys swam over from the city side, all the way across the river Des Peres onto this levee. They could have taken anything they wanted had these guys not seen them and put the light on them, because they could patrol it down here. I have seen one patrol last night. One patrol is all I seen, and I was up until three or four o'clock this morning.

ADAMS: Now, you wouldn't think looting would be a problem in a situation like that.

SMITH: No, you would think not. But people thrive on disaster.

ADAMS: How much higher do you think the water will come up on that porch where you are?

SMITH: It's got about an inch and a half. Actually, I think it dropped an inch or so last night, but this is the first crest. Now, the second crest will come between now and next week, and they expect another four foot, so we won't be on this porch this time next week. I don't know if we are going to go to the second floor or just get out.

ADAMS: What does the river smell like at that point, where you are?

SMITH: Kerosene or diesel fuel, and every now and then, you will get the stench of rotting protein from the worms floating around. You wouldn't believe the worms that were here yesterday. They're starting to clear out a little bit now.

ADAMS: I know you are in a situation where you'll have to scramble just to keep your head above water when a flood like this happens, but does it make you mad, does it make you angry, does it make you frustrated? How do you feel about it?

SMITH: Right now, I am actually a little confused because I don't think I've felt the full impact of it yet. See, my in-laws, who were here in the seventies for the flood, they know what to expect. I have kind of been going along with that, but it's new to me. The way it came on, my father-in-law tells me it's worse now than it was in the seventies. And this hasn't even finished with us yet. So I'm pretty dazed. I don't know what I'm getting into. I don't know what kind of help I can get from the government, or things like that. I have saved some things. Some things I haven't been able to save.

ADAMS: Is there any kind of help that you could get right now that you could use? Are you getting enough help?

SMITH: I think so far we have been pretty self-supportive here, with the neighbors and all, and we are getting plenty of food. We have got water. They bring us drinking water. I don't know if the county's even aware of it, but our water is on in this house. The rest of the area is down, but we can take baths. Every time I get in the water, or I'm forced to be in the water for some reason or another, I have to go take a bath.

ADAMS: You figure it's diseased? The water?

SMITH: They say it's got hepatitis in it, and you name it, it's probably in there. I can believe it with all these worms and stuff floating around.

Eighty-eight-year-old DAN FLOHR tells Linda Wertheimer about the Great Flood of 1927, when the Mississippi River was out of its banks, covering almost three hundred thousand square miles of land. Dan Flohr is a retired land surveyor who lives in Vicksburg, Mississippi. July 14, 1993

WERTHEIMER: Mr. Flohr, Vicksburg, as I understand it, was not flooded in 1927. Is that right?

FLOHR: That's right. We were on the hills.

WERTHEIMER: So you were looking down at the Mississippi?

FLOHR: Yes, ma'am. The city runs along the west edge of the town.

WERTHEIMER: What did it look like from the town?

FLOHR: There wasn't a lot to look at, just that muddy water over on the other side of the sea wall. And as far west as you could see, it was just water.

WERTHEIMER: What do you remember about the flood? You were a Boy Scout. Did the Boy Scouts get out and do anything?

FLOHR: What my assignment was, and what we did primarily was, when the people came from the flooded areas on the boats and the barges, we helped them load them up on the army trucks and take them out to the camps.

WERTHEIMER: I suppose that the people who came out of that flood must have had stories to tell.

FLOHR: Oh, sure. There was a black lady, and she had eight or ten children, and one of the youngest ones was missing when they got to Vicksburg, and, they were all distressed over it and crying and carrying on, like they can. It was some time later that a barge came in with people that had this one particular little boy that they didn't know who he belonged to, so we took him up there to the camp, and, sure enough, it was this woman's boy.

WERTHEIMER: Mr. Flohr, I wonder if you could describe it for me. Can you just sort of take your mind all the way back to all those years ago and think of what those barges looked like and what the river looked like and the people looked like?

FLOHR: The barges were uncovered barges. They went back into the backwater areas and just got these people and brought them out of there.

WERTHEIMER: How did the barges move? What powered them?

FLOHR: They were tied to the big riverboats.

WERTHEIMER: When you say "riverboat," what do you mean? You mean those big paddle wheels?

FLOHR: Paddle-wheel boats, yes, ma'am. There were steamboats in those days.

WERTHEIMER: They were bringing strings of barges loaded with people and their possessions down to Vicksburg?

FLOHR: They would go right across what had been fields with those big old steamboats. Now the Mississippi riverboats don't draw much water. They only draw about four feet of water. The water could be rather shallow and the steamboats couldn't go back in there.

WERTHEIMER: So those paddle-wheel steamers just could go right across somebody's farm and not even get caught?

FLOHR: That's right, and they did.

HENRY SWEETS tells Noah Adams how Hannibal,
Missouri, home of Mark Twain, handled the
Great Flood of 1993. Sweets is the director of the
Mark Twain Museum. July 1, 1993

ADAMS: When you look out the window of the Mark Twain
Museum, what can you see?

SWEETS: As one looks towards the river, the thing that is
most noticeable is when you look at the Illinois side, the far
side, you just don't see a shoreline anymore. There are many
trees, and the water is up around the bottoms of the trees, so the
trees are just floating out in the water, and Mark Twain com-
mented at one point in time that, speaking of the Mississippi,
"I've seen this river so wide that it had only one bank." That's
the feeling you get. You know where you are standing, but you
don't see where the other side is anymore.

ADAMS: Now you have in Hannibal a flood wall.

SWEETS: We built a flood wall that was completed just last
November. With the earlier flood this year and with this one,
we have now given it two tests.

ADAMS: It's holding?

SWEETS: It's holding so far.

ADAMS: It's high tourist season, or would have been, were it
not for the flood. Have people been coming?

SWEETS: The weekend that includes the Fourth of July in
Hannibal is National Tom Sawyer Day, and we expect huge
crowds, and I think we will have them. Many of the activities
had to be rescheduled because many of them are down closer to
the river, on the river side of the flood wall, which is of course
totally inaccessible right now. But nothing has been canceled.
Everything is going ahead, and I think we are still going to have

a pretty crowd of people here for the Fourth of July celebration.

ADAMS: Now, you would officially have to be an optimist in this situation?

SWEETS: We really haven't noticed a tremendous drop in our attendance so far this spring, even though we've had these long periods of flooding conditions. At the immediate situation, we are going to see some changes because there are highways around us that are being closed as water goes over the highways, so with people knowing that there is that type of flooding going on, I do expect that we are going to start dropping off some.

ADAMS: Earlier, you made reference to something that Mark Twain said about the bank of the Mississippi. Did he write much about flooding on the river?

SWEETS: At the time that Mark Twain was living in Hannibal, flooding really wasn't the problem that it is today. Since Mark Twain lived here, they have built the many levees along the river, which confine the river. And when the rainwaters come along, they are confined and they get much deeper. Mark Twain made some remarks at a dinner that was honoring his sixty-seventh birthday in 1902, and he spoke of a friend who lived just upriver from Hannibal at a town called Warsaw, Illinois. Speaking of the Mississippi there, he said, "Well, it was an emotional bit of the Mississippi. If it is low water, you have to climb up to the town on a ladder, and when it floods, you have to hunt for it with a deep-sea lead," referring to the fact that the river can vary so much from one season to another.

ADAMS: He would have probably figured that a modern-day flood would be a great chance for a writer to really tear into a bit of prose.

SWEETS: In his book *Life on the Mississippi*, Mark Twain was aware of efforts to build wing dams and to build some regulating chutes and to try to control the river, and his comment was pretty much that it was going to be futile because the river was too powerful and would overcome them. Today we do have pretty good protection in terms of a levee system up and down the river, but just this morning, a section of the levee broke north of Hannibal, and there are about a thousand acres of farmland that have gone underwater, so perhaps Mark Twain's prediction of being able to control the river still has some merit today.

MEGAN EDWARDS and MARK SEDENQUIST lost
their home and most of their inventory from their toy
business when the Los Angeles fire raged through
their neighborhood in October 1993. Several weeks
later, on Thanksgiving Day, they speak with
Noah Adams about starting over with practically
nothing. November 25, 1993

SEDENQUIST: In some ways it's kind of fun. In some ways
it's kind of tragic. It's like being right out of college again, only
with about twenty years of experience and life history behind
us.

EDWARDS: It's sort of a clean slate all of a sudden. Not the
way I would want to have a clean slate, but there it is. All our
options are open.

ADAMS: And you have no children?

EDWARDS: No, just one dog.

ADAMS: And how did the dog do?

EDWARDS: He was very scared the morning of the fire, and,
in fact, it was that dog that made me leave. He started crying
and almost screaming.

ADAMS: What kind of dog is it?

EDWARDS: A little white cockapoo named Marvin.

ADAMS: So Marvin was your warning system here?

SEDENQUIST: Marvin was.

EDWARDS: It was beginning to dawn on me that this was
getting a little too hot for comfort. But Marvin knew, and he
was saying "Let's get out of here."

ADAMS: Is there any object from that fire that was destroyed,
any family heirloom that you still think, after a month, is price-
less, that you really do wish you would have had a chance to
jump back in that fire and bring it out?

SEDENQUIST: Oh, sure. Lots of stuff.

EDWARDS: Lots of things.

SEDENQUIST: Not only our own life of collecting, but we had gifts and mementos that our grandparents and great-grandparents owned. There's a lot of accumulated stuff that we can't replace no matter what we had.

EDWARDS: With extreme difficulty a couple of months ago, we had moved in my grandmother's piano. It just made me very sad to think that if I hadn't moved that piano two months ago, it would still be where it used to be in Elsa's house.

ADAMS: I guess twenty years from now you will look back on this Thanksgiving, good or bad, and this will be the one you will remember.

EDWARDS: Yes, it will stand out in stark relief. I really am thankful that I am picking a turkey today and that I can and that I have a place to do it.

ADAMS: But you don't have your favorite cooking equipment there?

EDWARDS: No, and the cookbooks and the recipes left from grandmothers and other people like that, those are gone. That makes me kind of sad because she had great dressing recipes and things like that. I am sure other people in my family have them, but I had some in her handwriting.

SEDENQUIST: We had planned to have the Thanksgiving dinner at our house, but as soon as the fire burned that down, then we moved it to my folks' house. We are actually really enjoying the fact that today is Thanksgiving and thankful that we got the essentials out, which was us. We are going to really enjoy Thanksgiving.

CURTIS BOYD has performed abortions for twenty-five years and has been harassed and picketed during the course of his work. He spoke with Linda Wertheimer a day after Dr. David Gunn was shot to death by the abortion opponent Michael F. Griffin outside a family planning clinic in Pensacola, Florida. March 11, 1993

WERTHEIMER: Dr. Boyd, first of all, are you concerned about your own personal safety? Do you think something could happen to you like the attack on Dr. Gunn?

BOYD: Yes, I do have some concerns. I think many other health care providers do also, not just physicians. I think counselors, administrators, nurses, medical technicians, have all been subject to this harassment, and objects of the violence at times.

WERTHEIMER: What is it like to make the decision to keep going? You have been doing this for years. Can you just see a point at which you decide you can't deal with it anymore?

BOYD: No, as long as there is a need, I will continue. It's sometimes frightening, it's sometimes infuriating. But I think it's important that you know how deeply rewarding my work is, and I think that's one reason many people continue to provide it. I spent the first ten years of my professional life as a family practitioner in a small town in rural east Texas, and I tended my patients in birth and death, illness and injury. I loved my work and was, in turn, both loved and respected. But few of those patients, who were whole extended families I knew by name, thanked with the depth of feeling that women whom I have never met before, and will probably never see again, thanked me when I have completed their abortions. That kind of reaction, I think, sustains many people providing abortion services.

WERTHEIMER: When you say you have been threatened and harassed, could you tell us what you mean?

BOYD: The worst of this harassment began in the 1980s as a current upsurge. But through that period of time, I have always had picketing. But in addition to that, we have had Operation Rescue invade our clinic. On several occasions, we have had people break in, chain themselves to the furniture and the tables and vandalize. We have had the clinic burned, a bad arson on one occasion, on a Christmas Eve night. The next Christmas Eve, there was another small arson in which the fire was put out. We have had numerous death threats, handwritten notes placed in my mailbox at home. I have had threats by telephone, by letter, the whole gamut, most anything you can think of.

WERTHEIMER: I understand that a Wanted poster, very much like the one which pictured Dr. David Gunn, has been issued with your picture on it.

BOYD: Yes, that was passed out in a neighborhood, and I believe that my name is on their current list. They have a list, which is a frightening thing, of doctors that have been especially targeted. This is mostly Operation Rescue and various branch groups of Operation Rescue. They are now springing up, a number of them with different names, such as Rescue America, which is thought to be associated with Dr. Gunn's murder.

WERTHEIMER: Do you think the situation for you has changed at all with the election of President Clinton, and the president's decision to revoke some of the executive orders on abortion which have been put in place by President Bush and President Reagan?

BOYD: Temporarily that may be true. It seems that the level of harassment has gone up in the last few months. There is quite an escalation, I think, in the violence, and Operation Rescue has stepped up its level of activity, and those affiliated groups that I mentioned.

The gay veteran PAUL HARDMAN talks with Noah
Adams about his experience in the military. Paul
Hardman founded the Alexander Hamilton American
Legion Post 448 in San Francisco nine years ago for
gay veterans. January 27, 1993

ADAMS: Mr. Hardman, you are hearing all these complaints,
all these objections to Mr. Clinton's proposed lifting of the ban.
Do you see merit in some of the arguments?

HARDMAN: There is no merit in them at all. They are the
same arguments they used back in 1941 when they wanted to
lift the ban on African Americans serving in the military, and
they use exactly the same language, even "esprit de corps,"
"living in close quarters." Interestingly enough, they said it
would be OK. In those days they used the word *Negroes* to serve
parenthetically as "mess attendants." So it's nonsense.

ADAMS: Chairman Colin Powell of the Joint Chiefs of Staff
says this argument, this connection between the admission of
blacks and the discrimination against blacks in the armed services isn't comparable in this situation with gays.

HARDMAN: I would beg to differ with him. Prejudice is prejudice regardless of whether it's color or sexual orientation. In
my point of view, it's all a natural phenomenon, whether you
are black or whether you are gay or straight.

ADAMS: But the senior military leadership surely cannot be
ignored. Senator Dan Coats of Indiana says it appears that a
president without military background or experience is dis-
missing the advice and counsel of America's most distin-
guished military leaders.

HARDMAN: That's perfect nonsense. There always have
been gay people in the military service. The fact that they want
to recognize it today doesn't change the experience. The mili-

tary did not suffer because gay people were in the military. In fact, I think they benefited by it. Their own reports, which the Pentagon had prepared between 1957 and 1991, show that the homosexuals did quite well. And the most recent one that was done in June 1992 shows that, in many cases, homosexuals were superior in their military service, and the word *superior* is the word that's used in that Government Accounting Office report.

ADAMS: You mentioned you were in the service for six years. Where did you serve?

HARDMAN: In the Atlantic, the Pacific, and the Gulf of Mexico, in the South Pacific.

ADAMS: In the navy?

HARDMAN: In the navy.

ADAMS: And were you openly gay?

HARDMAN: No. We are talking about 1940 to 1945. You were discreet. You minded your own business, you did your duty and you don't misbehave and you succeed.

ADAMS: A couple of months ago on this program, we talked with David Hackworth, a retired army colonel, a highly decorated veteran of several wars. He said his personal experience is about twenty years out of date, but he does stay in touch. Here is an example he gave of the argument that you can hear within the military.

Recently, a first sergeant in a rival company in Korea molested a number of young eighteen-year-old boys. This first sergeant had twenty-five years service, a very big vested interest, but there he was in Korea in a situation where he couldn't go to the kind of surroundings that he wanted to go to and he couldn't control himself. It destroyed that company's combat effectiveness, not for a week or two, but for a long, long period of time.

Now that would be an extreme example. It probably speaks more to the fear if not the fact of what's going on now.

HARDMAN: You don't have people striking out against homosexuality unless they themselves are so insecure in their own sexuality. It isn't an issue unless you make it one.

ADAMS: Colonel Hackworth is talking about the military concept known as unit cohesion, though.

HARDMAN: He may be right and for his own point view, but I saw a program last night, *MacNeil/Lehrer Newshour*, where they had a thirty-year experienced submarine captain who had a totally different point of view, and he discussed the subject quite openly and quite logically. They had no trouble at all in his experience in the years that he was on this particular submarine; and he knew of people who were homosexual, but there was no conduct problem.

ADAMS: You do see the argument, though, that it could be disruptive in some situations?

HARDMAN: The only reason there would be any problem is if there weren't proper discipline. Discipline is the name of the game in the military. You just don't tolerate improper conduct. But you don't punish a class of people for what they naturally are, particularly if you want to get the benefit of their outstanding service.

ELIZABETH SUSSERE of Mesa, Arizona, and BRIAN LOCKE of Corinth, Mississippi, telephoned their senators, both of whom serve on the Senate Armed Services Committee, to voice their opposition to the lifting of the ban on homosexuals in the military. They told Robert Siegel why the ban should not be lifted. January 27, 1993

SIEGEL: I would like to ask Elizabeth Sussere first, what moved you to call your senator's office today?

SUSSERE: I am totally against lifting the ban on homosexuals, and I felt that it was really time to start speaking out, especially since this was going to be effective on a national level.

SIEGEL: What do you mean by "on a national level"? Why was that particularly troubling to you?

SUSSERE: Rather than individual states making up their minds how they want to handle certain issues, especially dealing with homosexuals, this was something that was going to be on a national level; and I didn't want this to lead to other things being decided.

SIEGEL: What other things might you be concerned about?

SUSSERE: I believe it would filter down to how children are taught in schools. I believe it would start affecting local legislation of certain bills of how to treat homosexuals, and I just feel it could have a very great impact. I did not want this to be passed on a national level without having individual people speaking, especially since so many voices are saying, "No, do not do this," and yet what I am hearing is that President Clinton seems very determined to keep this promise, even though he's broken others already, to keep this promise to pass this no matter what we say.

SIEGEL: Have you called your senator before?

SUSSERE: No, I haven't.

SIEGEL: This was the first issue that moved you in this way.

SUSSERE: Right.

SIEGEL: Mr. Locke, you are a former member of the service, spent ten years in active duty and reserves.

LOCKE: Yes, sir, I did. I spent four years in the United States Air Force at Keesler Air Force Base, Mississippi. Then I went on to college, and I served with the Tennessee Air National Guard and also the Army Reserve.

SIEGEL: What prompted you to call Senator Lott's office?

LOCKE: I believe that the president is making a major decision that is not representative of the United States. The majority of the people think the decision is going to be a detriment to morale, the efficiency of the military, especially the esprit de corps of the military. I felt that it was important for me to call the senator and let him know how I felt, as a member of the military, a former member of the military. Also, I grew up in the military. My father was a twenty-seven-year veteran of the United States Air Force, and I felt like this would be a major blow against the efficacy of the military.

SIEGEL: So when people speak of a military culture that people feel very strongly about in the service, you would be a product of that culture?

LOCKE: That's correct.

SIEGEL: Elizabeth Sussere, how would you answer the argument that what we are talking about here is an extension and, in the view of some, a natural extension of civil rights protection to individuals?

SUSSERE: I don't agree with that because I believe it is preferential treatment. When a man or a woman is walking into the military or even to a place of business, they are not wearing something that says what their sexual preference is or how they like to make love, no matter what type of sex it is. I believe coming out of the closet and having people come out and say that they are homosexuals and that they want to have certain rights, first of all, they are labeling how they participate in sex, and they are bringing it very much out into the open. They have their civil liberties protected, so why do they feel that they need to have their sexual preferences protected too?

SIEGEL: You are saying, if they would be discreet and not advertise their sexuality, there would be no problem?

SUSSERE: Right. I do not believe that they are really asking for us to be tolerant of them because there has been tolerance before. I believe that they are looking for our approval. For example, if someone were to have, like, Nazi views and they were to tell you this, you could be tolerant of them and just let them go their way, and say, "No, I believe you are wrong." But if that same person came to you, and said, "Look, I want to come into your place of business, I want to hang up my Nazi flag. I want to teach your children in school what my Nazi views are," that's a totally different subject. And I feel that's exactly the same way with the homosexual issue.

SIEGEL: Brian Locke, in all those years in the service, you must have known people or known of people who are homosexuals.

LOCKE: Yes, sir, quite a few that were known to be homosexuals, and they practiced their sexual preference. I was a barracks sergeant with about fifty men in one row of barracks, and it made the men very uncomfortable. The men, because of their personal upbringing, their religious upbringing, their sexual preferences, preferred not to be around these men. Therefore, it was very difficult for me to assign tasks to men when they were working with homosexuals. That's where I believe the efficacy or the efficiency of the military would be torn apart.

SIEGEL: How do you answer the argument that forty years ago people would have said the same thing about racial desegregation and it was up to people to learn how to work with those people?

LOCKE: Forty years ago and today, I believe, the homosexual issue is much the same. It is an aberrant lifestyle. When you start getting into the bedroom things, I think you are going too far. You can work with people. You can enjoy their company. You can do things publicly, but when you start mandating to accept their sexual preferences, I believe that the country or whoever's mandating it has gone way too far.

SIEGEL: If you were to be presented with a policy that simply ended any effort to try to root out who the homosexuals were, to try to probe and find out what people's private lives were, would you approve of ending that kind of effort and barring that kind of effort? No other guarantees, just that. Elizabeth Sussere?

SUSSERE: No, I believe you still have to decide who is coming into your military and who is going to be rooming with whom, and what type of person they are. You would not stop asking an officer what his character was and what type of person he was because that's important to his job and so is this.

LOCKE: I have to agree with Elizabeth. She is very eloquent and very well spoken, and she pretty much says what I believe from my heart.

The journalists ROBERT MACNEIL, of *The MacNeil/
Lehrer Newshour* on PBS, and TOM WICKER,
formerly of the *New York Times,* tell Scott Simon what
it was like to witness the assassination of President
Kennedy in Dallas on November 22, 1963.
November 20, 1993

SIMON: We have heard over the years, of course, those of us
a little bit younger but still old enough to remember it, certainly
know what a dangerous place Dallas was considered to be. Adlai
Stevenson had been attacked by a group of demonstrators just,
I guess, a few weeks before. Did you just assume it was the
report from a motorcycle? Was the whole notion of somebody
firing shots at a presidential motorcade inconceivable?

MACNEIL: It was so inconceivable to me. When the shots
were fired, I was in the first of the two press buses, right up at
the front, and I heard the shots, and then got the bus to stop and
got out. Even in the few minutes of running around, I didn't
believe Kennedy had been hit. My assumption was that some
individual had fired shots as a kind of protest, and that was fixed
in my mind. I got out of the bus. Then I ran around the corner,
and Kennedy's car had disappeared under the underpass, and I
noticed the police running up the grassy knoll. So I ran with
them, thinking they were chasing someone, a gunman. When I
got to the top there was nothing but empty railroad tracks there.
I figured I better find a place to phone and say what I knew. I ran
along the top of the grassy knoll, looking for a phone. The first
place I came to that looked as though it might have a phone was
the Texas Book Depository. Not knowing it had anything to do
with anything, I ran up the steps, and as I did, a young man came
out, and I said, "Where's there a phone? Where's there a phone?"

and he said, "You better ask inside." That's when I did that first report. It was just about three minutes after the shots.

SIMON: William Manchester, for one, established to his satisfaction that you, unbeknownst to you, encountered Lee Harvey Oswald.

MACNEIL: I discussed that with Manchester at the time. I have no way of knowing that the young man I stopped for and asked for a phone at the top of the steps was Oswald, because by not concentrating on him, I didn't have a clear image of him in my mind. Manchester went over the ground very thoroughly, and he told me that, as Oswald was interviewed by the Secret Service that evening, that he said that a young, blond, crew-cut Secret Service man ran up the steps and asked for a phone. I was young and blond and had a short haircut, and Oswald may have mistook me for that.

SIMON: I want to talk a bit if I could about the John F. Kennedy that we know and cherish to this day and about some of the changes in his image in the public mind that have occurred over the past thirty years. For example, I don't know how much was known about the state of his health, but we now know, of course, that it was not only bad, but that he was taking a number of drugs that can powerfully affect mood and even powers of judgment. This was, of course, a man who had the nuclear codes in a satchel next to his desk. Was the press responsible in not pursuing some questions about his health?

WICKER: I think so. It had been alleged during his 1960 campaign, I think, by the man who became vice president, Lyndon Johnson, or his staff, that the president had Addison's disease, which he very vigorously denied. I think to a large extent, the press was culpable in not following up, not examining, not questioning more closely that. But 1963 was a very different time from now. We had not yet had the disillusionments of Vietnam. We had not had Watergate. We had not had many of the things that have brought the presidency quite low in public estimation by comparison to what it was in 1963.

MACNEIL: Young people talking to me today say, "Why was

it never reported that the president was such a philanderer?" It wasn't the kind of thing one reported in those days, unless there was some egregious behavior that couldn't be ignored. If Judith Exner had come out in public the way the woman who alleged the twelve-year affair with Clinton did during the 1992 campaign, certainly the press would have covered that, and it would have been one hell of a story, and perhaps would have led to a lot of other questions and disclosures. But nobody did come forward.

SIMON: Let me explain that she was also the intimate companion of Sam Giancana, who was head of the Chicago Mob, and to say the least, this would raise questions about national security.

WICKER: I can't imagine any reporter, even in 1963 or 1863, for that matter, if he had proof that the president of the United States was involved with a woman, who at the same time, was involved with the Mafia, I can't imagine any reporter who wouldn't have printed that story. But we didn't have it. At least I didn't, and I don't think anybody did.

SIMON: Is it a little easier thirty years later to talk about this as being one of the biggest stories you ever covered.

WICKER: This kind of reminiscence comes along, not every year, but certainly on anniversary periods. You almost get to the point where your buttons are pressed, and you roll out whatever you have to say. But I recall on November 22, 1963, in Dallas, I was dictating my story to the *New York Times* from a telephone booth, and as I began to dictate my first words, "President Kennedy has been shot ...," I burst into tears. I had not expected to do that. I had not realized that I felt that way. I had not been a particularly deep, close friend or admirer of President Kennedy as a White House correspondent. It was just the absolute horrendous fact that somehow, this young leader, the president of the United States, had been cut down that way, in a way very few living Americans had ever known or could conceive. It was just an overpowering moment.

At 104 and 102, sisters SADIE DELANY and Dr. BESSIE DELANY live a life of quiet simplicity in a suburb just north of New York City. Their father, Henry, was a slave until he was six years old, before becoming the first elected black bishop in the Episcopal Church. Sadie became the first black woman to teach home economics in the New York City school system. Bessie became the city's second black woman dentist. The Delany sisters talk with Liane Hansen about their lives and their autobiography, *Having Our Say*, beginning with Bessie's memory of the imposition of the Jim Crow laws in 1896. She said it was the day everything changed, starting with taking a ride on a trolley in Raleigh, North Carolina. November 28, 1993

BESSIE: Of course we always ran up to the front and sat with the motorman because the wind would blow your hair and you felt free. He said, "You'll have to go to the rear of the car," although he knew us because we would go out there every year. I said, "Well, we don't want to sit at the back." And he said, "Well, it's the law. You have to sit in the back." Under protest I went back. It was nothing strange for me to protest anything I didn't like. And I am that way today. If I don't like it, I say, "I don't like that. I don't think that's fair. I don't think it's honest. And I don't mind saying so. I will contend it with you." I haven't changed very much, I don't think. Except that my mind is not quite as quick as it used to be.

HANSEN: There was one point in your life when you were young, you had graduated from college, and you were teaching, and you really almost got yourself lynched.

SADIE: Yes. I was going down to Brunswick, Georgia, to teach at Saint Athanasius School, and there was nobody around, and I had nice hair. It was kinky, but I liked that and so it pleased me. I have always had hair that went down to my waist or below. So I was in the waiting room, the colored waiting room.

BESSIE: You were changing trains.

SADIE: It was Waycross, Georgia, I will never forget it. I was sitting there, and I had my hair down. There were two other girls from New York who were coming down to go to Saint Athanasius. So I combed my hair, and this white man who was drunk came in. He thought he was going to have a little fun, but he picked the wrong person to have his fun with. So as soon as he saw me he began. And so I just rose up in my seat, and my hair was hanging down. I said, "You go back over in your department and play with your white women." I said, "I don't want any part of you." And he said, "Oh, the nigger bitch has insulted me." And he cried. It wasn't long before the people began to gather together. The two girls from New York left me, and I was there by myself. The station had a man who kept the station clean, a colored. He came, and said, "What did you do to that man?" I said, "I told him to go back and play with his own people. Don't come playing with me because I have no time for play." They were gathering out there like everything, but I didn't mind. I have never been afraid to die. I don't believe in any pussyfooting. If I tell you anything, it is so. And I think that my people helped establish America as much as yours, and maybe more. I have got as much right to it as you have, and I want my part. And I am going to fight for it and contend for it.

BESSIE: You don't always get it when you do that.

SADIE: No, but I let them know I have been there. At least I let them know I have an opinion, and I have a right to it.

HANSEN: How did you get out of this predicament with the mob that was gathering?

SADIE: My Heavenly Father took care of me just as he always does. It was time for the train that carried us to Brunswick, Georgia. It was time for it to come on, and these people were very much excited. But I do think that some of them realized that he was drunk. I hadn't done anything to the man. But I was all ready, and we got on the train and went on to Saint Athanasius.

HANSEN: Tell us how you got the job at Theodore Roosevelt High School.

SADIE: They had a list and you get on the list and it's the first three on the list. It's according to grade. They sent them to the high school, and they could select anyone. Naturally, they would select the highest. So they sent my name with the others. And there was a fellow, my brother's friend, who went down to the board of education, and they said to tell me to come and interview. He told my brother, "You tell Sadie not to go for that interview because if they find out she is colored they will take the next one that is white." I was at the head of the list, so when they wrote me to come, I just didn't appear. They thought nothing of it, and they appointed me. When school opened, I appeared that day. It was too late to do anything. I was appointed.

HANSEN: Do you think the world still needs to be changed, Bessie?

BESSIE: Oh, of course.

HANSEN: How would you do it?

BESSIE: The first thing I would do, I would say if people are wise enough to be able to get to be one hundred, after that no more taxes. That would be the first thing I would do. They have earned it. They ought not to have this responsibility of wondering, How in the world am I going to do this? Things ought to be easier for them if they live to be one hundred and have been honest and taken care of their civil duties, like they ought to. That would be the first thing I would do. The next thing, I think I certainly would try to have America do what it was planned they should do. America was built on the foundation that all men were created equal. I would try to put that more into practice.

HANSEN: How about you, Sadie? One of the reasons that you have said you have written this book is you want people to know your story and to change. "To help people," wasn't that your family motto? "Your job is to help somebody." What do you think needs to be changed in the world?

SADIE: I think that we could be kinder to one another, and I think we need a little more religion than we have.

BESSIE: Don't get me started on that.

SADIE: I am awfully afraid that they are going to be so disappointed when that time comes. It seems to me something ought to be done about that. They don't care a thing about religion.

BESSIE: Very important.

SADIE: We think along the same lines, but we have a different way of meeting together. But we agree fundamentally on what ought to be done, but we don't always agree how it should be done.

HANSEN: After all this time, what do you have to be thankful for?

BESSIE: Oh, just being alive.

SADIE: Everything.

BESSIE: Just everything. We don't have any complaints against the Almighty. I don't know why he works it out this way, but if it pleases him, I will make do with it.

SADIE: We are very happy.

BESSIE: We are. Lately I haven't had as much time to myself as I would like to have.

SADIE: But if you can help others, it's worth it, I think.

BESSIE: Well, I don't know. After you get to one hundred I think you ought to be allowed to do exactly what you want to do.

ENDERS

BILL HARNEY is an Australian aborigine, one of the Wardaman people, who runs tours in the town of Katherine, in Australia's Northern Territory. A traditional lawman, storyteller, interpreter of dreams, and a musician, he explains some of his people's customs: ceremonies called laws, marriage with mates old enough to be one's grandparents, strict rules against straying across the Wardaman's boundaries into the lands of neighboring aboriginal groups. He plays a pair of boomerangs as clapsticks and a hand-painted wooden trumpet called a didgeridoo and describes for Robert Siegel how the instrument is made and on what occasions it is played. October 8, 1993

SIEGEL: Now, tell me about your didgeridoo.

HARNEY: All right.

SIEGEL: It's a long, wooden tube —

HARNEY: Well, a didgeridoo is a long tree that we chop in the country, in the bush. First they use this on a burial site meeting. Then everybody get together, and they hold this big ceremony, and they do the dance, and then take the dead person's clothes, and that's when they destroy everything and bury him into the ground also. Then right after, they use a boomerang then in the night, to chase the spirits away.

SIEGEL: To chase the spirits away?

HARNEY: They chase the spirits away in the night. That's where the boomerang and didgeridoo work together.

SIEGEL: Now, the piece of music that you played for us on the didgeridoo, for what occasion might you play that at home? What would that music be used for?

HARNEY: It's a part for when the old fellow get married. In our country, the old men must get married to young girl.

SIEGEL: Old men must marry young women?

HARNEY: Yeah. One gal from fourteen year old, marry old man, round about seventy.

SIEGEL: Seventy-year-old men marry fourteen-year-old girls?

HARNEY: Fourteen-year-old girls. Later, when these old men die, the young girl goes back and marries young boy. But first, when she is with that old man, she learns all the laws and it keeps her under control.

SIEGEL: You're saying that the way that your people see to it that teenage girls learn how to behave well is they get married to old men?

HARNEY: Old men, yeah, that's right. Then also, young boy, eighteen-year-old young boy —

SIEGEL: Who do they marry?

HARNEY: He marry old lady. Old lady could be sixty, seventy-year-old. He still must marry because that's what the laws say. And when he's with the old lady, there's not the divorce or anything with the aborigine in the country. That's why when they marry young and old, they don't fight, because with the two young ones, if they fight, they break the law. That's why the young and old must marry all the way. But later when the old lady dies, the young boy, that's when he can go back and marry young one.

SIEGEL: I see. Now when you were a young man of eighteen —

HARNEY: I had eighty-year-old lady.

SIEGEL: You had an eighty-year-old wife, yes?

HARNEY: Yeah, eighty. And she was a wonderful old lady. I was only eighteen, and she taught me everything, what I wanted to see, and here I am.

SIEGEL: And you have three sons.

HARNEY: Yeah, three sons. After the old lady died, then I married the young one.

SIEGEL: The young one.

HARNEY: Yeah.

SIEGEL: But have any of your sons married yet?

HARNEY: No. But one of them is about twenty now. Young Billy is twenty. He already had a promised wife, but the old lady died before he even got married. And then with the aboriginal law, again you don't choose any girl.

SIEGEL: It's arranged.

HARNEY: It's arranged marriage, yeah.

SIEGEL: Do you marry someone in your second marriage whom you fell in love with, who is more your age, or is that arranged also?

HARNEY: Well, that's all arranged also. But it's what I call "nicking off" in the side. That's still operating like nicking off in the side.

SIEGEL: Nicking off?

HARNEY: Nicking off, yes.

SIEGEL: When you go off to the side?

HARNEY: When you go off and chase another girl.

SIEGEL: I see, one who is a little bit more your own age.

HARNEY: A lot of that's still around, but you mustn't be seen by anyone. If you get caught by someone, and you have been chasing another girl, then the big trouble starts.

SIEGEL: Ah! And then is there a law in that case?

HARNEY: A law, of course. A big boomerang flies every-where. Then at the big ceremonial meeting, they take him along and they give him a bit of understanding not to do that sort of thing. But you don't see much of that sort of thing because everyone is satisfied more or less with three and four wives.

SIEGEL: Why complain, you're saying.

HARNEY: Yes, why complain? [laughs]

SIEGEL: Let me ask you about the laws that operate for the Wardaman people. You are a lawman?

HARNEY: Yes, I am what they call a custodian with the group. Also I am a singer. I sing for the rain to come down, I could sing for the rain to go away, and also I could to sing for anybody who was sick. The spiritual song goes inside and gets rid of all the sickness of his body. Also there is no operating on an aboriginal lady. They always have some singer come and be with a woman who is giving birth. And the old man, the singer, brings the kids out. No operating.

SIEGEL: You mean when a woman is giving birth?

HARNEY: Yes.

SIEGEL: An old man would go and —

HARNEY: And sing to expand everything inside.

SIEGEL: So that the baby could come out?

HARNEY: So the baby can come out, yes.

SIEGEL: It sounds as though music is very important in a whole variety of activities. That is, as you say ceremonies about rain and also weddings, but in many different activities.

HARNEY: Yes, many different ones, yes. The guy that sings all of that to make atmosphere happy in all the world. It's the spirit of his song. The voice should go out in the air and make the whole land happy and you get all different season, food comes up, the rain comes up the right way, and all the leaves and stuff. If you didn't do that, the atmosphere, the spirits, would get real cranky and then make a big tornado. But we still have a song to stop that also.

SIEGEL: To stop the tornado?

HARNEY: To stop the tornado. If we get bad lightning, we still have a song to stop the lightning. He take notice of the song.

SIEGEL: Why is it so important to make sure that people don't go beyond the boundaries? Is this to keep other people out, or to keep people of your own group in?

HARNEY: It's to keep the own group in, to keep every individual, their own different tribes, in their own community. But if they want to cross over the border and just go in and out like they wandering around, that wasn't right, because they could be destroying their big ceremonial area and all this sort of stuff because they have lots of aboriginal arts in the country.

SIEGEL: Yes.

HARNEY: And if we went along, we mustn't see what to the heart they look like.

SIEGEL: You mustn't look at those?

HARNEY: Yeah, we mustn't look at them, unless we got it by

them, and they explain it to us. To just go look at them, we could get sick.

SIEGEL: If you see somebody else's, another group's art, you mean?

HARNEY: Yeah.

SIEGEL: On a stone or somewhere, you could get sick by seeing the spirits that are in touch there.

HARNEY: Yeah.

SIEGEL: So you have to stay within your group to be safe?

HARNEY: Yeah, more safer. You can't just go along and drink water in an another next-door neighbor place because it is spiritual in there also with that song, what they call it, a dreaming waterfall. If you drink this while walking, you can get sick from that water and die, because there's spirits in it. Or if you're walking away, just going away, you could just — spirits can pick up that water and then the water will all go dry.

SIEGEL: The water could disappear?

HARNEY: Disappear, yeah.

SIEGEL: So it's really important for you not to just walk around places that aren't part of your own group's land because it could be dangerous or it could destroy things?

HARNEY: You could destroy everything. That's why all these big laws, all of that sort of thing, the ceremony, and giving the young ones good discipline and a little bit of understanding about the original aboriginal culture. It's been handed over from generation to generation, and it comes right up to us now today.

MIKE MORTON wrote a computer program that makes anagrams of words and phrases. In recent years he has taken to making anagrams of political slogans, names, and catchwords. A month into the Clinton administration's first year, Mr. Morton reports from his home in Hawaii on what his program made of a number of current Washington names and phrases, starting with the phrase that had served the Clinton campaign as a reminder of priorities: "The economy, stupid." February 22, 1993

MORTON: There is "Dupe thy economist," "Shout my deception," sort of cynical stuff. Perhaps referring back to the races, "Hum despite tycoon." I guess that's Perot.

SIEGEL: We also asked you to try "Tax and spend."

MORTON: That really turned into nothing. The interesting one was "tax-and-spend liberal," which becomes "a bland, lax president."

SIEGEL: A phrase very important to the new administration should be "national service."

MORTON: That was quite a good one. There were a couple of foreign policy ones which were surprising: "Israeli covenant," which seems not to quite go with "Cairo's valentine." There's also "one Calvinist era," which I don't quite know what to make of.

SIEGEL: A phrase that's going to figure certainly in congressional debate over the new tax proposal is the "British thermal unit," because it's the number of Btus in various different fuels that will determine tax rates. Does "British thermal unit" yield anything?

MORTON: It seems to be a small thing, but it's apparently

going to cause trouble, because it turns into "this humble irritant."

SIEGEL: And the names for the leading figures in the new administration, we have one to add now really because Mrs. Clinton, after the election, said that she will be known as "Hillary Rodham Clinton."

MORTON: I found two that I liked. One was "I thrill no lady monarch." Also, completely incomprehensible to me but still interesting was "matriarch, hi, nylon doll."

SIEGEL: "Matriarch, hi, nylon doll"?

MORTON: Yes. The program spits these things out, and I pick the ones that come closest to making sense and that was about the best we could do for "Hillary Rodham Clinton."

SIEGEL: What did you get from "shared sacrifice"?

MORTON: That was perhaps the best of the bunch of buzz phrases since the new administration. "I chide crass fear." Presumably berating people who are worried about their taxes and nothing else. Perhaps a little more cynical is "Rich cadre is safe."

SIEGEL: "Rich cadre is safe"?

MORTON: Yes. Also, alluding to our new secretary of labor is "Sir Reich's facade," and last of this group was "I face hard crises," which really, I think, sums it up for Clinton or individual taxpayers.

When Sotheby's put up for auction a two-hundred-year-old cheese from Tibet, Briton SIMON PERRY, a member of the Cheese Appreciation Society, did not hesitate. He bought the cheese for the equivalent of fifteen hundred dollars. Perry lives in the town of Maidstone in the county of Kent where, by telephone, he discusses his acquisition with Noah Adams. February 3, 1993

PERRY: I've never been so determined in my life, and it was a fight to the death, as well, because the French were there, the Germans were there. There was a lot of heavy bidding.

ADAMS: And how did it go?

PERRY: I've got it. I've got it. It's here in my hand right now. I haven't let go of it since that great moment. I'll be taking it down to Maidstone later on, and we'll be cracking open a few bottles down there. There will be celebrations going on tonight, I can tell you.

ADAMS: But you're not actually going to eat the cheese?

PERRY: Well, it's tempting, I must say, but no, it's not really edible anymore because of its age. You see, it hasn't lasted very well. It's actually shrunk, as well. As I say, I've got it in my hand right now, and it's rather hard and brown. It's not bigger than about — what do you have, inches or centimeters over there?

ADAMS: Let's try inches.

PERRY: It's about a cubic brown inch, with a bit of string through the middle of it.

ADAMS: I'm just trying to figure out how you determined it was worth this much money, aside from the fact that it came to auction at Sotheby's.

PERRY: I was prepared to pay anything for it, really.

ADAMS: Why?

PERRY: Simply because of its collectible value. It's a once-

in-a-lifetime chance for me to bid for the Tibetan cheese, because it's one of the named cheeses. When I say "a named
cheese," you know that famous diamonds have names, like the
Pink Panther or something like that. This particular piece of
Tibetan cheese that came up was a named cheese because of its
age. You don't get very many cheeses that age, and it was called
the Eye of the Tiger. It's a very important thing to me, this piece
of cheese, and also to the others in my club. The French were
bidding against it, and we couldn't let it go over to France, that's
for sure. It's been in Britain for over a hundred years, and I didn't
want to let it out again.

ADAMS: In whose collection was it, recently?

PERRY: It was actually in the collection of somebody called
Martyn Stumbles, who is quite an elderly gentleman, but who
is certainly still alive. It was actually found in Tibet by his
father, Henry Martyn Stumbles. I think it predates Tibet. It's a
cheese with a history. I think it went down in the fall of Con-
stantinople in the thirteenth century. It's a relic.

ADAMS: Now, do you figure it was an especially good cheese
for the Tibetans many years ago?

PERRY: I think it's either a goat's cheese or a rancid yak milk
cheese. It's one or the other, and as I say, I have only just laid my
hands on it this morning, and so it will take a little while for me.
I will have to study it, show it to some other expert friends of
mine, and give it a good old sniffing, of course.

ADAMS: Would you have trouble if you went out for a cele-
bratory pint at a pub, there in London?

PERRY: I don't drink alcohol, no. I don't know what you call
it out there, but I drink what is called orange squash over here.
I don't think you can actually get it in America.

ADAMS: Some kind of orange soda.

PERRY: It's like an orange drink. You water it down.

ADAMS: But would you have trouble convincing your neighbor there, at the pub, that you had spent this much money on
a piece of very old cheese?

PERRY: I don't think I want to talk about it to anybody, just any Tom, Dick, or Harry in the pub, because, you never know, they might come in and steal it because it's quite precious to me. It's really something for the connoisseurs, really. I'm not really proud of the money. But the money is irrelevant. It's possessing it that is the most important thing.

GERALD STALKER of Athens, Georgia, tells Katie Davis about the day he noticed that one of his two plastic flamingos, the one he called Phil, was missing from the front lawn. Then, Stalker said, a letter arrived in the mail from Phil. December 4, 1993

STALKER: I opened it up, and it was from the flamingo. It was a picture of the flamingo in Oregon, at a place called Diamond Pass, Oregon. The letter said, "Gee, I hope you noticed I was missing. I went to sleep under the tree like I always did, and when I woke up I was here in Oregon."

DAVIS: And you have continued to get letters?

STALKER: I got one today, and the picture that I got in the mail today is him at the Golden Gate Bridge in San Francisco, but the letter is postmarked Eugene, Oregon. He's back in Oregon again.

DAVIS: And does each letter have a picture of him?

STALKER: Each letter has anywhere from one to three pictures.

DAVIS: How is he looking?

STALKER: Looks good, just like he did when he left.

DAVIS: And where else has he been?

STALKER: Let's see, Canada, New York, Washington, D.C. He has been to Las Vegas and then to California and now he is back in Oregon again.

DAVIS: Do you have any of his letters there that you could share with us?

STALKER: Let's see what I have got here laying in front of me. This is one of the letters that I got. This one is from Florida. It says, "Hi, guys, Florida's great. The weather's warm. I'm at my family reunion in Tampa. I got to see family that I haven't seen since moving to Athens. Take care. I'll write later, Phil." And there is a picture of the plastic flamingo standing in front of a group of real flamingos.

DAVIS: Now I understand he went to Hollywood, this flamingo?

STALKER: I don't know whether I've got that one here in front of me. But I got one where he was standing with a picture of him standing in front of the Hollywood sign on the hill.

DAVIS: So he climbed all the way up that hill?

STALKER: Evidently so, and the letter said that because he was the strong, silent type, he was hoping to land a part in a motion picture while he was there.

DAVIS: Did you know this flamingo had this much personality when it was sitting out there in the yard?

STALKER: Not at all. Believe it or not, the birds have stood out there for two years and never said a word.

DAVIS: Do you miss the flamingo?

STALKER: Sure I do. It was something I looked at every day for two years, and it's just like he's up and gone now. But I think eventually he will come back home.

DAVIS: Sounds like he will.

STALKER: The really hard part in all of this is trying to convince people that I don't know who has the flamingo. I don't know who took the flamingo, and I may never see the flamingo again. Everybody thinks more or less that this is set up. But once I show them the pictures actually postmarked from the places he is at, they say, "Well, I'll be dogged. Now, how about that now."

DAVIS: Because they know you haven't been to all those places?

STALKER: That's it.

DAVIS: Mr. Stalker, we're a national radio program, as you probably know, and if you could communicate with Phil, what would you like to say to him?

STALKER: Phil, come home in time for Christmas.

AMANDA ADLER, an epidemiologist writing in the
Journal of the American Medical Association, presents
convincing data to show that mud wrestling can
be unhealthy and offers a healthier alternative.
Her conclusions, which she described to Robert Siegel,
were based on an investigation undertaken after several
students who had engaged in mud wrestling at the
University of Washington, Seattle, campus came down
with a nasty rash. January 26, 1993

ADLER: These rashes somewhat resemble the rash one can
get from hot tubbing. We cultured the rash, but, much to our
surprise, found that it was growing a fecal organism rather than
a more typical skin organism. Then the students told us they
had all participated in a mud wrestling social event. So, given
the association between prone-form mud wrestling, particularly with organisms usually found in stool, we chose to find
out whether mud wrestling did cause a rash and, if so, what was
the source of contamination of the mud.

SIEGEL: How would you describe the rashes?

ADLER: They had red bumps, some of them with pus on top
of them, covering their arms and legs, also their bodies, but
generally sparing their faces, their necks, their hands, and their
feet. Of the fifty-three people who attended the event, twenty-
four cases were reported, of whom twenty-one reported had
mud wrestled. It seems that about eighty percent of the people
that mud wrestled were affected by this rash. Three of the students simply got in the mud and didn't wrestle, so we referred
to these students as "wallowers." Of these three, one of them
got the rash.

SIEGEL: Although a small sample, the majority of the non-
wrestling wallowers did not get the rash.

ADLER: This would seem consistent with mud bathing, in which rashes like this have not been reported to our knowledge. Mud baths do, apparently, harbor these kind of organisms, and it appears that the abrasion involved in wrestling probably had something to do with getting the rash.

SIEGEL: It's hard to speculate about the number of people who indulge in mud wrestling, so you don't know how great a danger is there. But you do say that one group at the University of Washington had hosted a Jell-O wrestling event from which no adverse dermatologic effects could be recalled.

ADLER: They had a great time. Presumably, Jell-O would be less likely to be tainted with manure than mud, so that's a good substitute, or any other less-alive substance that people choose to wrestle in would probably be entirely safe.

SIEGEL: I'm just curious whether the *Journal of the American Medical Association* was instantly receptive to your report or whether this took a little bit of prodding of the editors.

ADLER: No, it was warmly welcomed, and, with a few revisions, it was accepted.

SIEGEL: Have you heard from any of your fellow epidemiologists since the appearance of this?

ADLER: They think it's all great fun and chide me about the possibility of soiling my reputation.

KEN FISCHER's decision to retire to Florida and live on a sailboat was marred by one thing: his discovery that each year his boat would have to be lifted out of the water to have barnacles scraped off its bottom at considerable expense. He describes to Linda Wertheimer how he came up with a solution to his dilemma at a cocktail party after eating deviled eggs laced with Tabasco sauce. May 26, 1993

FISCHER: I've never had any experience with Tabasco sauce. When I bit into these eggs, all hell broke loose. My mouth was on fire. My eyes were watering, my nose was running.

WERTHEIMER: Well, now, Mr. Fischer, what I'm interested in is that moment where the two things came together. That's the difference between an inventor and somebody who just has heartburn.

FISCHER: After I got quieted down and before I left the party, I thought to myself, There's got to be something in this that could be useful for keeping barnacles off of the boats. So I started to make inquiries about them, and I went into a public supermarket and I bought a jar of this cayenne pepper that was made up in Hunt Valley, Maryland. I got to thinking that there had to be a way I can test this. So I got some double-faced adhesive and put it on a board, and I covered the board with this pepper, and I stuck it in the ocean, and three weeks later I checked it out. I could see on the back side that wasn't treated were tubeworms and some barnacles that decided to make this their home, but on the front side, where I put the cayenne pepper, they didn't. That's where I made the association. I figure if a human can't stand it, I'm sure that they can't stand it. Does that make sense?

WERTHEIMER: Apparently it does. I just think it's such a funny leap.

FISCHER: Well, a lot of inventions are funny.

GERALD CORMIER, whose tomato plant raised the roof, literally, in Kingsville, Ontario, speaks to Linda Wertheimer. August 25, 1993

WERTHEIMER: Mr. Cormier, I understand that you have a tomato plant that is trying to eat your house?

CORMIER: I won't say it's eating the house, but it looks like it wants to get taller than the house.

WERTHEIMER: How tall is this tomato plant?

CORMIER: As we speak, it's fourteen feet four inches.

WERTHEIMER: Fourteen feet! What are you supporting the thing with!

CORMIER: I had to use eight-foot-length two-by-twos. I had to use three. Then it grew to eight feet, and I thought, Uh-oh, so I added three more. Now I've got three more ready in case I need them. It looks like I may need part of them, anyway, because, as I say, it's fourteen feet now.

WERTHEIMER: Often when a tomato plant goes into stalk and leaf like that it doesn't produce as many tomatoes.

CORMIER: Oh, my dear lady, you should see the tomatoes on this thing! It's just loaded. There is a picture of me in our local paper, and you can see the amount of tomatoes that are on it.

WERTHEIMER: What is the variety?

CORMIER: Just your regular cherry tomato.

WERTHEIMER: Cherry tomatoes!

CORMIER: If we don't get frost, this plant will produce for quite some time yet. We will have plenty of tomatoes for the winter.

WERTHEIMER: How do you pick tomatoes off of a plant that is fourteen feet high?

CORMIER: I've got a ladder. I use a ladder. Eventually I will be picking them off the deck I hope.

WERTHEIMER: It's now reached the deck of the house?

CORMIER: Yes, it's gone through the floor. I have had to cut part of the floor out.

WERTHEIMER: Do you think it's really worth it to cut a hole in your deck?

CORMIER: Oh, sure.

WERTHEIMER: Why not cut the top off the plant?

CORMIER: Oh no! Why do that? It's healthy. It's producing, and there's plenty growing season left. Why not let it go? The floor can always be patched.

WERTHEIMER: To what do you attribute your success as a grower of giant tomato plants?

CORMIER: I am not certain. I have got a few little tricks that I used. I have grown them eleven-foot before, and I have grown them eight foot six, like your regular beefsteak tomatoes. I just don't overwater. I don't overfertilize. I try to use as much rainwater as I can. I collect rainwater, and I use it versus tap water, and I use a fertilizer that you can get in any hardware store. I won't mention any names, of course. That would be free advertising. I don't crowd it, either. And I let it have lots of room and lots of sun, of course.

....

And speaking of tomatoes, the amateur historian
MIGUEL SIERRA explains to Linda Wertheimer that the
annual tomato fights in the Catalan town of Bunyol,
Spain, began as a form of political protest. Depoliticized
in 1993, they became instead a social occasion that
attracted twenty-five thousand youths to Bunyol.
The NPR correspondent Claudio Sanchez interprets.
August 25, 1993

SIERRA: Describing this has two aspects. First, what we see
is just a huge number of people together. And then what you
have is just this large mass of people celebrating as one, and all
are behind the idea of the freedom and the joy of the world.

WERTHEIMER: Now, what I don't understand is that everybody throws tomatoes, but do they throw the tomatoes at each
other?

SIERRA: Yes, because, after all, this is like a battle. Girls
against boys. Of course, in the past, the other part that young
men from Bunyol have taken advantage of is that they can
actually use this to approach girls and flirt with them and caress
them.

WERTHEIMER: A food fight as a way to make friends!

SIERRA: But it is, in essence, a war of tomatoes.

WERTHEIMER: Well, now, how did this get started? Where
does this tradition come from?

SIERRA: This is strictly a tradition of Bunyol. It has had a
long history. It started in 1945 and it started as a rebellion, or as
a way to rebel against the Franco dictatorship, because during
those days, young people felt repressed. They felt they weren't
allowed to enjoy anything. Parties and celebrations were pro-
hibited, so at one point the young people started throwing tomatoes at the authorities, at the priests. This was, of course, the

result of brutal repression, but after a while it became a way for the entire community to express its discontent. It became a very established and very commemorative activity for us.

WERTHEIMER: It seems to me that a tomato fight which involves hundreds of thousands of pounds of tomatoes must leave a terrible mess!

SIERRA: Of course. But the architecture of Bunyol lends itself to this, because there's an aqueduct that is nearby that literally runs through the city and that aqueduct allows us to set up many pumps or many machines that will pump water and simultaneously spray and bathe the people participating with water while they throw tomatoes. Of course, another byproduct of all this is that because the tomatoes are smashed against so many of the buildings and walls, the seeds remain on the walls and soon, at some point, we see the sprouts coming from these walls.

....

In an NPR stairwell, CAROL VAUGHN, a performance
artist, describes to Alex Chadwick her plan to tap-dance
down the 897 stairs of the Washington Monument,
stopping along the way to perform a little piece on each
of the monument's 50 landings. She is an accomplished
dancer and said she could do it easily, but she was
unable to obtain a permit for the performance from
the National Park Service. Her motto is "I ain't afred
of stairs." October 23 and 30, 1993

CHADWICK: What is all this about?

VAUGHN: Tap dancers in the 1990s need to find their own
voice, their own style, and traditionally tap dancers have only
danced on stairs. Fred Astaire did it. Bill "Bojangles" Robinson
did it. So, as a tap dancer, I had to do it, and what better staircase
than that one.

CHADWICK: Thousands of people are injured every year
walking normally down those stairs. Aren't you a little worried?

VAUGHN: No, that's because they're not tap dancing down
the stairs.

CHADWICK: Really? You think it's going to be safe. Didn't
you have to ask the National Park Service, which runs the
Washington Monument, if you could do this?

VAUGHN: Actually, I applied for a permit, and I was denied.
But the head of the Department of the Interior said he didn't
object to my doing it, he just wasn't going to issue me a permit
to do it. So I am doing it anyway.

CHADWICK: So you're going to go over to the Washington
Monument, take the elevator to the top, presumably, and get all
the way down?

VAUGHN: You're allowed to go down the steps. You used to

be allowed to go up and down on foot. You're only allowed to go down and only allowed to go on a guided tour, which is so boring your brain crashes in on itself. I'm going to liven it up.

CHADWICK: Really? Are you going to go with the guide, though? With a bunch of other people?

VAUGHN: Yes.

CHADWICK: Do they know?

VAUGHN: No. It's guerrilla theater. Actually, it's more like chimpanzee theater. It's not that serious.

CHADWICK: On each landing, you are going do a little piece. Would you do a sample here of what you are going to do?

VAUGHN: Sure, I'd be glad to. On the first landing, I'll probably do "Shuffle Off to Buffalo," which goes like this. On the second landing, I think I'll probably do a timed step. On the third landing, I think I'll do "Clinton on Gays in the Military."

CHADWICK: How do these steps compare to the Washington Monument, do you think?

VAUGHN: I'm sorry to say, but they are inferior.

CHADWICK: They are? How come?

VAUGHN: The Washington Monument has much wider steps, and they are also deeper. My little feet have a lot more room to do their thing.

CHADWICK: Have you figured out what to do in case the guide calls for the police, and says, "Look, I've got a mad tap dancer on my hands."

VAUGHN: If the audience will promise not to tell, here is exactly what my plan of action is. I plan to go up in the elevator with the tour group and hang toward the back of the pack. As soon as they round the very first corner, I'll sit, and I wait for about fifteen minutes. Then I'll continue down on my own. There's a chance that one of the park police will come down. But otherwise, I'm anticipating smooth sailing down those steps.

CHADWICK: All right. Where are we here? We're between four and five. Shall we tap-dance on down to the fourth floor?

VAUGHN: I think we should.

CHADWICK: OK.

VAUGHN: You're tapping with me?

CHADWICK: I'm not really much of a dancer. So I'll watch.

VAUGHN: All right.

A week later CAROL VAUGHN returns to report on her attempt to tap-dance down the Washington Monument steps.

CHADWICK: Did you make it?

VAUGHN: Yes I did, but the Park Service was tipped off by listening to National Public Radio, and they were waiting for me.

CHADWICK: Oh no. What happened?

VAUGHN: There was an immense monster of a Park Service official there from Public Affairs, saying, we've been tipped off this is going to happen and I want to let anyone on this tour know, if you do tap-dance down, we will arrest you immediately.

CHADWICK: God, you're kidding.

VAUGHN: The guard said, and this is a direct quote, "The feeling is that small things like this only lead to bigger ones." First you have dancing, next thing you know, they'll be singing, and then who knows what else. Then they had us all show our feet to make sure that there was no one in tap shoes.

CHADWICK: You had to show your feet before you got on the elevator?

VAUGHN: Before you get on the elevator, you have to do sort of a dog-dropping minuet to show that you had nothing on your feet. So, as luck would have it, when we got to the top, he disappeared. On went the shoes, and we had a nice, very gentle tour guide taking us down. Who was very much in the spirit of it.

CHADWICK: So how long did it take you?

VAUGHN: An hour and ten minutes.

CHADWICK: That's very good, I guess.

VAUGHN: And when I emerged, there was a paddy wagon and four motorcycle cops waiting. So I doubled back, whence I came, took my shoes off, and merged with a group of Japanese tourists and walked out the door free as a breeze.

....

Twenty-two-year-old KLINT FREEMANTLE of Napier, New Zealand, went up in a small plane for his seventh skydive. With his family watching on the ground, he jumped out of the plane at thirty-five hundred feet and started counting to five. That was when, as he tells Noah Adams, his parachute was supposed to open automatically. August 11, 1993

KLINT: I got to the count of four. You're supposed to count to five and then look and check your parachute, and I looked up and it just wasn't opening for me, so I looked down at my reserve handle and gave that a pull like you're supposed to do and then went back into my fold position, and that automatically cuts away your top parachute and it opens your second one so no tangles occur, and I looked up and that one wasn't opening either. At that stage, I didn't know the top one was tangled in it.

ADAMS: OK, let me figure this out. The main parachute just didn't deploy?

KLINT: It came out, but it didn't open up properly.

ADAMS: OK, and then the emergency chute got tangled up with the main parachute? And you said to yourself?

KLINT: Basically, I thought, That's it. I'm a goner. I thought I was going to die right then and there.

ADAMS: What did you do then?

KLINT: Thanks to my father teaching me not to panic in situations like that, I looked up and saw the lines were twisting up and the parachute was spinning quite quickly, so I spun my arms and knees and body and tried to untwist the main parachute line, and I managed to untwist one, but then it just went back into its spin and did it again.

ADAMS: And then what happened?

KLINT: I struggled with it as much as I could until I looked down and realized I was going to land in a duck pond.

ADAMS: In a duck pond?

KLINT: In a duck pond, yeah. All the ducks were all taking off by then. I just stopped struggling with the parachute. I knew it wasn't going to work. I just turned onto my back and started undoing my harness. I thought, Well, if I'm going to live through this, there's no way I'm going to drown in a duck pond when I hit the bottom.

ADAMS: What made you think at this point that you were going to hit this water and be OK?

KLINT: The chutes were up above my head to slow me down. I wasn't going at terminal velocity or anything. The guys say I was going probably about fifty miles an hour.

ADAMS: Oh, I see, you were going a bit slow.

KLINT: Yes.

ADAMS: So you go into the duck pond, what? Feet first?

KLINT: No, spinning around on my back, and I hit, basically, bum first.

ADAMS: Bum first? How bad did it hurt?

KLINT: It didn't. I was pumped up with adrenaline and all that sort of thing going through me. I wasn't expecting to hit the water. I thought I had a couple more seconds before I hit and I just went whack into it.

ADAMS: And then what did you do?

KLINT: I stood up. It was only knee-deep. Looked at my arms and legs to make sure they were all still there. I put my hands above my head, and went, "Yoo-hoo!"

ADAMS: Wow, that's quite a story! Are you going to go sky-diving again?

KLINT: Yes.

ADAMS: Could I speak to your dad?

KLINT: I'll put him on right now.

TERRY FREEMANTLE: Yes, good evening.

ADAMS: Terry Freemantle, Noah Adams here. That moment when you saw your son coming to earth —

TERRY: It took quite a long time. Seconds become minutes when things are happening like that, and I could see the malfunction of his first parachute. That really is no big deal, you've got your second one. You just get rid of it, but when the second one went up and got tangled up in the first one, then I started to think something's not too good here. But then Klint is the type of guy that would be showing us how good he can fly these things because he's a bit of a daredevil. I thought he was possibly mucking around a wee bit. Everybody was starting to get a bit agitated down on the ground, including jumpmasters that were down there. Klint had two little powder puffs about a third of the size of the parachute he should have had, and he was spinning very vigorously clockwise. In the Southern Hemisphere things go clockwise, whereas in the Northern Hemisphere they normally go anticlockwise.

ADAMS: I've heard that.

TERRY: I thought he was still just mucking around, and so I started thinking to myself out loud, Come on, Klint, stop mucking around and get on with it, but when he got down to a fortyfive-degree angle from where I was watching, I could see that he was in bad trouble, and these jumpmasters, one in particular, made a run for it and grabbed a cell phone and dialed straight through. "Get an ambulance!" My daughter beside me, Klint's sister, Sarah, was sort of making gasps, and she was quite disturbed, and so I started running across the field because I knew he was going to hit, and if he hit I would probably be shoveling him up with a shovel to put him into a box. When I got over there, lo and behold, there was Klint standing up in the middle of this damned duck pond, pulling in the chutes as if nothing had happened.

ADAMS: So you actually didn't see the impact in the duck pond.

TERRY: Two-thirds of the way across the Napier Airfield Park, I was watching him all the way to the ground. I just saw what looked like dust go up, and I thought, Well, it's either pollen from rushes or he might have been crashing into sand. I thought, Man, he's just going to be a crumpled heap when I get there, but of course it was water splashing. He landed in about knee-deep water. It's a sanctuary estuary where the ducks and swans and other waterfowl are quite free to do their thing, where nobody's supposed to disturb them except the parachutists.

ADAMS: Do you think that the two of you are going to go back up?

TERRY: I am. But Klint, not because he is frightened to, but he actually made a pact with his fiancée, and before that particular jump, he said, "Well, I'm going to stick to that, Dad, and did say to her that would be my last jump." But that's not because he wouldn't want to. He wouldn't be too frightened to jump out again, but he had promised his fiancée, and he's going to keep to that. That's fair enough.

ADAMS: He credits your training in helping him maintain his composure.

TERRY: That's very nice of him to say. I wouldn't particularly say that myself. We are into the outdoors a lot over here. We do make river rafts and we go river-rafting on some very wild stuff that's killed people. We also do scuba diving, which does kill people, but to us it's just our outdoor living. We're outdoor people. I'm pleased that he was cool enough and calm enough to do everything he was taught and he survived. It sort of gives me goose pimples now just thinking about it.

The restaurateur ERIC STROMQUIST of Zeebento
in Portland, Oregon, talks with Neal Conan about his
un-fortune cookies that are anything but sweet.
March 10, 1993

CONAN: Where did this "fun" idea come from?

STROMQUIST: That's a good question. I'm a seriously disturbed person, and I think it's been loitering in some recess of my mind for years.

CONAN: And reading these un-fortunes shows many aspects of your disease manifesting themselves. "The town isn't big enough for the both of you." "A fetish for rubber underwear will bring you shame."

STROMQUIST: Like I said, I'm disturbed.

CONAN: What ever happened to the slogan, "The customer is always right"?

STROMQUIST: "The customer isn't always right" is the truth of it. I have worked in restaurants for probably seventeen years, and I'm not going to live in fear of offending people.

CONAN: Have you offended anyone, so far?

STROMQUIST: Oh yes.

CONAN: Give me some typical reactions.

STROMQUIST: A typical reaction, the one I'm looking for, is a smirk. But we have had a couple of people that were angry.

CONAN: Walked out, and said, "I'll never eat here again."

STROMQUIST: I did have one woman do that.

CONAN: Her problem, from your point of view?

STROMQUIST: No sense of humor.

CONAN: Are these un-fortune cookies, on the other hand, attracting some people?

STROMQUIST: Sure they are. It's a combined effort of classic marketing, to differentiate yourself from the competition, and it's in part an effort to get people to laugh. I am kind of a silly person anyway, and I like laughing. I think humor is a great lubricant for life, and I think people take themselves and life way too seriously.

CONAN: Be honest for a minute, now. Are you one of those people who might, in your wallet somewhere, have a real fortune from a real fortune cookie tucked away somewhere?

STROMQUIST: I really don't, although occasionally, my wife will stick them on the refrigerator, which is kind of embarrassing when guests come over. But we now have a few un-fortunes to match.

CONAN: Any stuck up on your refrigerator?

STROMQUIST: "You're no Jack Kennedy" is my personal favorite, and I'm not sure why. But we have that one. And "You are well liked, despite your table manners." Also, "You have a nose for the football" seemed to tickle her for some reason.

CONAN: Do you hire special writers, or do you do this yourself?

STROMQUIST: I actually do it myself.

CONAN: People have a flair for some things.

STROMQUIST: And I'm afraid that's my cross to bear.

TORILL BROCK-SEBERG is a senior vice president of the Lillehammer Olympic Organizing Committee. She talks with Bob Edwards about a campaign to make Norwegians smile in time for the 1994 Winter Olympics. Part of the campaign was the development of a device called a "smile holder," which forces even the most reluctant mouths to turn upward. December 9, 1993

BROCK-SEBERG: Norwegians have been accused of being very sloppy with service, and in order to get this campaign started, we invented this kind of hook, which should learn Norwegians how to smile. It's really a true hook. It's made out of plastic with an elastic band, and you put it around the back of your head and in your mouth and then you smile. This was a gimmick in order to get the campaign started.

EDWARDS: Do Norwegians have trouble smiling?

BROCK-SEBERG: Norwegians don't have trouble smiling, but we can always smile a little more, and we are looking at what happened in Calgary when everyone in Calgary wore this button. One said, "Smile, you're a tourist attraction." Instead of making a button, where we put something similar on the button, we said we make this kind of device in order to show that Norwegians also could smile, and it's important to smile when you get visitors and when you get tourists and when you get so many different kinds of people coming to Norway, because smiling is an international language.

EDWARDS: Don't Norwegians have a reputation for being a little dour?

BROCK-SEBERG: I wouldn't say so, but Norwegians are a little bit shy. I think that Norwegians have been living quite up north. We're not so used to getting so many visitors, so I think we are rather shy, and not very spontaneous perhaps, but once you get to know us we are smiling and nice and quite friendly people.

EDWARDS: You mentioned the service. Now, what else besides the lack of smile would characterize the service of Norwegians?

BROCK-SEBERG: It has been accused of being a little slow, and we haven't always put the customers in the center. Instead, we perhaps have been more concerned with ourself instead of seeing that the customers really got what they wanted. But we are changing. We wanted to make the Olympics do something about this, saying to the Norwegian people, "This is really an opportunity to show what Norway is like in the 1990s," showing that we can be as good as anyone else in giving service to foreigners, to visitors, to people wanting to come to this country and make business with us.

EDWARDS: Are people smiling more now, or are they going to wait for the Olympics?

BROCK-SEBERG: I don't know. I think they might wait for the Olympics. It's quite dark and cold in Norway at the moment, but we are practicing to smile when you come to see us during the Olympics, and we will hope that the Olympics will have such an impact that we'll keep smiling for the next years to come.

EDWARDS: Tell me a Norwegian joke.

BROCK-SEBERG: A Norwegian joke?

EDWARDS: Sure.

BROCK-SEBERG: Translated into English?

EDWARDS: Sure.

BROCK-SEBERG: OK, I'll tell you a Norwegian joke. We usually tell jokes about our neighbors, and the Finnish Olympic Committee decided they wanted to go to St. Moritz in order to apply for the Olympics, and it was quite a party before they went down there. And so when they got to St. Moritz they didn't have much time to prepare themselves, so the Finn president of the Finnish Olympic Committee, he just started to reading the application. And he started to read it like this:

"Oooh, oooh." And then this little clerk went up to him, and said, "Mr. President, Mr. President, it's not common to read the Olympic rings."

EDWARDS: That's very good. Well, I think you're making a good start here.